The Work/Life Dichotomy

Recent Titles from Quorum Books

The Work/Life Dichotomy

PROSPECTS FOR REINTEGRATING PEOPLE AND JOBS

Martin Morf

Q ————————————————————

QUORUM BOOKS
New York · Westport, Connecticut · London ——————

Library of Congress Cataloging-in-Publication Data

Morf, Martin.
  The work/life dichotomy.

  Bibliography: p.
  Includes index.
  1. Personnel management.   2. Labor productivity.
3. Work environment.   I. Title.
HF5549.M625 1989   658.3'14   88–35739
ISBN 0–89930–421–4 (lib. bdg. : alk. paper)

British Library Cataloguing in Publication Data is available.

Library of Congress Catalog Card Number: 88-35739
ISBN: 0-89930-421-4

First published in 1989 by Quorum Books

Greenwood Press, Inc.
88 Post Road West, Westport, Connecticut   06881

Printed in the United States of America

The paper used in this book complies with the
Permanent Paper Standard issued by the National
Information Standards Organization (Z39.48–1984).

10 9 8 7 6 5 4 3 2 1

To Donald, Rita, and André

Contents

Exhibits

Preface

The two categories of work and life addressed in this book are broad and overlap with many other dichotomies. Sigmund Freud contrasted civilization with instinct. Joseph Campbell distinguished between the machine and the state on one hand, the enterprising individual on the other. Michael Maccoby relied on the dichotomy of head and heart. Philosophers have had much to say about the classical world of reason and the romantic world of feeling, perhaps even passion.

Work is activity typically done in public and for the public. In the work sphere we know we are under scrutiny. We present ourselves as reasonable, as reliable machines, as creatures imbued with the values of our civilization. There is no demand for revolutionaries and artists in the work sphere. In marked contrast, we tend to go many different ways in our personal lives. Here we allow our feelings and basic convictions to govern our actions and we do what we want rather than what society, corporations, superiors, and employers want.

We are not only looking at a dichotomy here. In the industrial society, the worlds of work and of life—in the sense of real, private, personal life—are separated by a wide gap for the majority of people. Worse than that: The demands they make on us often clearly conflict with each other.

This raises questions about how to bridge this gap on both the level of society and that of individuals. The title of the book refers to the reintegration rather than the integration of work and life. In pre-industrial societies, work and life were, and are, a single set of activities.

The matter is less clear in the case of the life span of the individual. On this level one can make a case for both reintegration and integration, but the gap is perhaps most marked for mature adults who begin to question the purpose of their work activity in the larger scheme of leading a meaningful life. One can imagine adult employees who have done the same work for decades pondering earlier stages of their development when work was a real challenge and activity in which they learned and through which they became socialized.

This project had its beginnings in an article on the future of work first presented to an extremely bright group of students at the University of Osaka in 1982 and eventually published in *The Futurist* and several books of readings. This led to a more thorough analysis of work in a book titled *Optimizing work performance: A look beyond the bottom line*, published in 1986. In the same year, five colleagues from Japan, Canada, the United States, and Switzerland agreed to participate in a symposium on the topic *Toward a reintegration of work and life*, which I organized for the 21st International Congress of Applied Psychology held in Jerusalem. This provided the final stepping stone for the present effort.

I am grateful to the colleagues who participated in our symposium. They were Frank Auld, Ronald Burke, Felix Frei, Toshio Iritani, and Jyuji Misumi. Takao Watanabe, then of the Canadian Embassy in Tokyo, and Akira Kobasigawa, my colleague at the University of Windsor, patiently introduced me to Japanese culture, indulgently let me misinterpret it, and gently tried to stop me from going too boldly in the wrong direction. Opinions will differ on how well they succeeded. Conversations with colleagues at the Swiss Federal Institute of Technology in Zürich led to a restructuring of the entire book. My department head at Windsor, Robert Orr, did everything he could to make my life easier during the final stages of writing.

Help from colleagues notwithstanding, errors no doubt remain and are my responsibility alone. This is a generalist's book. A large canvas is covered with heavy strokes. Specialists in industrial and organizational psychology, management science, anthropology and ethnology, Japanese Studies, economics, and education will not always be pleased. If this effort generates some discussion and succeeds in pulling together some ideas from different disciplines on a fundamental issue, I will consider it to have attained its major objectives.

_____ PART 1

WORK AND LIFE ON THE LEVEL OF SOCIETY

The Gap Between
Work and Life

WORK: A CRUEL NECESSITY?

Between 6 A.M. and 9 A.M. millions of Americans find their way to the
workplace by car, on foot, by bus, in crowded subways and commuter
trains. They usually are not in a happy mood. After an evening or
weekend in the relatively permissive life sphere—at play, discharging
family responsibilities, pursuing educational, political, and perhaps even
religious activities—they have to prepare for a shift into the much colder
work sphere. Television, popular literature, and rock lyrics pervade the
personal and private life sphere with messages like "you can be anything you want to be." The work sphere, in stark contrast, demands
that the majority of people be satisfied with simple jobs, often jobs in
which they produce the same item or perform the same responses a
hundred or a thousand times every day.

The context within which most workers experience work as a cruel
necessity or as a necessary evil is that of the industrial society in its
later stages, as it enters a post-industrial stage. Psychologist Robert Dubin (1973) describes this context as one of "multi-equal institutions." It
seemed to Dubin that the "productive institution" (i.e., the factory)
had lost its dominating role at the expense of institutions like the family, alternative education institutions concentrating on socialization rather
than occupational competence, and consumer organizations ranging from
department stores and shopping centers to Nader's Raiders. He argued
that where earlier societies had been "focal institution societies" in which

one institution dominated the culture, modern societies sport many equally important institutions.

These institutions are, still according to Dubin, quite independent of each other because they are physically and temporally separated, and functionally and organizationally different. For example, the workplace is away from home; we work at certain times of the day and during our life span, and play at other times and life-span periods; the workplace and the family or health club meet different needs; and the workplace is probably organized hierarchically like the army while the home may be a tumultous or *laissez faire* democracy.

For many workers the contradiction between the individual- and freedom-oriented values governing personal life and the specific demands of the workplace for exact knowledge, punctuality, prescribed and repetitive performance, and even standard dress and hairdo, produces a conflict which makes work barely tolerable. This conflict creates stress and reduces work satisfaction. Sometimes directly, but most often indirectly, it also lowers work motivation, performance, and productivity. Such effects are costly on the level of the dissatisfied worker as well as on the levels of work organizations and an economy that must cope with increasingly intense competition from Asia and Europe.

This book's underlying theme is that work motivation, job satisfaction and, above all, satisfaction with one's life in general, are lower than they could and should be because of the marked gap between the work sphere and the sphere of personal life in the United States. It is argued that the industrial past of the United States has produced this gap, that its post-industrial future may provide ways of bridging it, and that far-sighted efforts to raise work motivation and job satisfaction must deal with the question of the reintegration of work and life. This suggests a focus on job design that increases job scope rather than scientific management; humanistic organization theory rather than structural organization theory; and a focus on the maintenance of organizations and their personnel, which goes beyond performance and productivity as they are reflected in the famous next quarterly bottom line.

An Overview of the Work and Life Spheres

Both the work sphere and the life sphere as conceived here assume distinct forms on the macro-level of society and the micro-level of the individual. On the level of society, the work sphere overlaps almost completely with sociologist Daniel Bell's (1976) techno-economic structure of private and public work organizations producing the goods and services a society requires. On the micro-level, the work sphere includes the working conditions and work tasks which impinge on a particular individual, that individual's perceptions of these conditions and tasks, as well as his or her values pertaining to work. The work sphere of an individual is typically a reflection of society's work sphere. Work is generally something imposed by society and done for society. It is collective and public activity. Thus, the work sphere is associated with society rather than the individual.

The life spheres of society and of the individual are somewhat more heterogeneous and difficult to define. Here the salient starting point is the individual. The life sphere of the individual encompasses personal and private concerns and the conditions that relate to these concerns, either because the individual brings them about, chooses to be where they prevail, or because they happen to prevail. On the level of society, the life sphere encompasses conditions and generally held values that foster individual growth and development regardless of economic consequences. Although society may offer opportunities that enhance personal and family (i.e., non-work) life, the life sphere is basically the concern of the individual.

The macro- and micro-level perspectives of the work and life spheres meet on the intermediate level of the work organization. The work organization as we know it currently is more a part of the work sphere than of the life sphere. Its primary concerns are productivity and profit. It is not usually concerned about the welfare of its people anymore than the law requires. But it has implications for the life sphere of its workers, it could and should be more concerned with the life sphere, and it can afford to be concerned with it in a post-industrial society no longer dependent on relentless and backbreaking labor from workers. In short, the work organization is part of the work sphere and of society, but some of its aspects could be concerned with the life sphere and with the individual worker to whom it matters. Thus work organizations could play a crucial role of reintegrating work and life in the coming post-industrial society.

Exhibit 1–1 presents some of the major features of the two spheres as they present themselves in the form of material conditions and as cultural or psychological conditions in society in general, in the work organization, and on the level of the individual worker. The objective of this chapter is to provide an overview that sets the stage for separate analyses of the relationship between, and the prospects for reintegration of, the work and life spheres on the macro-level of society and the micro-level of the individual.

Material and Cultural Conditions

An important distinction made in Exhibit 1–1 between material and cultural or psychological conditions needs elaboration. Sometimes it is fairly straightforward. In the case of Bell's techno-economic structure it

Exhibit 1–1

Conditions Characterizing Work and Life Spheres on the Levels of Society, the Work Organization, and the Individual

Level	Work Sphere	Life Sphere
Society		
Material conditions	Constraints (sphere of necessity)	Absence of constraints (sphere of liberty)
	Demand for personnel	Material conditions conducive to educational activity
Cultural conditions		Cultural conditions conducive to educational activity
	Collective industrial values	Collective post-industrial values
	Materialistic determinism	Cultural determinism
Organization		
Material conditions	Routinized jobs	Humanized jobs
	Traditional organizational demands for personnel	
Cultural conditions		Innovative organizational demands for personnel
	Structural organization theory	Humanistic organization theory
	Performance-oriented values	Maintenance-oriented values
Individual		
Material conditions	Fixed work tasks	Flexible demands of family, political structure, self
	Specific training requirements	Material conditions promoting the development of a particular individual
Cultural/ psychological conditions		Cultural conditions promoting the development of a particular individual
	Personal industrial values	Personal post-industrial values, assumed life roles, identity
	Perceived sources of dissatisfaction	Perceived sources of satisfaction of growth needs

is clear that we are dealing with a set of material conditions: resources, manpower, equipment, even capital. In the case of Eric Trist's (1973) industrial values we are dealing, as we will see shortly, with cultural conditions. Even in these apparently straightforward cases, values may be the result of material conditions, while material conditions may have been brought about by specific and motivating values.

Often the distinction between material and cultural conditions is more complicated. Both are objective conditions, that is, objectively observed conditions. In other words, they can be studied scientifically in that observations about them can be replicated by different independent observers.

An important aspect in which they differ is the ultimate source on which observations about them are based. Material, physical, or economic conditions are based on observations about the environment of the reporting observers. They are more likely to be noted by environment-oriented scientists, such as the radical behaviorists in psychology. Cultural or social conditions are ultimately based on introspective evidence, for example, on reports made by individuals about their attitudes and values.

Cultural conditions too are objective in the sense that they are observed by outsiders, for example, scientists who survey rising and falling anxiety levels of populations in response to news of nuclear power plant catastrophies. The scientist's data are objective, the fact that 10 percent of the sample reported high anxiety levels can be verified by a second scientist. The ultimate observations in this case, however, are subjective. This implies also that they are necessarily about people. Person-oriented cognitive psychologists are more likely to deal with cultural conditions than environment-oriented behaviorists.

Difficulties in actually making the distinction between material and cultural conditions are illustrated by the condition which is referred to in Exhibit 1–1 as the *absence of constraints*. It is listed as a material condition, although whether the absence of something can be regarded as material in any sense may be debated by persons of a philosophical bent. Similarly, is *demand for personnel* a material condition? Demand sounds like a psychological construct; however, it is also directly based on unfilled jobs, a material condition.

A final observation regarding Exhibit 1–1: It contrasts material conditions and cultural or psychological conditions. On the level of the individual, the focus is on individual cognitions (values, ideas, perceptions) rather than cognitions held by a group, a collectivity. What is cultural on the level of society thus is, once assimilated, psychological on that of the individual.

THE WORK AND LIFE SPHERES OF SOCIETY

"The techno-economic order," according to Bell (1976), "is concerned with the organization of production and the allocation of goods and services" (p. 11). A major part of this techno-economic structure is the private business sector, and the objective of business is to make money. Even in the case of nonprofit organizations, the main objective usually is to produce, be on target, reach objectives. It is not deemed to be the work organization's or employer's concern to make workers happy. While many employers utter such thoughts as "our people are our most valuable resource," and while the personnel manager has moved up in the organizational hierarchy and become the director of human resources, not enough American work organizations actually take care, expend time, and devote large sums of money to nurturing long-lasting goodwill among their employees.

In part, the problem is the difficult relationship between those who run American work organizations and the workers of these organizations. Owners and managers on one side, and labor on the other, tend to have quite different ideas about what is in their interest. The American preference for the adversarial system of resolving disputes, in which each side hires the best lawyers and does everything possible but still legal to prevail, does not help to improve relations.

An even larger aspect of the problem is the spirit of scientific management which continues to dominate the workplace. Costs are reduced and output is increased by simplifying work, by routinizing the worker's operations, by reducing the skills and knowledge required to do the job. Investing in hardware that produces visible results quickly is generally regarded as more efficient than investing in complex and difficult human workers with a variety of growth needs. The employer's paycheck buys the worker's soul for an eight-hour day. During these eight hours most workers enter willingly but not happily the sphere of relatively routine work, which is very different from the sphere of their personal lives.

The latter, the sphere of their personal lives, overlaps with what Bell calls the culture. While most anthropologists define culture as the different modes of adjustment a particular society has evolved, including the modes of production developed to meet the needs arising within the sphere of necessity, Bell (1976) restricts the term to the sphere of liberty, leisure, discretion. As far as he is concerned, the culture is part of the sphere of personal, private life and excludes the techno-economic structure embodying the values of the world of work. Bell's culture is oriented toward self-realization while the techno-economic structure or economy strives for efficiency. In his less charitable moments, Bell suggests that hedonistic self-gratification rather than self-realization was the moving force within the American culture of the 1960s which he analyzed.

Bell (1976) defines culture as "those efforts, in painting, poetry, and fiction or within religious forms . . . which seek to explore and express the meanings of human existence in some imaginative form" (p. 12). The development of a culture in Bell's sense requires that the members of a society ponder "the existential situations which confront all human beings" (p. 12), that is, that they reflect on archetypal situations like death, birth, crisis, and parenthood. Reflection leads to interpretation. A fatalist culture might interpret death as something to be accepted without futile resistance, a Christian culture might celebrate it as the beginning of real life, at least for the virtuous, far from this vale of tears.

A society's interpretations of the meaning of significant situations, its ways of perceiving them and coping with them, may be escapist, silly or profound and they may be transmitted to future generations and disseminated within the society by a variety of media. These media include literature, painting and sculpture, music, newspaper stories, cartoons, comic strips, ways of dressing and speaking, film and, above all, television. The anthropologist's culture in general and Bell's culture in particular thus have content and are transmitted by the media, but as Marshall McLuhan (1964) observed, the media are themselves a part of the content of the culture, that is, they are significant features of the environment that we have to adjust to, cope with, and reflect on. The medium is at least part of the message.

While Bell (1976, pp. 37, 87) stresses the "disjunction" or gap between the techno-economic structure and the culture, he is ultimately concerned about three conflicting spheres governed by incompatible "axial principles." The third sphere is the polity, focusing on the legitimate exercise of power with the consent of the governed, on the right of citizens to be either represented on decision-making bodies or to participate directly when decisions are made through bargaining and negotiation. This political sphere, as we will see in Chapter 10, is another important aspect of the life sphere which directly conflicts with the generally authoritarian work sphere.

Marx's Spheres of Necessity and Liberty

What Bell calls "techno-economic structure," Karl Marx calls "realm of necessity" and what Bell calls "culture," Marx calls "realm of freedom" (Marx, 1981). The realm of necessity is the domain in which people are driven by extrinsic forces: the need to feed and house themselves and their families. Necessity compels the worker to labor under unpleasant conditions and to accept the constraints imposed in the work sphere.

There is something compelling and concrete about deficit needs like hunger and the need for shelter, and the realm of necessity can be thought of easily as a set of material conditions, that is, conditions that actually exist "out there" rather than only in the human mind. The corresponding realm of liberty has a less material air, but the absence of material conditions imposing restraints is perhaps itself a material condition.

There are many constraints in the work sphere. They are obvious in the case of the firstline worker performing routinized functions. Managers too, however, operate under constraints: deadlines, assigned tasks, critical paths, decisions dictated by probabilities of outcomes and their costs and benefits. Whatever else the techno-economic structure may be, it is generally a structured domain. It is its constraints which strike and annoy many workers when they approach the plant or the office in the morning.

The constraints imposed by work organizations on their employees are the result of an ultimate constraint on the organization itself: the bottom line. Even if the bottom line is defined liberally to include effects on the environment and on the long-term viability of the organization, effects which are beyond the concerns of the accountants, it dictates fairly clearly what has to be done.

While lofty strategic decisions may be made by flexible gamesmen (Maccoby, 1976) in the boardroom, the day-to-day operations are handled by bureaucratic structures that issue regulations, assignments, and schedules. The world of work is quite generally a world of prohibitions and duties, of "don'ts" and "musts." A bricklayer cannot suddenly make a visit to the local bar without disrupting the construction project. The console supervisor of a power plant cannot leave her dials unattended. The aircraft mechanic must know the particular engine he is testing and his hand must be steady when he puts in delicate wiring.

The techno-economic structure is a complex system, consisting of many interdependent elements. These elements range from picks and shovels to telecommunication systems, computers, and robots. The village smithy was a one-man operation; the design and production of a new car involves thousands of people, hundreds of raw materials, complex machinery, specialized knowledge about design, production, and consumer demand. This complex system must be carefully structured if it is to function efficiently and if it is to avoid mistakes.

Errors within the techno-economic structure usually have concrete consequences, and these can have ramifications. If the mechanic did not consult the right manual and if he was not fit and attentive, the pilot and his passengers may be in trouble. Many a lawyer is making a good living from such ramifications.

Additional constraints in this sytem are imposed by its environment: Raw materials may be limited, workers with clearly defined skills have to be located or trained, clients who do not pay their bills may reduce cash flow to a cash trickle.

Exactly which of these constraints should be regarded as constraints on the macro-level of society, the intermediate level of the work organization, or the micro-level of the individual is not always easy to determine, and the choices made in Exhibit 1–1 are somewhat arbitrary.

Demand for Personnel Versus Educational Opportunities

As noted earlier, the demands for personnel on the part of society's work sphere are based on actual jobs that are not filled, thus they can be considered as based on, or even as, material conditions. The demands for workers and managers, bringing to the job certain motivational dispositions and abilities, shape the supply side of the equation: society's schools.

These schools are referred to as the "education system." This, however, is an unfortunate term. A careful differentiation between education and training as these terms are usually used suggests that the schools constitute a training, not an education system.

The schools are themselves a particularly important aspect of the techno-economic structure. They are institutions structured to fulfill a mission dictated by the society or public which finances them. As a result, learning activity within them is rule-bound, constraining, and meant to achieve definite objectives such as the successful inculcation of basic industrial virtues like punctuality and reliability, and basic industrial skills such as the ability to read simple instructions on how to use a tool or an office machine.

This structured training system must be sharply contrasted with the learning activities that are less dictated by the extrinsic demands of the workplace and more by intrinsic, private, or personal needs to understand and develop. Although the structured training system of schools and programs is usually called the "education system," it is useful to reserve the term *education* for the learning activities of the second kind, those associated with private concerns of the life sphere.

The distinction between training and education is made clearly by R. S. Peters (1965): Training is always a means to something else (such as earning a living) while education is an end in itself. Training is clearly practical, related to the real world, while education concerns less tangible goals such as wisdom, higher level of awareness, personal growth and development. Education is the pursuit of an ideal never attained, but intrinsically rewarding every step along the way.

Educational activity is seen here as activity that leads to insight and understanding, and as activity that cannot be planned and structured because it happens to be in large part the result of fortunate accidents. True, some environments are more likely to let fortunate accidents happen. Such environments include certain types of schools that foster curiosity more than salable skill. They may also include jobs that offer challenge, although education is more associated with the life sphere than the work sphere as it is organized today.

Some say that education is associated with leisure. The Greeks certainly saw a close relationship between the two. The word *school* comes from the Greek *schole*, a word meaning *leisure*. To the Greeks, schooling was sitting around, discussing, meditating, discovering. In other words, it was something Americans do not currently have much use for. Perhaps this ought to make us pause, sit around, and discuss what we mean by education today.

Education as defined here can take place at any time and anywhere.

It is subtle and informal. In contrast to training, it is unstructured, it does not predictably take place in institutions, it is not governed by externally formulated objectives, and it is not pursued by standard and structured means. It takes place as one passes through a variety of more or less stimulating environments: schools, jobs, marriages, personal crises. But an environment that stimulates educational activity in one person may stifle it in another. There are people whose insight and awareness deepen and expand in jail, there are others on whom no wisdom at all rubs off in a university library.

All of this suggests that education is a micro-level process by which individuals shape themselves with help from the environment in order to cope with issues arising in their life sphere, while training is both macro-level activity of interest to the techno-economic structure of society and meso-level activity engaged in by organizations to meet their specific needs for trained workers.

The opportunities which the environment provides for the self-initiated process of education within and for the life sphere may take the form of material or cultural conditions. Society may provide generous scholarships so people can sit under trees and read Plato instead of in toll booths collecting tokens and small change. Such financial support is material in nature by most standards. Society, or at least some of the subcultures within it, may also espouse values conducive to the reading of philosophical wisdom. The Jewish communities of many societies strongly espouse such values, ensuring cultural conditions that are likely to encourage their people to attain high levels of education.

Industrial and Post-Industrial Values

This brings us to two features of the work and life spheres that are cultural rather than material conditions: the type of value systems that characterize the two spheres and the type of prevalent view about what primarily causes what.

In North America and Europe, a particular set of values, designed to maximize the chances of survival in a world in which manna does not fall from heaven to satisfy our deficit needs, are characteristic of the entrepreneurs and managers of the techno-economic structure and some of their more ambitious workers. These values are sometimes collectively referred to as the "work ethic" or the "Protestant ethic." They are the product of a Europe revolting against traditional (Catholic) Christianity and busily engaging in trade, innovation, investment, and in the beginnings of modern industrial activity. Trist's (1973) industrial values of achievement, independence, self-control, and endurance are encompassed by the work ethic characteristic of the industrial society.

As the industrial society makes way for the post-industrial society in which much of the essential work is done by automated systems, the industrial values are making way for post-industrial values. This has a major bearing on the relationship between work and life spheres since post-industrial values are much more compatible with personal concerns than the industrial values that mainly served the needs of society and business. Trist argues, for example, that achievement is in the process of yielding to self-actualization, self-control to self-expression, independence to interdependence, and endurance of distress to "capacity for joy."

Economic and Social Determinism

Exhibit 1–1 distinguishes between material and cultural conditions. It is one thing to classify conditions as material or cultural, it is another to regard one or the other of these types of conditions as primary, as initial, as more important, as giving rise to the other type. The latter judgement puts us into the camp of either the material determinists or the cultural determinists. Material determinism is the tendency to regard material, physical, or economic conditions as primary. Cultural determinism assigns primacy to cultural or social factors such as values. Religious values have played a particularly large, and not always happy, role in people's belief systems about what causes what.

Be they materialistic or cultural in nature, such belief systems are themselves cultural conditions of our work and life spheres. In this context one tends to speak of economic and social determinism. Economic determinism is more directly associated with the work sphere than the life sphere, while the contrary could be argued for social determinism.

Anthropologist Marvin Harris (1981) is one of the better known exponents of economic determinism. He argues that what shapes our basic values are the ways in which we handle the problem of putting food on the table, clothes on our backs and roofs over our heads. Material or economic concerns thus lead to the cultural values of society and to the values of individuals. Both in turn affect primarily our perceptions and behaviors in the life sphere.

The Marxists' dialectical materialism postulates that the irreconcilable conflict between proletariat and bourgeoisie generates the tension that drives historical evolution, and that this conflict is the result of material (physical, economic) conditions. Bertold Brecht, the German playwright, sums up the primacy of economic and material conditions in the pithy phrase "First comes grub, morality afterwards" (cited from Meakin, 1976, p. 6). Psychologist Abraham Maslow (1954) postulated growth needs which enter into play only after the basic deficit needs

like hunger and physical security have been attended to. Pierre Teilhard de Chardin (1959, p. 63) writes "To think, we must eat."

The social determinists, on the other hand, see the life sphere as
cause and the work sphere as effect. The German sociologist Max Weber (1958) argued around the turn of the century that the work ethic is
also the Protestant ethic, that it had its origins in religious values and
beliefs. Sigmund Widmer (1984), Swiss historian and former mayor of
the city of Zürich makes a convincing case for the position that his city,
and many others like it, evolved in the early Middle Ages because they
were religious centers. In his view, economic activity followed religious
activity and the city expanded as artisans and food-producers were
needed to feed and house pilgrims, monks, and nuns.

Materialistic and cultural determinism are not necessarily incompatible if we keep in mind the role of scarcity and affluence. In times of
scarcity, economic considerations, and that means the work sphere
concerned with basic needs, are likely to dominate. In times of affluence, as in the still fairly affluent United States of today, social considerations, that is, concerns emanating from the life sphere, are likely to
be strong, at least among those who have succeeded in getting a slice
of the pie.

THE WORK AND LIFE SPHERES OF WORK
ORGANIZATIONS

By definition, the work sphere dominates within the work organization. Ultimately it is the system's output that counts, hence the work
organization is concerned with collective productivity. The shipping
department cannot ship unless the sales department obtains orders.
The activities of many employees must be scheduled to maximize the
bottom line under given conditions. As technology becomes more sophisticated, each employee's understanding of it becomes more frag-
mentary and the task of coordinating this fragmented expertise becomes more difficult. Decisions tend to be made by groups of managers,
by boards and committees, since no single person has all the information required to make informed choices.

Among the material conditions of the organizational work sphere,
routinized jobs and traditional organizational demands for personnel
loom large. Among its cultural conditions is structural organization
theory, which stresses hierarchical organization and task orientedness,
and which explicitly or implicitly underlies many decisions made within
an organization. Among them also are the organization's basic values,
which typically stress performance, productivity, and profit.

Of course, a work organization should be concerned about more than
short-term productivity. It should be more concerned about the life

sphere, a sphere which already intrudes into its concerns in such areas as retirement planning, on-site recreation facilities, and the development of alternative work schedules that take into account the employee's nonwork needs (Mankin, 1978). It could humanize its jobs, look for personnel that will be more than reliable machines, base action on humanistic organization theories and focus not only on immediate productivity, but also on the maintenance of its human and material components, which are necessary conditions of productivity in the long run.

Routinized Versus Humanized Jobs

Scientific management is one variant of structural organization theory, as we will see in Chapter 10. This approach, associated with the engineer and efficiency expert Frederick Taylor, aims at breaking work down into routine jobs that can be done by workers with little training. It thus implies job design that decreases job scope by restricting the range of physical and cognitive activities the job requires.

The opposite of work simplification and routinized jobs is a "humanized" job. The term "humanization of work" comes from Europe. It refers to job design that increases the scope of jobs by making jobs more demanding and challenging. Such jobs may increase stress for some workers, but it is assumed that most people wish to function on the job as they do in their personal life, as decision-making and reasonably autonomous beings.

Traditional Versus Innovative Demands for Personnel

One would expect work organizations to hire people who fit the available job slots. The jobs, and hence the organization, do indeed demand certain motivational dispositions and abilities. The unfilled jobs and the demands they generate are material conditions of the organizational work sphere. This is especially evident when the unfilled jobs are routinized jobs designed on the basis of strictly economic considerations. An example of a material condition is thus a worker's place along an assembly line close to levers and switches that have to be operated.

Sometimes personnel are hired first, and the jobs are created later. This is unorthodox and innovative, and likely to work only under fairly specific conditions for organizations, although this is what happens when individual entrepreneurs start a project. Here the life sphere comes first, the needs of the work sphere second. People choose to do what they want, or they are selected to do what they want if that looks profitable in the long run. In the case of the entrepreneur we are no longer talking about demand for personnel, but about demand for certain kinds of work and opportunities. Values enter the picture and we are looking at cultural rather than material conditions.

Structural Versus Humanistic Organization Theory

The school of organizational theory that focuses on performance and productivity is structural organization theory (Bolman & Deal, 1984). As we will see in Chapter 10, structural theory focuses on the one best way to do a job or job tasks, and the one best way to organize the positions corresponding to these jobs within an organizational hierarchy or structure. Its opposite among organization theories is humanistic organization theory which puts the workforce first (e.g., Bolman & Deal, 1984, p. 65), usually because it is understood that the workforce assures long-term productivity if it is well cared for, sometimes because of the belief that technology has solved production problems and that work organizations now should increasingly play the role of stimulating learning environments. No doubt the latter view would be regarded as premature by many.

Performance- Versus Maintenance-Oriented Values

Structural organization theory is usually espoused by authoritarian managers whose primary concern is immediate performance and productivity. On the other side of the fence are managers espousing humanistic organization theory focusing on the nurturing and maintenance of the organization in general and its people in particular. The performance-oriented manager is only concerned about the work sphere. The maintenance-oriented manager is willing to take into account the life sphere of workers.

Different variants of these two managerial styles have been described by a large number of researchers (see, for example, Certo & Applebaum, 1983). The two styles reflect the cultural conditions embodied by the organizational theories with which they are associated: the tough-minded performance or the tender-minded humanistic values of groups of managers, of management teams, or of an organizational culture.

THE WORK AND LIFE SPHERES OF THE INDIVIDUAL

In some respects the work/life dichotomy is more complex on the level of the individual than on those of the work organization and society in general. As we saw, cultural conditions become psychological ones when we talk about the individual. Furthermore, these psychological conditions are characteristics of the person rather than characteristics of the environment. Finally, where there is a person, there is behavior. Person characteristics both determine and are shaped by behavior. In a sense the work and life spheres are no longer just different parts of our environment, of the society in which we live. On the level of the individual, they include aspects of the environment, the person, and the person's behavior.

To take an example: Harry D. is a convenience store operator. His work sphere encompasses the store, the industrial values like need achievement, which makes him spend twelve hours a day in it in the expectation of future wealth, and his work behavior itself, which involves making small and big decisions. He changes as a result of making these decisions. For example, he might become more expert at identifying situations in which a decision should be made on the spot and others in which it should be delayed.

Harry's life sphere dominates on his day off, say Monday. A reliable acquaintance looks after his store. Harry spends time with his two young children and his wife at home because he attaches great significance to having a family, to being a father. He washes the car, engaging in a routine activity which relaxes him. He even reads a book about matters beyond the store, such as religion or death, which raises his level of consciousness.

Both Harry's work and life spheres clearly include aspects not only of the environment, but also personal characteristics of Harry as well as aspects of his behavior. We will return to the behavioral aspect in Chapter 9; in this chapter the focus remains on the material and cultural or psychological conditions shown in Exhibit 1–1.

Fixed Tasks Versus Flexible Demands

We saw that the work sphere of society is characterized by constraints. The same is true of the work sphere of the individual. Here it is specific conditions which impinge on particular people that are of interest. Most jobs are fairly routine. Specific tasks have to be executed: bottles inspected, passengers driven to airports, rugs rolled and shipped.

The life sphere also makes demands. A child has to be fed, a home cleaned, a car taken to the garage, and the lawn mowed. However, there is more choice here, the demands are more flexible. One can leave the field, say "no!" or "not now," delay things. The window can be repaired next week. The child can be left in the hands of a capable aunt. In addition, the demands of the life sphere are usually the result of relatively freely made earlier choices: the choice to have children, to buy a house, and so forth.

This difference between fixed tasks and flexible demands of work and life sphere, respectively, applies only in general. There are many exceptions. For example, the self-employed worker probably has more choice in the work sphere than the handicapped person in the life sphere. Nevertheless, for the majority of workers work is more constraining than life.

Training Requirements Versus Conditions Conducive to Educational Activity

A part of a particular individual's work sphere is the training demands made by the job, career, or employer. One has to fit into one's slot within the techno-economic structure. What may be required ranges from the specific motor skills of a seamstress to the ability to apply the Performance Evaluation and Review Technique (PERT) to a major construction project. It may also range from a patient disposition to an aggressive go-getter attitude.

Meeting such demands may in turn require attending a three-hour workshop on the use of the latest photocopying machine or pursuing a three-year liberal arts program offering many options. However, the training requirements tend to be more like the workshops on photocopying than the liberal arts program. They are usually designed to meet the employer's needs and the employee's work sphere interests, rather than the employee's personal, private, most central interests. They are creatures of the work sphere and one would not expect them to be otherwise.

On the other hand, the educational opportunities, both material and cultural, discussed on the level of society impinge on the individual's life sphere. The scholarship given to Jane C. to pursue Greek philosophy changes her material conditions and may lead her to an entirely new outlook on life, perhaps dialectical in nature and dominated by the notion of *arete* or excellence. The cultural values transmitted to Harry D. as a child are cultural determinants which, once they are assimilated by Harry, become psychological determinants which may impel him to seek self-fulfillment in the business world.

Roles and Personal Values in the Work and Life Spheres

Roles we assume and values we adopt are person characteristics, the person now moves into the forefront of attention. Since the person often sees work as something that is externally imposed, something done because one's basic deficit needs leave one little choice, and since he or she tends to identify with the life sphere rather than the work sphere, the life sphere also becomes the primary object of interest at this point. We have moved from the work sphere of society, at the top left corner of Exhibit 1–1, to its diametrical opposite, the life sphere of the individual represented by the bottom right corner.

A society may espouse industrial values, as the United States did in the 1950s, or post-industrial values, as many Americans did in the 1960s. However, these values are not necessarily adopted by the individual, just as many educational opportunities provided by society do not become actual opportunities for a particular individual. There may even be conflict between the values held by society and those held by the individual. In short, we must distinguish between personally held and collective industrial and post-industrial values.

Within the life sphere the individual is likely to have a reasonably consistent set of values and a sense of identity or self. True, people tend to identify with their successes in the work sphere and their careers. However, such identifications turn out to stand on clay feet when things turn sour, the stock market crashes, the job is declared redundant. The real identity of the individual is rooted in the life sphere. It is within that sphere that we ultimately say "This is what I am. This is what I like." The sense of self is more likely to be inspired by the media, by Archie Bunker or Heavy Metal, than by the handsome trainer sent by the Xerox Corporation.

In fact, the real self is likely to be left behind as we go to work to play assigned roles as calm mediator, efficient photocopy machine operator, or docile assembly-line worker. We forget about the roles we assumed ourselves in the life sphere, the roles of conservative source of wisdom or loud, raucous mass of self-expressive ectoplasm. We may not be successful. Conflict is likely under these conditions, both within and between our work and life spheres. Here is where the gap between work and life is particularly evident.

Dissatisfaction in Work and Satisfaction in Life

We tend to be dissatisfied with the work sphere and satisfactions tend to be associated with the life sphere. Of course, the family, the video machine, the vacation in Greece can be disappointments, but in general we have greater control over the life sphere than the work sphere and can thus often organize it to provide more satisfaction.

Maslow's (1954) distinction between deficit and growth needs is useful here. Deficit needs are tissue needs. They are either physiological, like hunger and thirst, or have some recognizable physiological basis, like the need for security. They arise when something—water, food, minimal comfort provided by shelter—is missing. They play a crucial role in the work sphere; without them most people would be sitting on the beach rather than sweating in factories.

Growth needs are described as uniquely human needs. They are far removed from physical processes that we understand. Robert White (1959) calls them neurogenic rather than viscerogenic, based on what goes on in our brains rather than our stomachs. They include needs to learn, to develop, to "grow." Employers are not concerned about their employees' growth needs. They have a different function: to create wealth. The growth needs are thus associated with the employee's life sphere rather than the work sphere.

Frederick Herzberg and his colleagues (Herzberg, Mausner, & Snyderman, 1959) have argued that dissatisfaction is the result of unmet deficit needs, while satisfaction is the result of met growth needs. That does not surprise anyone. However, they also argue that meeting deficit needs does not produce satisfaction and that failure to meet growth needs does not produce dissatisfaction. In their view, giving workers more money does not make them work harder or exhibit greater loyalty as a result of greater satisfaction, and the person who does not have the opportunity to nurture a talent as a still life painter will not feel, except perhaps for some vague ennui, dissatisfaction.

The analysis by Herzberg et al. is controversial but it contains enough intuitively acceptable truth to be taken seriously. It suggests that the work sphere is associated with perceived dissatisfactions and resulting stress, while the life sphere is more likely to offer opportunities to meet growth needs and hence satisfaction.

This brings us to the end of the overview of the work and life spheres of society, of work organizations, and of individuals. It appears fruitful to deal with the two spheres on the macro-level of society and micro-level of the individual, and to treat the work organization as a middle level on which the two interact or interface. The work organization is primarily an aspect of the work sphere. But it has implications for the life sphere of its workers. Furthermore, work organizations should be more concerned with the life sphere, and, according to some, they can afford to be concerned with it in a post-industrial society no longer dependent on relentless and backbreaking labor. Work organizations can thus play a crucial role in efforts to reintegrate work and life in the coming post-industrial society.

If the work organization is the level on which the micro-level of the individual and the macro-level of society interface, the subject matter divides itself into two parts: work and life on the level of society and on the level of the individual. Thus the two parts of this book. On each of the two levels we have to look more closely at each of the two spheres, at the relationships between them, and at the possibilities for bridging the debilitating gap between them.

2

Tools, Machines, and Computers

Chapters 2 to 5 deal with the work sphere on the macro-level of society. There is, of course, more to it than the material and cultural conditions which represent it in Exhibit 1–1; nevertheless these conditions provide some idea of its nature. Since the work sphere is primarily concerned with material needs, it is the two material conditions listed in the Exhibit which are of particular interest: the constraints dictated by the collective objectives of meeting primarily material needs and the demand of the productive system for, and supply of, personnel. Collective industrial values and materialistic determinism, where the latter is a way of looking at the world, exemplify the cultural conditions of society's work sphere. They will appear less prominently in the discussion.

BELL'S THREE STAGES OF SOCIETY: FROM ECONOMIC TO SOCIAL CONCERNS

The work sphere is the starting point of this book since, if Brecht, Marx, Harris and other materialistic or economic determinists are right, "grub comes before morality," that is, the work sphere addressing our material needs comes before the life sphere addressing the less urgent higher level needs for self-fulfillment and growth.

The first step is thus to look at the work sphere of society in the context of three widely recognized steps of social evolution: the pre-industrial, industrial, and post-industrial stages. What form does the

Exhibit 2–1
Aspects of the Pre-Industrial, Industrial, and Post-Industrial Stages

Aspects	Stages		
	Pre-Industrial	Industrial	Post-Industrial
Concerns	physical	economic	social
Source of power (Bell, 1973)	land	capital	knowledge
Technology (Bell, 1973)	tools	machines	telematics, computers
Nature of work (Arendt, 1958)	labor	work (machino-facturing)	action (social)
Rhythm (Arendt, 1958)	nature	machine	self
Place of work	farm, cottage	central plant, central office	electronic cottage, virtual office

work sphere assume in these stages and how does the relationship between the work sphere and the life sphere change as a society evolves through them?

One of the best ways to understand something is to find out how it came about. Three types of elements appear particularly useful in understanding the development of the work sphere, that is, of Bell's techno-economic structure. These are its tools, its machines, and its electronic information processing and transmitting equipment centered around computers, optical fiber transmission channels, and robots.

One can argue that as society evolves through the pre-industrial, industrial, and into the post-industrial stages, its attention shifts from basic physical concerns about survival, to economic concerns about surplus production and security, to social and psychological concerns about meaningful relationships and self-actualization. The old issue of material versus cultural conditions arises in a third form here. Up to this point we have differentiated between material and cultural conditions and between the belief that material conditions have priority over cultural ones, or vice versa. It turns out that we also have to distinguish between physical (clearly material), economic (fairly obviously material), and social (cultural) concerns of society.

This shift is shown in Exhibit 2–1 based on Bell (1973). According to Bell, land was the source of wealth and power, and the hand-held tool (the hoe, the axe, the plow) was the principal means for fashioning an environment more conducive to physical survival in the pre-industrial or agricultural society. The industrial society resounded with the clanging and whirring of machines, its source of wealth was the factory generating the goods available for sale and exchange in a local, national, or international economy. Bell calls the current post-industrial stage both the "knowledge society" and the "service society." Its principal source of wealth, power, or influence is information, its characteristic instrument is the computer, its concerns are primarily social and the majority of its workforce is occupied in the service sector.

Philosopher Hannah Arendt's (1958) distinction between labor, work, and action is also relevant here. Labor, as she sees it, is executed to the rhythm of nature. It is "forced upon us by necessity" (p. 157) and makes bare subsistence possible. Work in Arendt's sense is often referred to as manufacturing, but one ought to call it machinofacturing— making by machine. It is "prompted by utility" (p. 157) and surrounds us with things that have a certain permanence. It is executed to the unforgiving rhythm of the machine. Action implies the presence of others, it is social in nature and each act may be the beginning of something new and unexpected. It is, in some way, executed to the rhythm of the self. Labor, work, and action thus seem to characterize the pre-industrial, industrial, and post-industrial stages of society.

Exhibit 2–1 also suggests that the nature of the place of work has changed across the three stages. In the pre-industrial society most work was done on the farm or in the cottage. Of course, in the emerging towns and cities, merchants and craftsmen also pursued their commercial objectives. In the industrial society, work is done in large-scale central plants and office buildings, where major power sources can be tapped and where supervisors can keep an eye on employees and exercise control.

In the post-industrial society alternative places of work are emerging. There are trends toward a decentralization of the workplace. Some corporations distribute their workforce over satellite work centers in the suburbs. Some people work at home on computers connected to other computers; their home has become an *electronic cottage* (Toffler, 1980). This does not necessarily mean creative and happy keyboarding in bucolic surroundings or complete integration of work and life spheres. Much of the work done by the new homeworkers is routine updating of repetitive insurance and medical records so vital in this information society (Morf & Alexander, 1984).

In the pre-industrial or agricultural society work and life were one. For the feudal serf, life was probably mostly work. For the free farmer and artisan, jumping off the pallet with a song on his lips and ready to tend his animals or create another sword or cabinet, work was perhaps mostly life. In the industrial stage, work and life became divorced. During the present transition from industrial to post-industrial stage, the prospects for the relationship between work and life are unclear.

There are forces which currently tend to increase the gap. For many managers, the new electronic technology that drives the transition merely provides the means to automate the office; to routinize, centralize, and monitor relentlessly the work of information processing. For some idealists, it raises expectations that traditional, compulsory, and routine work will soon be done by robots, computers, and electronic communication systems, leaving people free to concentrate on personal development and the pursuit of gratifying experiences. Such unrealistic expectations make even moderately routine work unbearable. In either case, the gap between work and life is accentuated.

On the other hand, the new technology raises the possibility of assigning all routine work to machines and, in the European phrase, of "humanizing work" so that more competent workers will intelligently pursue the nonroutine cases that currently confound our information systems.

It is important to focus on these opportunities offered by the new technology and the current transition to the post-industrial stage for reintegrating work and life into a more harmonious larger system. On the macro-level of society this should encourage a culture, in the anthropologist's broad rather than Bell's circumscribed sense, that is not wracked by conflict between two of its most important subcultures. On the micro-level of the individual worker it should reduce the conflict between external demands imposed by "them," "the company," etc., and personal needs to grow and develop, to be one's own authentic self, or at least to be left alone.

THE WORK SPHERE AS STRUCTURE

If there is one thing that differentiates the work sphere from the nonwork spheres of society, it is the fact that it is highly structured. The work sphere exhibits certain types of structure and it exhibits these types of structure to a noticeable degree. It is contended here that it is this structuredness that sets the work sphere apart from the life sphere and produces the gap and even clash between them. As Exhibit 1–1 showed, the work sphere imposes constraints. It prescribes behavior from how we dress to what motions we execute and what we produce. In the life sphere, the sphere of (relative) liberty, we make our own decisions. The life sphere is less structured and less inclined to dictate and impose external prescriptions and demands.

The term *structure* is difficult to define, but it connotes immediately things like stability, limits, and expectations of restraint. By examining the contexts in which the term is used one can acquire a more specific sense of what it means.

Sometimes the term refers to a number of parts arranged in definite ways. A building is a structure, a number of stones, logs, or bricks arranged to form rectangular walls, and so forth. The Latin word *struere*, from which the word *structure* evolved, refers to such an organized set of elements forming a building. Structure in this original sense connotes something static, stable, and tangible.

There are those who define structure more abstractly as a set of relations. The stable or static thing here is not the elements, but the relations among them. Structure in this sense may assume the form of a mathematical system, for example, the system of real numbers is a structure. Robert Pirsig (1975, p. 93) explains structure in this sense in simple terms. He notes that operators produce structure, that the operator *contains* leads to hierarchical structure, that the operator *causes* leads to chain structures, that other examples of operators leading to different structures are *exists*, *equals*, and *implies*.

Still others go a little further and emphasize the organization, pattern, or form of a set of elements constituting a structure. Perhaps this is the sense of the word we have in mind when we talk about the structure of the body, of the social structure, and of cognitive structures.

Definitions of structure thus focus on elements or parts, on relations among elements, and on the pattern of elements and relations viewed as a single whole. The common aspect of different definitions seems to be the implication that the degree of structure depends on the number of different classes of elements or parts, and on the number and types of relations among them.

A cubic foot of gas has little structure: There is only one class of parts—molecules of certain chemical elements or compounds—and there are no discernible stable relations that constrain the behavior of these parts. The molecules are in a state of high entropy, that is, a state of low structuredness, and their behavior consists of the random Brownian movements familiar to students of high school chemistry.

The modern techno-economic structure on the other hand, consists of many different elements. Depending on one's frame of reference, these elements include the different sectors of the economy, the different types of work organizations, the occupations the workforce fits into, and the tools, machines, and computer systems that constitute its technology. There are many stable relationships among these elements, for example, consumer-supplier relationships, expected roles and functions of individuals in different positions ranging from firstline worker to owner, the relationships between the tools, machines, and computer systems comprising an assembly line or a larger productive system such as a number of production and supplier plants.

TOOLS AND PRE-INDUSTRIAL SOCIETY

We now turn to the question of how this modern techno-economic structure, our work sphere, came about. Since "grub comes before morality," it has a very long history.

The study of prehistoric times reveals the startling fact that the antecedents of many familiar features of European settlements, and hence of American rural settlements founded by European immigrants, go back thousands of years. In Britain, farmers have grown cereals for more than 5000 years. Between 3000 and 5000 years ago they started to build hamlets consisting of rectangular timber houses, to raise domesticated cows and pigs, to use oxen to pull their plows. The first artisans as we still know them today—stonemasons, carpenters, blacksmiths and wheelwrights—started to ply their trades in Britain more than 3000 years ago. In Europe it is possible even today to stumble on a sleepy hamlet that has not changed much since prehistoric times. It may, of course, sport the odd discarded Coca Cola bottle, rock music may blare from some transistor radio, someone may even have installed a gasoline pump.

The pre-industrial and agricultural stage of social development started more than 10,000 years ago in the Middle East and it has by no means ended for the majority of the world's population. Even the United States still constituted a largely pre-industrial society as little as a century ago. The majority of its population was engaged in agriculture, fishing, and forestry. Its chief resource was its land, its economy was based on what its people could extract with hoes, shovels, and nets from land and sea.

In short, the pre-industrial or agricultural society had a rudimentary techno-economic structure made up of tools, farming implements like the plow, farmers and artisans. At least in its medieval European form, it had its managers: the nobility and the officials representing its usually fairly straightforward and possessive interests.

This rudimentary techno-economic structure "organized production" and "allocated goods" and some basic services. More concretely, it put food on the table with a certain predictability for relatively large populations. While the hunters and gatherers who had preceded the agriculturalists were apparently quite capable of feeding themselves in a few working hours per day (Sahlins, 1972), their mode of production required large territories and low population density. What was new about the techno-economic structure of the agriculturalists was its ability to feed and clothe much larger and denser populations.

Civilizations emerge when there is surplus manpower, when a certain proportion of the workforce can meet the subsistence needs of the entire society. If a part of the potential workforce can handle all the necessary agricultural work, there are some people left who can pursue something else. These people can specialize with confidence that those needs which they do not attend to will be met by the efforts of fellow citizens. Thus, innovative and literate civilizations of Antiquity grew out of the conserving and illiterate stone-age farming village. These new social structures engaged not only in the labor necessary for subsistence, but also in "work" in Arendt's sense. Pyramids, temples, palaces, roads, and aqueducts were built and have survived until our time.

The surplus manpower no longer needed in the fields usually evolved into specialists: scribes, warriors, priests, architects, supervisors of work gangs. More than that: The surplus manpower also evolved into workers with highly specific functions that sound modern indeed. As early as the 4th century B.C., the Greek historian Xenophon observed that:

> it is, of course, impossible for a man of many trades to be proficient in all of them. In large cities . . . one trade alone, and very often even less than a whole trade, is enough to support a man . . . There are places . . . where one man earns a living by only stitching shoes, another by cutting them out, another by sewing the uppers together. (Cited from Mossé, 1969, p. 79)

Close to a thousand years after Xenophon, the inhabitants of the city of Rome were fed by a complex state-run organization that supervised shippers transporting wheat from Africa, dockers and weighers in the ports of Ostia and Porto, boatmen who shipped the wheat upriver to the city, millers and bakers who processed, baked and distributed bread in the city itself. At that time, during the decline of the Roman Empire, tradesmen like these were not free to leave their jobs since the increasingly troubled Empire badly needed both their labor and their taxes (Mossé, 1969), although at least the number of actual slaves among them was much smaller than it had been during earlier centuries in Greece and the Roman Empire.

The transition between Antiquity and the Middle Ages was characterized by turmoil and poverty. Often there was no authority in sufficiently good shape to administer and govern, and where there was such authority the taxes it levied were confiscatory. In the words of historian Colin McEvedy: "It is a telling measure of the burden of taxation that in the last century [of the Roman Empire] the free-holding peasantry voluntarily liquidated itself . . . In return for title to the peasant's land, the landowner guarded the civil interests of his client and as far as possible shielded him from taxes" (McEvedy, 1967, pp. 8–9).

In the slave-holding societies of Greece and Rome, and in the feudal system of early medieval Europe there was little need to hold work in high esteem. Slaves or serfs were destined to labor, and the Bible told the grumbling and toiling masses in no uncertain terms that "if any would not work, neither should he eat" (2:Thessalonians 3:10).

As the Roman Empire crumbled and the Dark Ages engulfed Europe, Christianity kept a few flickering lights of civilization burning in isolated monasteries. From some of these, specifically from the monasteries of the Benedictine monks, emanated the first European version of the doctrine that to work is to be virtuous. The followers of the fourth-century monk, St. Benedict of Ursia, charged into the world with the battle cry *ora et labora* ("pray and work"). A new spirit was abroad which eventually, together with other factors, led to the rise of the spirit of capitalism, the Protestant ethic, the Industrial Revolution and industrial society.

MACHINES AND INDUSTRIAL SOCIETY

The value system characteristic of the techno-economic structure today is industrial, and the industrial stage which generated it in Western Europe and the United States emerged with the development of more effective use of energy sources like wood, water, and wind to power machinery like grain mills, water pumps in fields and mines, trip hammers for crushing iron ore and bellows for smelting it. The roots of industrial activity go back very far, but the fall of the Roman Empire and the emergence of medieval Europe are a major transition after which industrialism as we know it gradually emerged. It exploded into full bloom in the middle of the eighteenth century in Britain.

The feudal system provided *ad hoc* government in a Europe too ravaged by endless conflict and insatiable Roman tax collectors to generate centralized and well-organized government. Jacques Heers (1965) describes the northern Europe of the ninth century A.D., for example, as " 'a few oases of culture' lost in the immense 'deserts' of forest, marshes, and mountain meadows" (p. 10), and he notes that the "tool made of iron [was] still a luxury" (p. 19). During the feudal period in post-Roman Europe, subsistence was still or again the major concern and there was little of the specialization Xenophon had observed in classical Greece.

But wealth increased, power became more centralized, and larger political entities took the place of the feudal lord's fief. The rural population became more mobile and the towns emerged as centers of trade and manufacture. Guilds of tradesmen and craftsmen had flourished in Antiquity, but they rose to particular prominence in the northern Europe of the Middle Ages. They constituted the major power base in most towns and cities of the period and their members often occupied the highest posts from mayor on downwards. They regulated commercial activity and the quality and standards of production. Their most lasting function was to train apprentices and turn them into journeymen and masters of their trade.

The medieval master craftsman's pride in his work was probably not something completely new. But the advent of "free labor" was. For the first time in the history of northern Europe there were sizeable numbers of men and some women who were not obliged to work for a feudal baron or other master and who had some choice in what they would do to feed themselves. For the first time there was a reasonably mobile workforce not unconditionally ready to sweat any more than necessary. An ideology of work was required to convince them that work is a worthwhile activity and perhaps even that work is more than a means to the end of putting food on the table. The work ethic of Weber, which preceded the Industrial Revolution by a few centuries, is the work ethic of the middle class, or at least of those with the freedom to choose among ways of feeding themselves and, sometimes, of becoming rich.

Not everyone was, or is, in that happy position. During most historical periods, the majority labors because it has no choice. It is here that the gap between work and life, the world of one's own drudgery and that of the privileged who hunt pheasant and play polo, becomes a chasm. If anything, the advent of the Industrial Revolution increased the numbers of those who had no choice but to work on the employer's conditions.

Those who have no choice also have a work ethic, one imposed on them. It is the work ethic of the working class, an ethic dictating docility, reliability, willingness to endure. It is espoused because it qualifies one for a job. It reflects necessity rather than freedom and it compelled most people to work long before the Industrial Revolution.

Britain's Industrial Revolution changed with dramatic swiftness the social structure, the nature of work, and the standard of living. A new age of power (steam, water) and machinery (spinning machines, steam engines) had dawned. The United States and continental Europe soon followed the British lead but with somewhat less speed and somewhat less upheaval. Industrialization in the United States was, however, characterized by an even greater reliance on mechanization than in Britain. Michael Argyle (1972, p. 28) suggests that this was due to a shortage of labor and an abundance of land. But an additional factor must have been the innovativeness and enterprise peculiar to America.

A century and a half ago, the French traveller Alexis de Tocqueville wrote:

Future events, whatever they may be, will not deprive the Americans of their climate or their inland seas, their great rivers or their exuberant soil. Nor will bad laws, revolutions, and anarchy be able to obliterate that love of prosperity and spirit of enterprise which seem to be the distinctive characteristics of their race. (de Tocqueville, 1963, vol. 1, p. 432)

This energy and enterprise manifested itself in the forerunners of today's "captains of industry," in the Carnegies, the DuPonts, the Mellons, the Rockefellers, the Vanderbilts and many others. They were tough and determined, and not unduly charitable toward their workers and customers. They laid the foundation of American power, a fact that is reflected by the universities, foundations, museums, research institutes, art galleries, foundations and even a few chapels that bear their names. They were the catalysts that mobilized Americans into the activity which produced industrial giants like Pittsburgh and Detroit whose factories and steel mills were instrumental in stopping the enemy in two world wars.

The new industrial cities were not places of sunshine and rich vegetation, and their inhabitants were not delighted by their work. Few have expressed the effects of assembly-line work better than the French novelist Louis-Ferdinand Celine. When the protagonist of Celine's *Journey to the End of the Night* proudly points out his educational background to a company doctor screening job applicants at one of Detroit's auto plants, he is told: "We've no use for intellectuals . . . What we need is chimpanzees" (Celine, 1934, p. 223).

Chimpanzees abound in Aldous Huxley's vision of the Brave New World, in which test tube babies are nurtured and conditioned on conveyor belts to be epsilons, simple creatures superbly suited for routine work; in which time is measured in "years of our Ford," and in which V.I.P.s are addressed as "your fordship" (Huxley, 1946).

Smokestacks, foundries, and giant factories are reminders of an industrial past whose economic activities appeared to be a positive-sum game in which the winnings far outweighed the losses, and which serenely ignored the social costs that often balance economic gains. We are now more aware of these social costs. Health endangering fluids and gases ooze out of thousands of haphazardly used landfill sites throughout the country. Acid rain kills lakes in vast parts of the eastern United States and Canada. Millions of workers, treated like chimpanzees, are cynical and unmotivated.

In dialectical fashion, these factors have generated their own opposites: movements to protect the ecosystem, to curb the American lust for driving oversized and overpowered cars, to give the workers more rights and responsibilities. One thing seems clear: In America, the industrial society, that is, the traditional techno-economic structure and work sphere, peaked some time ago.

THE TWO WORK ETHICS OF INDUSTRIAL SOCIETY

The Industrial Society and the work ethic are usually associated with each other, and the work ethic is usually thought of as that described by Weber, that of ambitious entrepreneurs. We saw in the preceding section, however, that there are really two quite different work ethics:

those of the middle class and of the working class (see MacMichael, 1974).

The Alienation of the Working Class: Matter over Mind

The work ethic as tool. Employers of the 1870s instructed their workers in a manner that sounded quaint until the recent discovery of drug testing by intrusive managers not entirely respectful of the workers' sensitivities and need for privacy. For example:

Working hours shall be 7:00 A.M. to 8:00 p.m. every evening but the Sabbath. On the Sabbath, everyone is expected to be in the Lord's House.

Or:

All employees are expected to be in bed by 10:00 P.M. Except: Each male employee may be given one evening a week for courting purposes and two evenings a week in the Lord's House. (Both passages cited from Bass, Shackleton, & Rosenstein, 1979, p. 82)

Fifty years apparently did not bring about much change in employer attitudes. In the 1920s, Sir Frederick Williams-Smith, general manager of the Bank of Montreal, recommended to employees such virtues as temperance, concentration, occasional introspection, care of the body, punctuality, and work. Of work he said that it is "the open sesame to every portal" and on temperance he advised that "if you touch stimulants before you are twenty-five years of age you are a fool" (cited from Newman, 1975, p. 101).

Another eager advocate of the Protestant ethic was the prolific nineteenth century British churchman Charles Kingsley. In his *Town and Country Sermons* he wrote:

Thank God every morning, when you get up, that you have something to do that day which must be done, whether you like or not. Being forced to work, and forced to do your best, will breed in you temperance and self-control, diligence and strength of will, cheerfulness and content and a hundred virtues which the idle man will never know. (Kingsley, 1969, vol. 21, p. 273)

Kingsley (1969, Vol. 1, p. 253) even burst into poetry:

> He that does not live by toil
> Has no right on English soil

This must have been an attempt to nip in the bud what in the 1960s became famous as the "British disease"—the tendency of truculent labor and inept management to bring the entire country to a halt once in a while and slow down its economic activity most of the time. More generally, attitudes like those of employers and clergymen of the late nineteenth and early twentieth century give one the feeling that the Protestant ethic could easily be turned into a tool of exploitation, that the pursuit of virtue may sometimes have been a pursuit of a docile workforce. Reverend Kingsley sounds as fervent a proponent of virtues that will benefit the entrepreneurs and owners as some industrial and organizational psychologists in America do today.

Marx's alienation. Given the exploitation of workers fostered by the Industrial Revolution, it is not surprising that joy in one's work was not universal. While Weber and his followers concentrated on the positive attitude to work of the entrepreneur, Marx addressed himself to the negative attitude of those who toiled for the entrepreneur. In one of his earlier statements on the subject, contained in his *Economic and Philosophic Manuscripts of 1844* (Marx, 1975), he distinguished between the workers' alienation or estrangement from their products, from the production process, and from their own selves.

The workers are separated or alienated from the product of their efforts for a number of reasons: it is indistinguishable from the products of their fellow workers engaged with them in routinized and mechanized production, it is seized immediately by the employer and dispatched to the market, and the individual worker's role in the production process is limited to specific and repetitive operations. Again and again, Marx points out that, unlike the craftsmen of the Middle Ages, industrial workers can neither identify with nor be proud of what they produce:

the worker is related to the product of his labour as to an alien object. . . . The alienation of the worker in his product means not only that his labour becomes an object, . . . but that it exists outside him, independently, as something alien to him. . . . [The] life which he has conferred on the object confronts him as something hostile and alien. (Marx, 1975, p. 272)

Perhaps more concrete is the alienation from the production process:

labour is external to the worker, . . . in his work, [the worker] does not affirm himself but denies himself, does not feel content but unhappy, does not develop freely his physical and mental energy but mortifies his body and ruins his mind. (Marx, 1975, p. 274)

But the ultimate alienation was the workers' alienation from their own selves. The production process from which they were alienated robbed them of the opportunity to lead really productive lives, in the sense of allowing them to express themselves in their work, to take pride in it, and to form images of themselves as persons of worth leading meaningful lives:

. . . [the worker] only feels himself freely active in his animal functions—eating, drinking, procreating, or at most in his dwelling and in dressing-up, etc.; and in his human functions he no longer feels himself to be anything but an animal (Marx, 1975, pp. 274–275).

In Marx's view, the workplace was a dreary and often cruel place of exploitation, and since the workers had no energy left for constructive pursuits beyond the work, the life sphere was not much more comforting.

Addressing issues on the macro-level of society, Marx argued that material conditions producing, and produced by, the system of production, the bourgeoisie, capitalism, or what we refer to today as the techno-economic structure, shape the nonwork values of a culture (e.g., Marx, 1859. See Tucker, 1972). In general, scarcity prevails and Exhibit 2–1 generally reflects a process of change initiated and determined by economic factors.

The Work Ethic of the Middle Class: Mind over Matter

Cultural conditions such as religious ideas and values play a major role in Weber's analysis of the work ethic of the middle class. The material conditions dictating values to the working class recede. Two of the figures whose ideas and values particularly attracted Weber's attention were the Protestant reformer John Calvin and the American statesman and patriot Benjamin Franklin.

Calvinism. Weber argued that religious values associated with Protestantism have been a major determinant of the rise of capitalism and hence of the major form of production adopted in western industrial societies. Specifically, he attributed to the Calvinists a need to act like individuals predestined for salvation. This entailed constant, disciplined, and organized effort and the attainment of visible achievements constituting signals to others and oneself of one's happy destiny. As Weber wrote, for the Calvinist

good works . . . are indispensable as a sign of election. They are the technical means, not of purchasing salvation, but of getting rid of the fear of damnation. Thus the Calvinist . . . creates his own . . . conviction [of salvation]. But this creation cannot, as in Catholicism, consist in a gradual accumulation of individual good works to one's credit. [It must consist of] . . . a systematic self-

control which at every moment stands before the inexorable alternative, chosen
or damned. (Weber, 1958, p. 115)

This seems to place Weber squarely on the opposite side of the fence
from Marx. Where Weber apparently thought that Calvinists imbued
by religious zeal created a free enterprise economic system, the Marxist
position is that the capitalist economic system shaped the religious values of the bourgeoisie.

In *The Acquisitive Society* the economist R. H. Tawney (1952), a disci-
ple of Weber, further developed the idea that cultural determinants are
the primary movers. Studying the second half of the sixteenth century,
he saw a major shift from "activities . . . which [embody] . . . the
idea of social purpose" (p. 9) to individualism, from a focus on common ends to one on individual rights. Individuals and hence society
came to value acquisitiveness. In Tawney's view, acquisitive individuals shaped the capitalist system of production and its attendant excesses and exploitation.

Calvin preached a doctrine of predestination: Everyone belonged either
to the elect or the damned. While there was no way one could change
one's status and no way of even telling whether one belonged to the
lucky or the unlucky group, it was nevertheless of critical importance
to show one's faith by acting as if one had no doubts and as if one
lived in a state of perfect grace. The best way to accomplish this was
to immerse oneself in worldly affairs and to lead a life of effective,
hard, and well-organized work. According to Weber, Calvin did not
trust feeling; he attached importance to the objective, concrete, usually
material results of work. For the English Puritans, cousins of the stern
Calvinists, work had an added attraction: It was the favored ascetic
technique to ward off the "unclean life."

The Calvinist work ethic is not easy to understand. One explanation
that may help, however, is that offered by historian Arnold Toynbee
(1955, vol. 5, pp. 615–618) in a note on *Fatalism as a Spiritual Tonic*. He
argues that deterministic or fatalistic creeds are symptoms of social dis-
integration leading to violent action in flagrant but merely apparent
contradiction to the belief that everything is already settled, that human effort will not change things. The reason the contradiction is merely
apparent is that predestinarianism is a "pick-me-up" for people who
are externally controlled, that is, who have lost faith in their "own
power to control events." Predestinarianism is "an attempt to fortify a
weakening human will by making the bold assumption that this human will is coincident with the Will of God or with the Law of Nature. . ." Toynbee notes that this process is illustrated not only by the
Calvinists, but by groups and movements as diverse as the Jewish
Zealots, Arab terrorists, the Janissaries of the Turkish Empire, the

Mahdists of the Sudan in the nineteenth century, and even the less extreme and nonreligious Marxist and liberal movements of nineteenth-century Europe.

American pragmatism. In the American patriot Benjamin Franklin, Weber saw the embodiment of the spirit of modern capitalism, a capitalism that is not just concerned with the judicious use of capital for the sole purpose of increasing it, but that is also a set of rules, an ethic, telling people how to live. In his *Necessary hints for those that would be rich* and in his *Advice to young tradesmen*, Franklin opined that:

time is money . . . credit is money . . . money is of the prolific, generating nature. Money can beget money, and its offspring can beget more . . . After industry and frugality, nothing contributes more to the raising of a young man in the world than punctuality and justice in all his dealings . . . The sound of your hammer at five in the morning, or eight at night, heard by a creditor, makes him easy six months longer . . . (Cited from Weber, 1958, pp. 48–49)

Internal control. Rapid British industrialization between 1760 and 1830 was the result of many factors: the new machines in textile production, the steam motor, wealth concentrated in few hands at a time of low interest rates, a rural population of tenants driven off the land by wealthy land owners interested in meeting new demands by raising sheep and so forth, and increased agricultural productivity. But among the immediate factors, Weber's Protestant ethic must have been crucial. It is hard to imagine the Industrial Revolution without a large number of eager entrepreneurs who have adopted the work ethic and who are trying to get their workers to adopt it.

The Protestant ethic or work ethic of the middle class comes in different variants and the entrepreneurs of the Industrial Revolution were not typically Calvinist predestinarians. On the contrary, they were what psychologists today call "internally controlled" (Rotter, 1966). They expected their efforts to result in just rewards. Ironically, this belief that one actually determines one's outcomes or fate is very likely the product of having been rewarded for working hard in the past by external agents placed there for, and acting on the basis of, reasons beyond the lucky learner's control. Entrepreneurs reap rewards and see them as the result of their meritorious efforts. The less fortunate who rarely are reinforced are more likely to be "externally controlled," that is, to believe that what happens to them is the result of chance and generally bad luck (Rotter, 1966).

The worldview of the successful entrepreneurs is thus likely to be a little distorted. From their vantage point, those condemned to sweat in factories have just not tried hard enough to better themselves and to become internally controlled entrepreneurs themselves. Their belief that people get what they deserve facilitates exploitation. And exploitation there certainly was. It included child labor, substantial fines for actual and even alleged lateness, contracts that bound the employee but not the employer, low wages, grimy factories, and twelve-hour workdays.

Where the work ethic of the working class is associated with necessity and economic determinants, that of the middle class is associated with cultural determinants, dictated by mind rather than matter, and— at least as it has evolved since Calvin's difficult predestinarianism— with a certain freedom of choice.

COMPUTERS AND POST-INDUSTRIAL SOCIETY

Long before it had passed its peak, the industrial society began to evolve into something new. The number of goods-producing jobs decreased while that of service and information-processing jobs increased. By the early 1970s, Bell (1973) proposed that the United States had become the first society to enter the post-industrial stage. By this he meant that more than half of its workforce was engaged in service and information work, and that it was no longer primarily concerned with the production of goods. The most important commodity today is said to be knowledge or information, and this makes the information-processing and information-storing computer a symbol of our time.

Of course, we are not completely out of the industrial stage yet. It is not exactly clear where the production of goods ends and the providing of services begins. The company psychologist provides a service when he or she develops and offers an Employee Assistance Program to alcoholic and drug-addicted employees. However, is the major objective of such programs to increase productivity, that is, are such service programs in the service of the production of goods? Furthermore, technology is not necessarily a horn of plenty. After all, in 1973, the very year Bell announced "the coming of post-industrial society," the Organization of Petroleum Exporting Countries (OPEC) administered a powerful shock to the industrialized world by tripling oil prices. Finally, productive capacity is one thing, ability to maintain and rehabilitate an environment ravaged by high levels of industrial activity is another.

Nevertheless, we are clearly in a transition to a new order in which the production of industrial goods need involve only a small number of workers supervising, maintaining, and improving the operation of automated factories. For one thing we seem to have little choice but to work smarter. An environment on its last legs provides few resources. That calls for effective information management and energy allocation and provides one impetus shaping the post-industrial knowledge society. Another is the increasing size of the human population and the attendant difficulties of keeping track of people and their, sometimes criminal and violent, interactions.

Thus we may be placing our bets on the knowledgeable professionals who are to the post-industrial, knowledge-based society what the shamans, medicine men, druids, and priests were to societies which preceded it. They are the minority that have the brains and training to deal with complex electronic data processing equipment, advanced substantive and methodological knowledge, and the mushrooming statutes, regulations, and legal precedents that govern the increasingly complicated relationships between individuals, between institutions and individuals, and between society and its physical environment.

In this post-industrial society, work is likely to be a mixed blessing for the expert minority of the available workforce. The post-industrial work sphere may reward with a sense of power as well as with ulcers this elite group which has to be consulted on everything from whether it is alright to eat apples once sprayed with pesticide X, to how to raise our infants so they will not sue us for parental malpractice some time in the future.

For workers in general, and even for the elite of technocrats of the post-industrial future, work will likely remain an essentially structured activity with clearcut demands made by the collectivity and by physical constraints which, at least during working hours, take precedence over personal needs and impulses. The challenge, from the perspective of this book, is to identify possibilities that are offered by the current transition toward a post-industrial society to bridge the gap which opened between work and life in the industrial society.

3

Demand and Supply in the Labor Market

BRAHMAS AND HEREFORDS?

Incident in a supermarket: A customer brings in a big dog. Big dog sniffs at vegetables and shows keen interest in the meat counter. Other customers are upset. The law says "no dogs in food stores." A nonroutine situation exists which amuses and fazes the staff of the store. Cashiers shrug their shoulders and roll their eyes. Young men stop boxing groceries and laugh. Big dog, tail wagging vigorously and saliva dripping from its fangs, keeps making a nuisance of itself.

But from his inner sanctum emerges the top man, the store manager. Briskly explaining the law and politely inviting the customer to return anytime without the dog, he hustles the offending owner-dog pair through the door.

In the United States you must go to the top if you want action, help, or information. Supermarket cashiers do not know what to do about a dog slobbering on the lettuce. The electronic automation revolution has transformed them into "slippers," employees who slip each item over the optical scanner registering the price. Salesclerks and even their supervisors do not know where the products they sell come from. The car salesman does not know how the car he is trying to sell was rated by *Consumer Reports*. Bank tellers look bewildered if you ask them for what purposes they want you to sign three impressive documents to make one simple transaction.

But, if you can catch them, you will find that there are people, the experts and managers at the top, who know what is going on. According to Peter Gillingham (1979), the workforce consists of docile Herefords and independent, spirited Brahmas. The workplace appears to demand many people with low levels of ability willing to accept routine work at low rates of pay and a smaller elite with high levels of ability, knowledge, and skill.

Like all figures of speech, the Hereford/Brahma metaphor gets a point across by oversimplifying. The economic reality is obviously more complex. One can think of the work sphere as consisting of two major subsystems: the production system of work organizations within which actual work activity takes place and which produces goods and services, and the training system which attempts to equip people with the motivational dispositions and the abilities required by the production system. Human resources are demanded by the first and supplied by the second. This chapter takes a look at some general relationships between demand for, and supply of, human resources.

NEED VERSUS DEMAND

Demand must not be confused with need. The two are usually related, but there can be demand without need and there often is need without demand. For example, a wealthy and slightly peculiar community in southern California might experience a strong demand for day care centers for French poodles, but few people would seriously think that this demand is based on a real need. On the other hand, there may be a great need to transform inner city wasteland into attractive business areas and parks, but the absence of funds may prevent this need from being translated into a demand for gardeners, laborers, and construction workers who will bring this transformation about.

Weak and strong needs and weak and strong demands generate a 2×2 contingency table representing quite different societies. A society characterized by weak needs and weak demands bears a certain resemblance to a Buddhist who meditates and transcends all needs and tensions and who refrains from making any demands. Burma, as described by Frederick Schumacher (1973), was an example. Schumacher depicted it as a Buddhist Garden of Eden in which "small is beautiful."[1] Fertile and rich pharaonic Egypt was a society periodically characterized by weak needs and strong demands: The latter emanated from its divine rulers and resulted in the pyramids. Strong needs that are directly translated into strong demands are probably typical of an expanding economy, but lately a fourth contingency, that of strong needs coupled with weak demand, has been of more general concern. The need for social services is strong. Many Americans are homeless, for example. Given the large deficit, the financial means to provide the needed services, hence the demand for them, are relatively weak.

The distinction between need and demand is useful in considering the question of whether technology will replace large numbers of human workers and usher in an age of voluntary or involuntary leisure for many. The German sociologist Ralf Dahrendorf (1982) argues that we are facing the end of the work society and the American economist Wassily Leontief (The New Economy, 1983) says flatly that "human workers will go the way of the horse" (p. 62). As far as most fairly routine work is concerned, human labor simply cannot compete, in the view of Dahrendorf and Leontief, with technology.

It appears that the demand for workers will decrease, in spite of the tranquilizing fiction offered by some that the more we produce, the richer we will be, the more we will buy, and the more jobs will have to be created. So far at least, technology has primarily been introduced into the workplace to reduce labor costs and increase productivity. One does not reduce costs by hiring more workers. One tries to increase the productivity of the best workers by amplifying their activities with computers, telecommunication systems, and robots, and one terminates, dehires, outplaces, or declares redundant the others.[2]

While technology thus reduces the demand for workers, the need for workers may remain constant or even increase. New needs are generated by energy-consuming and environment-polluting technology itself. Regulating human behavior has become a complex business, as is indicated by mushrooming bureaucracies and tax return forms beyond the comprehension of even the average employee of the Internal Revenue Service. The increasing proportion of old people increases the need for caregivers. As we will see in Chapter 4, this means that given the right conditions, such as sufficient wealth generated by automated work, new demands for human workers are likely to emerge.

DEMAND AND SUPPLY MATRICES

Ways of Looking at Demand

The instigating stimulus of activity in the labor market is some kind of demand. What do employers want done? The demands generated by the tasks to be done can be looked at in different ways. We can ask: What kinds of workers are required? Sometimes general categories are useful: routine workers, workers who will do moderately complex tasks, managers and professionals. Usually we are more specific and think in terms of occupations here: tile setters, plumbers, electricians. We can also approach demand in terms of worker characteristics rather than workers. Again, two possibilities arise: Demand can be looked at in

terms of broad motivational dispositions and abilities or in terms of
specified motivational dispositions and abilities required at specified
levels.

For example, a small construction firm might need a number of
workers to handle moderately complex jobs: brickmasons, stonemasons, tile setters, and plumbers. The employer is looking for adequate
levels of vocational skills reflecting manual dexterity, perceptual-motor
skills, and so forth. For example, his tile setters have to perform satis-
factorily on tasks such as cutting tiles to fit small spaces in corners and
around pipes, aligning tiles, calculating areas and the number of whole
and part tiles which will fit into them. The employer might also look
for high levels of loyalty and a certain moderate level of endurance. A
moderate level might do since union regulations and perhaps even the
employer's inherent humaneness set limits to the onerousness of the
tasks workers are expected to perform.

Motivation and Ability

There are some important differences between motivational dispositions and abilities, the two main categories of human resources in demand. Abilities are more directly determined by the demands of the
work environment. Students are quite willing to acquire those abilities
for which employers will pay. Motivational dispositions are to a greater
extent a function not only of demands of the techno-economic structure, but also of the life sphere and other factors.

It is useful to keep this difference in mind when one looks at the
ways in which a society's training system meets the demands of the
techno-economic structure. Such systems foster both motivation and
ability, but in practice the focus is on the development of ability because motivation is more difficult to manipulate or engineer. It is also
more deeply rooted in the biology of individuals and their early development within the life sphere in general, and within their families in
particular.

As a result, it is with respect to ability that the most specific questions of supply and demand are asked. On the macro-level which is
under discussion here, the question of interest is: What kinds and levels of abilities does the techno-economic structure demand and what
kinds and levels of abilities does the training system supply? Demand
and supply can be represented by a matrix whose rows represent different demands and whose columns represent different sources of supply or different "products" supplied.

Exhibit 3–1 represents a generalized demand × supply matrix for
ability. The demands of the work sphere for motivational dispositions
are not formulated with sufficient explicitness, and hence not met in

Exhibit 3-1
Generalized Demand × Supply Matrix for Ability

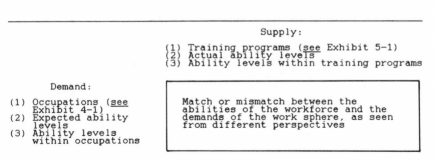

```
                                        Supply:
                                  (1) Training programs (see Exhibit 5-1)
                                  (2) Actual ability levels
                                  (3) Ability levels within training programs

        Demand:
                                  ┌─────────────────────────────────────────┐
(1) Occupations (see              │ Match or mismatch between the            │
    Exhibit 4-1)                  │ abilities of the workforce and the       │
(2) Expected ability              │ demands of the work sphere, as seen      │
    levels                        │ from different perspectives              │
(3) Ability levels                │                                          │
    within occupations            └─────────────────────────────────────────┘
```

sufficiently obvious ways, to warrant such representation. That is probably why the so-called *congruence models* seem to focus exclusively on the fit between a worker's abilities and the ability requirements of a job (see O'Brien, 1986).

The Economic and Educational Perspectives

Labor economists are, of course, economic determinists. They focus on the demands of the productive system, that is, they see demand not only as the thing which instigates labor market activities, but as the factor which determines or should determine supply in general. As noted in Chapter 1, in times of relative scarcity, their viewpoint is more likely to be widely adopted. Scarcity and hence necessity mean that the dictates of the productive system are taken seriously. In times of scarcity people need jobs and are prepared to acquire the specific skills required to get them. Schools cut "frills" like liberal arts and focus on vocational skills.

Even in times of scarcity, the demands of the productive system tend to be fairly undifferentiated: A firm is likely to say it needs fifty plumbers and ten custodians. The focus is on kinds of abilities. As long as basic requirements are met, the level of ability is not likely to play a major role. The economist's demand × supply matrix is thus a matrix of demands for people in various occupations (or groups of occupations) by training institutions and programs designed to fill these demands.

It is their relatively undifferentiated emphasis on clearcut kinds of abilities rather than more subtle levels of ability that led economists (Berg, 1971, Freeman, 1976) to speak of the "overeducated American" at a time when the schools were sharply criticized for producing illiterates. To the typical economist and employer, literate custodians are overeducated because they may be bored by pushing a broom and may demand wages commensurate with their unwanted talents.

Educators, on the other hand, tend to be more open to the possibility that supply affects, or should affect, demand. This reflects the fact that they tend to be social determinists. Given social conditions that have led to a large body of literate college graduates, perhaps janitorial work should be upgraded into maintenance engineering requiring diligent reading of manuals, technical literature regarding the various health hazards posed by different construction and cleaning materials, awareness of basic legal rules helpful in avoiding law suits from injured clients.

This point of view is more likely to prevail in times of relative affluence when even the business world is more willing to go along with certain frills. It prevailed during the affluent 1960s, the time of the counterculture. Also, educators are more likely to focus on levels of ability than economists. Their view tends to be more quality oriented and level of ability is a prerequisite of high quality performance. The educator's demand × supply matrix is likely to be a matrix of optimal ability levels by actual ability levels which the training system supplies.[3]

The economist's focus on kind and the educator's focus on level are both considered when one looks at the range of ability levels required within each occupation or occupational group on the demand side of the matrix, and at the range of ability levels generated within different educational institutions or programs. The ability levels within an occupation could be indicated as a proportion of highly trained to hastily trained workers, or as average levels of skill that are required, hired, or sought. Similarly, on the supply side, the proportion of graduates that have attained different levels of ability might be a more refined indicator of supply than the mere number of graduates from different programs. The demand × supply matrix thus becomes one of demanded ability level within occupations or occupational groups by supply of high and low ability level workers generated by training programs ranging from graduate courses offered in ivy-covered halls, to lifelong formal and informal on-the-job training opportunities.

For example, a particular labor market may require a small number of highly trained master plumbers, and many plumbers who know the basic operations of the trade and who will work under the supervision of an engineer or master plumber. The component of the training system trying to meet this demand is an apprenticeship system. Union and other concerns may dictate that every graduate of the program is fully trained. The result is a mismatch between demand and supply. Furthermore, this mismatch becomes apparent only when both kinds and levels of ability are considered.

THE RECIPROCAL RELATIONSHIP BETWEEN DEMAND AND SUPPLY

More often than not actual or perceived scarcity prevails and demand is cause and supply is effect in the labor market. If the techno-economic structure requires riveters, as it did during World War II, and engineers, as it did in the wake of Sputnik, demand tends to push up wages and salaries and people flock to the jobs to be filled. In addition, society finds ways to assign people to the jobs that need to be filled. The expectation that others and perhaps even oneself ought to do what is useful is cultivated in times of need, such as war or some other threat. Job allocation is the rule under these conditions (Stafford & Jackson, 1983). Economic determinism reigns supreme.

In better times, particularly in democratic societies, the labor market is less driven by employer demands and more by people's demands for work activity that suits them (Stafford & Jackson, 1983). Social determinism and the educator's viewpoint become more influential, the thought that the supply of variously trained and educated individuals be accommodated by the economy is entertained seriously by governments and academics and, of course, the available individuals looking for work commensurate with their talents and skills. Supply becomes cause and demand becomes effect. It becomes apparent that the relationship between the economy's demand for workers and the training system's supply of trained workers and managers is reciprocal.

However, the variable of scarcity versus abundance (Katz & Kahn's (1978) scarcity versus munificence) is not the only factor that determines whether demand or supply acts as cause. The interaction between demand and supply is more complex.

For example, regardless of affluence, low supply may lead to low demand. Howard Bowen (1974a, 1974b) points out that with fewer people available to do the laundry and the cooking, the economy responded by means of washing machines and TV dinners. These products reduced the demand for household workers. High supply may also lead to high demand: Instead of allocating available jobs, society may create the jobs demanded by entry-level workers. Or, as in the case of the Roman Empire, the availability of cheap labor may remove any incentive to innovate and change. This in turn ensures that the available cheap labor will continue to be in demand. As F. J. Wiseman notes: "For a long time . . . the economy of Rome had been cushioned against shocks by the plentiful supply of cheap slave labour . . . the answer to the need for larger constructional jobs . . . was not the discovery of new techniques, but the direction of even more hands to use the old ones" (Wiseman, 1956, p. 74).

The point of this very general introduction to the reciprocal relationships between demand and supply in the labor market is that the work sphere seeks to match people and jobs on the macro-level of society. We are looking at one aspect of a very general problem here: that of matching people and jobs not only on the macro-level of society, but also on the levels of the work organization and personal concerns.

The problem is familiar to us on the level of organizations whose human resource departments spend most of their time and effort on selecting and training people to fit available jobs, and whose engineers and industrial and organizational psychologists redesign jobs to fit peoples' abilities and needs. Of course, individuals struggle constantly to optimize the fit between themselves and their job, through accommodation or assimilation (Piaget, 1952).

In this chapter the focus has been on the match between people and jobs on the national level. It leads to questions like: Are there enough jobs for all Americans who need or want to work? Are there enough challenging jobs for the large proportion of young Americans graduating from colleges and universities? Are there enough highly trained American tradesmen to fill demanding jobs requiring complex though unglamorous vocational skills? (Morf, 1986). Hopefully, this chapter facilitates a better understanding of the mechanisms that have produced a mismatch between people looking for meaningful work helping them to attain their life objectives, and a work sphere of jobs that have become increasingly automated and routinized.

NOTES

1. At the time of writing a popular uprising and brutal repression by the army have disrupted the Buddhist serenity Schumacher attributed to Burma.

2. Our rich vocabulary for denoting this process speaks volumes about its importance today.

3. This distinction between the economist's and the educator's point of view is discussed by O'Toole (1977, p. 114). See also Morf (1986, p. 124).

4

The Demand for Personnel

THE COMPLEXITY OF JOBS

The Hereford versus Brahma metaphor of the previous chapter certainly reflects too much truth for comfort. Many Americans feel that theirs is a nonegalitarian society in the process of becoming more nonegalitarian (see also Chapter 8). However, at least for the time being, the world of work offers more than routine and elite or complex jobs. Many jobs involve a range of fairly complex and challenging tasks and lie somewhere between the two extremes.

It is not easy to classify jobs in general and it is even less easy to classify them in terms of a particular criterion like job complexity. There is a great variety of jobs to begin with, and each job is to some extent what the job holder makes of it. For example, some employees are innovative and bold and expand the scope of their jobs, making them more complex. Other employees constantly and defensively point out that "this is not my job."

Pies can be divided in different ways. The nature of a classification system depends largely on its purpose. For purposes of reporting summary statistics on education level, number of people employed, etc., the U.S. Department of Labor distinguishes between types of workers. Sometimes it does so within each of ten different industries ranging from agriculture to public administration (e.g., U. S. Bureau of Labor Statistics, 1983). The main types of workers are white collar workers, blue collar workers, service workers and farm workers. This way of dividing the pie tells us little about job complexity.

For purposes of employment counseling, the U.S. Department of Labor has produced the *Dictionary of Occupational Titles* (U.S. Department of Labor, 1977) which classifies thousands of jobs or occupations into primary categories, divisions, and occupational groups. Strictly speaking, jobs are positions in a work organization, and the occupations of the Dictionary are job types. The occupation *cloth printer*, for example, comprises many positions (jobs) in many work organizations. It falls into the primary category of machine trades occupations, more specifically into printing occupations, and ultimately into printing machine occupations.

The Dictionary indicates for each occupation the degree of involvement with data, people, and things by means of a three digit code. The lower a digit, the higher the level of involvement. Thus the code 000 should indicate the most complex job imaginable. For *cloth printer*, the code is 382 indicating that it requires compiling data, taking instructions from and helping people, and operating and controlling activities involving things.

The Dictionary's codes constitute useful indicators of job complexity, but they do not directly serve the purposes of this chapter. What is needed here are average complexity levels for broad job categories. Computing these from the Dictionary's data would require some questionable assumptions.

For present purposes of considering the demand for workers who can fill jobs ranging from routine to highly complex, a number of sources (e.g., Hall, 1975; Harvey, 1975) suggest a third classification system along the lines shown in Exhibit 4–1. It is clearly not perfect; some occupations or jobs end up in more than one category, and one can debate into which category many of the example jobs or occupations shown should be placed. What is of interest here is that one can meaningfully talk about three categories of jobs differing in job complexity.

These three categories of jobs are sometimes thought of as differing in the degree to which they are challenging or demanding. Complexity is the term relied on here because it is the most neutral and probably the most valid label. Any job done well is certainly demanding and probably challenging. Even describing jobs as simple and complex poses problems. Managerial and professional jobs are not necessarily more complex and are not necessarily executed by people with higher ability levels than many moderately complex jobs (and perhaps even some routine jobs). The driver of a fire truck or a policeman, for example, may require skills as finely honed as those of a professional engineer and make decisions as important as those of most managers.

Of course, in the real world, jobs are distributed continuously over

Exhibit 4–1
Three Levels of Job Complexity

Routine Jobs

Unskilled workers

Examples: hotel maid, farm laborer, assembly line worker, freight-handler, household servant.

Semi skilled workers

Examples: Waiter/waitress, assembly-line worker, process operator (in chemical plant, etc.), bartender, delivery personnel, construction laborer, farm laborer, maintenance worker, cabdriver.

On-the-job training frequently sufficient.

Moderately Complex Jobs

White collar workers

Examples: Secretary, telephone operator, receptionist, computer programmer, computer operator, flight attendant, cashier, bookkeeper, office machine operator, mail carrier, shipping/receiving clerk, bank teller.

Training requirements vary, often obtained in proprietory schools. Tendency (growing weaker at this time) to identify with management rather than a union (especially if there is a chance of upward mobility).

Skilled blue collar workers and foremen

Examples: TV repairer, auto mechanic, aircraft mechanic, tool and die maker, printer, farmer, heavy equipment (e.g., crane) operator, stonemason, electrician, carpenter, cook.

Traditional training: long and regulated apprenticeships, increasingly training at junior college and technical school. Workers generally identify with strong unions.

Work tasks are defined by people other than the worker. On-the-job training considered adequate.

Complex jobs

Professional jobs

Examples: doctor, lawyer, nurse, teacher, policeman/woman, professor, engineer, psychologist

Generally accountable to self-governed professional association of peers. (Licensing regulations, codes of ethics, etc.) Typically require university-level training.

Managers, administrators of public organizations ("officials"), and proprietors (entrepreneurs).

Examples: Personnel manager, CEO, store owner, city administrator, farmer.

Accountable to employing organization, except for proprietors. Jobs which intrinsically involve decision making. Typically require university-level training.

---

the range from routine to complex jobs. Exhibit 4–2 is meant to be a plausible representation of the current distribution of jobs over this continuum. There are data which bear on this distribution but they are complex and beyond the present scope. All that is needed here is a general impression. While this job distribution mainly reflects demand, the number of people holding a particular job is also limited at any point in time by the number of people motivated and able to do so. That latter number is likely to increase when demand is high, and it drives up wages and salaries. As noted earlier, demand and supply are interdependent quantities.

Exhibit 4–2
Demand as Hypothetical Percentages of Jobs Differing in Complexity

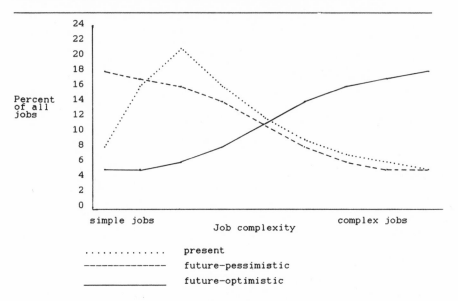

One thing seems clear: The current job distribution is positively skewed; there are many routine jobs, a sizable number of moderately complex jobs, and a minority of professional/managerial jobs. Exhibit 4–2 also shows possible future job distributions. These will be relevant to the last section of this chapter.

ROUTINE JOBS

There is a strong demand for workers to fill routine jobs. A few years ago *Time* pointed out that MacDonald's employs more people than U.S. Steel (The New Economy, 1983), and steelworkers in Pittsburgh and other centers of the industrial belt were told to move into the service sector and don a fast food chef's hat. Technology is automating jobs that once required complex, and hence expensive, skills. It is creating new jobs in the service sector that require few skills. Employers want to routinize work where possible and, apparently, would bring about a society of Herefords and Brahmas without qualms.

The Work Ethic Demanded of the Working Class

According to a notice posted on a Job Search Center bulletin board set up for jobless former steelworkers in the Monongahela Valley, "85%

of being hired is because your (sic) likable" and "15% of being hired is because your (sic) skilled" (Corn, 1986, September).

This message contains an important truth: Employers are very interested in the motivational dispositions of job applicants. Although it is ability we can measure most accurately and match best with the demands of the job, personality is usually more in demand than skill. To most employers a suitable employee is one who has the right attitude toward the free enterprise system, toward the objectives of the firm to earn profits and the duty of employees to contribute toward such profits. As James O'Toole has pointed out: "In the final analysis, employers hire people with whom they are comfortable" (1977, p. 125).

Depending on the jobs to be filled, the techno-economic structure looks for specific motivational dispositions. For routine jobs, docility and endurance are what is required. The assembly line workers in demand are those who accept orders and execute them relentlessly even if their backs are acting up, for example, those workers who are imbued by MacMichael's (1974) work ethic of the working class.

Routine Work and Basic Abilities

The attitude of the archetypal old-fashioned employer recruiting routine workers is summed up by the doctor of Celine's novel quoted in Chapter 2: "What we need is chimpanzees."

True, most employers profess to venerate education almost as much as motherhood. In practice, however, they are not at all impressed or interested in whether the applicant or employee for routine jobs is proficient in the things schools have traditionally taught. Since jobs are not designed to be learning environments that permit those who do them to constantly become more expert in their field, and since the basic skills transmitted in the schools are essentially the tools for further learning which is not really expected to take place on the job, these basic skills are not particularly necessary.

An interesting and detailed study done for the Ontario Economic Council in Canada repeatedly comments on the willingness of employers in banking, retail sales, manufacturing, and office services to hire young workers just out of schools in which they had learned next to nothing (Hall & Carlton, 1977). In the banks, the "demand on the teller and clerk for writing competence comes close to zero" (p. 178), "it would appear that the writing done on the job application form was the main writing assignment for most of the incoming retail workers" (p. 182). Interviews with new office workers "provide an account of dismal experiences with English and mathematics in secondary school. . . . On the other hand, their current employment makes almost no demands on any skills developed in secondary school" (p. 185).

The authors of the study conclude that "what stands out is the readiness of employers to employ students with lamentable academic records. Despite these, the students manage to handle the jobs effectively" (p. 186). The message seems clear: Routine work and school have very little to do with each other. Most observers assume that this means that the schools must become more relevant and vocation-oriented. But no matter what the schools do, they will not be relevant as long as the many routine jobs made available by the techno-economic structure are deskilled jobs.

Routine Work and Vocational Skills

The American attitude toward vocational skills is, and has been for a long time, less positive than that of the Japanese and many Europeans. American managers, applying the scientific management techniques of Frederick Taylor and others, tended to simplify and routinize jobs rather than to make them more challenging and satisfying by enriching them. They engineered skills out of the work. The semiskilled operators of their factories were in fact less well trained and less skillful than the so-called "unskilled" farm laborers of the generation that preceded them (Braverman, 1977).

American managers and engineers have been the pioneers in replacing old-fashioned, independent, skillful, and costly craftsmen with semiskilled operatives and conveyer belt production systems. This tendency is potentially even more marked today in many places as computers, telecommunications, and robots increase the possibilities of devising intelligent production systems and information processing systems that sometimes only need an attentive screen or dial watcher.

The recent movement toward career education might at first sight suggest that there has more recently developed a demand for vocational skills. In some jurisdictions, legislation and policies have been formulated with the objective of ensuring that no student leaves the schools without a salable skill. However, the proponents of career education were politicians and government officials worried about how to keep unemployed youth from being cast aside and causing social unrest. Thus it is negative reasons which account for the touting and, sometimes, funding of career education projects. This makes the demand for career education and vocational skills somewhat artificial and may help explain why it has seldom led to sustained and successful training programs.

The United States faces a serious problem as a result of this emphasis on deskilling and routinizing jobs and the concomitant lack of real and positive demand for highly developed vocational skills. Vocational skills are essential for both social and economic reasons.

High levels of vocational skills have a marked effect on the quality of life offered by a society. This can be true even of the most routine jobs. The life of the average hotel guest is materially improved by hotel employees who recognize and report dangerously damaged electrical outlets and frayed cords. It is also improved by bartenders who can diffuse incipient brawls and maintenance workers who can read the labels on the many containers of cleaning substances with which they are expected to work.

High levels of vocational skills can also have positive effects on the workers who possess them: They can increase self-esteem, they motivate workers to develop their skills further and to take pride in the work they do. Admittedly this is less true of alienating and routine work than of more challenging work but, as we will see in Chapter 11, even routine work can have positive effects on the worker.

To sum up: Technology is reducing the number of relatively complex jobs, that is for example, many jobs in the steel industry and in middle level management. It is creating new routine jobs, such as those in the food-handling business. Employers are using technology to routinize work wherever possible; they have succeeded in changing into routine work many occupations that were only recently considered to be highly skilled. Secretaries have become keyboarders sitting all day in front of computer screens, car mechanics have become Volkswagen transmission or Chevrolet brake repairers. To fill this abundance of routine jobs, employers demand mainly a docile willingness to labor. Although they usually insist on a high school graduation certificate, they sometimes value it as evidence of the ability to sit still and get along in an authoritarian system rather than as evidence of proficiency in the basics of writing, reading, and doing arithmetic. The jobs have largely been routinized so that only minimal levels of vocational skills, acquired cheaply and quickly, will be required.

MODERATELY COMPLEX JOBS

What about the demands generated by jobs which are neither routine nor managerial or professional? We have seen that this is a larger group of jobs than one might suspect, in view of the onslaught of scientific management and high technology on the nature of work. The work of auto mechanics, farmers, crane operators, hospital attendants, paramedics, policemen, busdrivers, cab drivers, and many others simply cannot be routinized to the same extent as the average production job or clerical job. In these jobs there will always be surprises and a need to interact competently with other people.

From the point of view of motivation, these jobs probably demand a judicious mixture of docile willingness to endure and initiative, independence, and enterprise when the surprises occur. In terms of ability, these jobs do require basic skills to read reasonably complex work manuals and material used in training courses, and they usually require distinct vocational skills. Security personnel must be able to distinguish potential intruders and choose among available options. Sales people must be able to respond appropriately to questions and recognize different closing signals.

MANAGERIAL AND PROFESSIONAL JOBS

In the case of the minority of the workforce constituting the professionals and managers, the Brahmas, there can be no doubt: From them the work sphere demands a high level of ambition and initiative and of expertise, knowledge, ability, and skill. The nurse must be able to distinguish different types of medication and to hit a vein with a needle. Teachers must know the subject matter they are supposed to teach and have the skills to prevent mayhem from breaking out among the little angels or macho adolescents to whom they are supposed to teach it. Here it is the work ethic of the middle class that is demanded, and increasingly complex and pervasive technology calls for sophisticated workers, managers, and professionals who control, maintain and develop it.

The profusion of different and not immediately compatible hardware and software calls for people who not only can use computers, but who understand them, can connect them to other computers, to networks, and to peripheral devices by patching available software or writing new programs. The regulatory environment spawned by technology and increasing population density has also become more complex. Toxic substances have to be disposed of more carefully, defective products can lead to multi-million dollar damage claims. Executives are surrounded by bevies of legal advisers, every initiative can have ramifications in the most unexpected places.

It seems likely that the highest levels of expertise will continue to be in great demand. Professional skills, abilities, and knowledge are at a premium. This appetite of the techno-economic structure for high level expertise has led to periodic rushes to the professional schools: medicine, law, business, etc. These rushes have sometimes led to a flooding of the market with graduates. Such fluctuations aside, the techno-economic structure is interested in the most talented 20 percent of the workforce. They are the only ones who know what to do about a slobbering dog in the produce section of a supermarket without provoking a law suit from a disgusted customer or from dog owners whose mental health has been irreversibly impaired by the brutal eviction of their beloved four-legged friends.

FUTURE DEMANDS FOR PERSONNEL

This chapter has looked at demand for "human resources" within the work sphere. On the most apparent level this means demand for workers who fit jobs differing in complexity. Within each of the categories of routine, moderately complex, and complex jobs, it means demand for specific levels of specific motivational dispositions and abilities.

Demand, in whatever sense the term is used, is of course subject to change. It is not clear what long-range effects technological change and other factors, such as increases in population size, will have on the occupation structure and on the job distribution. Which occupations will require more workers? In which ones will workers be laid off? Which occupations will demand higher levels of motivation and ability, which ones will require merely routine activity? The reader interested in detailed statistics is referred to one of the periodic studies of George Silvestri and J. M. Lukasiewicz (1987) of the U.S. Bureau of Labor Statistics. They have addressed these questions in studies based on clearly stated assumptions and projection procedures.

Exhibit 4–2 can serve as a starting point. In addition to a curve reflecting current demand, it also presents a pessimistic and an optimistic scenario. According to the former, technology will deskill the majority of jobs as machines become more intelligent, as we move from the merely electronic third wave into the cybernetic fourth wave of industrialization (Raymond, 1986). According to the optimistic scenario, technology will continue to take the drudgery out of work and generate wealth that will allow human workers to concentrate on decision-making and supervisory roles during relatively short working hours. The most likely scenario, however, is one between those envisioned by the pessimists and the optimists.

No doubt many occupations will continue to focus on our subsistence needs. These needs are most likely to be translated into demands: We have to eat, clothe ourselves, and maintain a roof over our heads. Silvestri and Lukasiewicz (1987) predict that the largest numbers of new jobs will be created in the occupations *retail sales* and *waiters/waitresses*. There are those who say that we can't all make a living selling hamburgers to each other (see The New Economy, 1983), but far more people are certainly selling hamburgers than ever before. Basic subsistence activities such as buying food and cooking it have become "monetized," that is, they are done by paid workers rather than by unpaid housewives. This trend is likely to continue.

More people will probably be occupied in regulation. As the population increases and people live closer together in ever-larger cities, the opportunities for inadvertently stepping on each other's toes increase, especially when everyone's actions are amplified by the use of equipment that can have dramatic effects. Almost everyone drives a car and has the power to inflict not only damage, but death. Any half-baked adolescent has it within his power to inflict a rock concert on the neighborhood by merely positioning his stereo "boom-box" on the steps of his house.

Rapid change compounds the problem of regulation. Statutes and rules have to be interpreted in the context of new situations, frequently they have to be reformulated. For example, many workers traveling daily to downtown offices may soon be electronic homeworkers. What rights will they have? Will these isolated workers be able to form unions? Will they be treated as employees or as independent entrepreneurs (responsible for their own tax and pension payments)?

Thus there may be a great demand for workers engaged in the devising, interpreting, transmitting, and applying of regulations. The trend that made taxation and customs regulations impenetrable to ordinary mortals is likely to get worse. Accountants and lawyers, and perhaps para-accountants and para-lawyers are likely to flourish. Civil service personnel may expand to enforce ever larger numbers of statutes and regulations as society continually finds it necessary to prescribe behavior in new situations and under changing conditions. Many new positions are expected to open for lawyers (Silvestri & Lukasiewicz, 1987).

Laws, rules, regulations, etc., are not only becoming more complex, they also cover more aspects of our lives. In some places a permit is required to leave the road in case you might start a fire or get lost. Increasing numbers of people are tapped for bodily fluids to determine whether they have ingested banned substances or whether they have AIDS. We may face a future in which permission will be needed to sit underneath a tree to chew a blade of grass.

Once upon a time, somebody carved a few dolls and sold them. Today children's toys have to meet exact specifications that are established in government laboratories by means of complex apparatus permitting exact measurement of stresses and their effects. These tests include the "pull test," the "push test," the "drop test," and so forth. If the testing of toys keeps many people busy, one can only imagine the job opportunities that exist for regulating such major industries and such infinitely more dangerous products as the car industry and the car.

Ever-larger numbers of people seem to be engaged in the business of offering financial services. There will be more accountants and auditors (Silvestri & Lukasiewicz, 1987). Our cathedrals of work are the bank towers gracing downtowns from New York to Los Angeles. They house thousands who earn a living by transferring funds. Their clients may include average citizens, but large numbers of them deal with corporations. When one large company takes over another, millions of dollars in commissions are generated for hundreds of brokers, lawyers, and investment bankers, although no tangible new wealth has been created.

In some areas new types of technologists may be needed. One such area of expanding technology application has been medicine. Doctors no longer grab their black bag and jump on their horse-drawn buggy to respond to an emergency. Instead, whole teams of specialists and assistants are required to handle health technology ranging from ambulances to artificial hearts. Perhaps teams of technologists will descend on the small plots of remaining arable land to extract from them yields large enough to feed entire cities.

Enforcement, alas, promises to be a growth area as well. There are officials who hint darkly that while medical costs have been a major threat to public solvency in the past, it may be the costs of maintaining law and order that will be the major threat to relative solvency in the future. Twenty years ago there were no security officers at airports scanning bodies and baggage; today they are everywhere. Drug testers may constitute a new and large occupation in the future; they would have to be highly trained since erroneous results lead to the loss of reputations and jobs.

Thus thousands of new jobs have been created by the tendency of people to step on each other's toes deliberately or to consume substances that make them unreliable and dangerous on the job. The future may bring larger jails and jobs for more policemen, prison guards, social workers, psychologists, and psychiatrists engaged in the task of ensuring that violent and psychotic behavior are kept under control. There may be more jobs for people manning electronic surveillance equipment.

The most promising area of job growth may be what sociologist Brigitte Berger (1976) has called *people work*. There are demographic factors which suggest this possibility. While there are fewer children needing care and help, there will be far more older people than today. The "graying of America" may generate stronger needs for health personnel, helpers, social animators, etc. Since senior citizens will be a large block of voters, their needs are likely to be translated into demands. Silvestri and Lukasiewicz (1987) project rapid growth in such occupations as medical assistants, physical therapists and aides, home health aides, physician assistants, and occupational therapists.

As work becomes physically less demanding, bodies need to be exercised more. The physical fitness business may be one area of people work that will expand. Similarly, as more work is done in the "electronic cottage" there may be increasing demand for people engaged in improving social fitness. Such animators and trainers might compen-

sate for the lack of social contact experienced by many electronic cottage workers far away from the water cooler, the lunches at the corner
tavern, the Wednesday night bowling game with fellow workers.

Perhaps as the behavioral or social sciences progress, new types of
people work will emerge. One could imagine landlords hiring psychologists to administer tests of introversion versus extraversion so the in-
troverts can be assigned to a quiet wing and the extraverts to one that
will rock to the music of wild parties every night.

These are just some examples of new or increased demands for different kinds of abilities that may be demanded by the work sphere of
the future. Some occupations will disappear, new ones will emerge.
These demands of the work sphere may not manifest themselves in
the form of the traditional "job," however. Most workers today are
employees who occupy a fairly fixed niche in the structure of the work
organization. A certain stability and predictability are associated with
these niches. In the future there may be fewer such niches. More people may be entrepreneurs running their own small operation providing
some service or tangible item; more may be *intra*preneurs who work
for a particular corporation on a project basis rather than a fixed and
frequently less than optimal forty-hour work week.

Rapid technological change may even make the notions of vocation
and occupation obsolete. As many people find that their knowledge,
abilities, and skills have to be updated constantly, learning and working may merge for them. All of this means that the job situation is in
flux and that it is quite possible that the optimistic future distribution
of jobs across the spectrum of job complexity, challenge, and meaningfulness is the one that will actually materialize.

5

The Supply of Personnel

THE SCHOOLS

Graduation at Anytown High

It is graduation day at Anytown High. Long rows of chairs have been arranged in the gym by the custodial staff. The graduating students are lining up in a hallway. Parents, relatives and friends take their seats in the back rows. Ornate chairs grace the podium, ready to support the portly frames of distinguished dignitaries. A band plays rousing and solemn music as the procession of graduands moves along the center aisle.

The principal leads the procession into the gym. Distinguished guests, the teachers, and the students follow. The graduands are welcomed "to the ranks of educated men and women." The principal is described as "this leader among academic leaders, this man of action, wisdom, discernment, and judgement." The principal says that times are tough, the taxpayers are not generous for reasons he is sure everyone in the gym understands. But the school has pulled through.

More polished prose echoes from the rafters as gracious personages outdo each other in displaying humility by protesting that the compliments heaped on them by other speakers are exaggerated and in displaying generosity by heaping even more eloquent praise upon everyone in sight. In the process Anytown High is described as "this institution which enjoys a prestigious sports and academic reputation,"

"this leading institution among the city's high schools," and "this locus of intellectual enlightenment." The students, it is declared, have
behind them "years of assiduous toil" and are now ready to receive
their "well-earned and richly deserved recognition and to embark upon
careers which will no doubt entail roles of leadership."

This only partly hypothetical graduation ceremony tells us much about
America's training system. The activity taking place is clearly regarded
as important. It symbolizes the role of the school as the core institution
of the training system and it certifies that young people have acquired
basic skills and the restraint and patience required to sit on the school-
bench six or more hours per day. In the course of what philosopher
and educator Alfred North Whitehead (1929) called the "stage of precision," the school, as part and instrument of the techno-economic work
sphere, has imposed the classical virtue of following rules—grammati-
cal, mathematical, and ethical—on children who entered it in the throes
of the spontaneous and creative, but undisciplined, "stage of ro-
mance." It socialized them, restrained them, "civilized" them to the
best of its ability and in the process prepared them in some ways to
meet the demands of the techno-economic structure.

Basic Skills and Abilities

The rhetoric generated on this occasion also draws attention to the
low level of academic achievement attained in American schools. It does
so by denying that there is a problem. "Our graduates are the best"
may be what some parents want to hear, but most people know it isn't
so. The schools are under attack. American students are said to have
low levels of linguistic and mathematical skills and to be ignorant about
geography and history, especially when they are compared to their
Russian, Japanese, and German counterparts (e.g., Fiske, 1987a, 1987b;
Rohter, 1986). One recent report of a Presidential Commission asserted
that a foreign power could not subvert the United States more effectively than do its own schools; it considered the "nation at risk" because the schools are not doing their jobs (National Commission on
Excellence in Education, 1983).

Have basic skills declined? Horror stories abound which illustrate how
the schools produce graduates who are illiterate, innumerate, and un-
acquainted with basic historical and geographical facts. Employers
complain that they have to expend substantial resources to teach their
workers basic skills that should have been taught in the schools (e.g.,
Rohter, 1986). The American workforce is unfavorably compared to the
better trained workforces of Japan and Germany.

This does not necessarily mean that there has been a decline in ability levels. While ability levels are low today, they may have been as

low or even lower in the past. There are those who note that adult illiteracy has never been eradicated and that the older generation is not always an inspiring example. A Ford Foundation study has reported that an estimated 64 million Americans are unable to cope with such everyday tasks as addressing an envelope (St. John Hunter & Harman, 1979). Larry Rohter (1986) cites a comprehensive University of Texas study according to which there were, in 1980, 23.2 million illiterate white adults, 7.8 million illiterate black adults, and 5.1 million illiterate Hispanic adults in the United States.

Furthermore, there is truth to the observation that complaining about the illiteracy of students is "the oldest literary tradition" (Barzun, 1954, p. 46). The blunt H. L. Mencken, for example, wrote in 1926 that "the great majority of American high school pupils, when they put their thoughts on paper, produce only a mass of confused and puerile nonsense" (cited from Lyons, 1976, p. 33). "I really debate," writes Stephen Judy, "the notion that there has been a dramatic decline in basic skills acquisition. You'll find the basic skills crisis resurfacing about every 20 years. It dates back to the 1880's when Harvard first discovered that students coming in were illiterate" (cited from J. Harris, 1977, p. 12).

In fact, the "basic skills crisis" dates at least to the Middle Ages: The medieval philosopher Thomas Murner addressed himself to what he considered to be "soft youth" that was pretty weak in Latin (see Ong, 1958, p. 85). In all probability similar complaints were uttered by Roman, Greek, Hebrew, Egyptian, and Sumerian educators.

Ability levels may even have increased for some groups. The "best and the brightest," the future or potential Brahmas, are trained at least as well as they were twenty or thirty years ago. They are headed for, or are enrolled in, demanding programs of the professional and graduate schools and they are as qualified as previous generations of students to occupy the elite jobs. Furthermore, this well-trained minority comprises a larger proportion of the population: More doctors, engineers, managers, etc., are trained per capita than in the past. They may not know much about Kant or Socrates, and they may regard history as bunk and literature as the domain of the slightly peculiar, but they are professional football player types, aggressive and eyes on the ball, who have learned to simulate complex processes on computers, to analyze and synthesize systems, and to apply decision theory and linear programming to problems that arise in the techno-economic structure. They will join the experts to which the majority must turn for expensive advice on everything from selling a house to brushing one's teeth, and who design airplanes as large as ships, send men to the moon, and develop and apply medical equipment that can practically reawaken the dead.

At the other end of the spectrum, there are probably fewer children who do not go to school than there were thirty years ago, and perhaps fewer illiterate adults who never had the opportunity to learn how to read and write.

Nevertheless, we cannot dismiss the horror stories about illiteracy, inability to handle numbers, and plain generalized ignorance about anything that has not been directly received from the TV screen in the last half-hour or so. The assumption will be made here that there *has* been a decline in ability levels in the case of young people who are not headed for the demanding professional schools and who do not belong to the poor and otherwise disadvantaged that would simply have been ignored in the past.

The shortage of basic skills. Whether we postulate an actual decline of ability or not, levels of basic abilities are certainly not astoundingly high. A *Time* cover story cites a study by the U.S. Chamber of Commerce which found that "35% of corporations surveyed had to provide remedial basic-skills training to new employees" (The New Economy, 1983, p. 62). According to Literacy Volunteers of New York, "New York area businesses are forced to spend $1.5 billion annually to train employees in the basic skills" (Rohter, 1986). A recent report on the first National Assessment of History and Literature (Ravitch & Finn, 1987) suggests that "something is gravely awry," that "our eleventh graders as a whole are ignorant of much that they should know" (p. 200). The authors describe themselves as "deeply uneasy about what it portends for these boys and girls, for the society they will inhabit, and for the children *they* will rear" (p. 203). Law suits have been filed against schools on behalf of graduates, alleging that they failed to teach the plaintiffs how to write and read sufficiently well to be able to understand simple written instructions and to fill out job application forms (Is a Board Liable, 1973).

Remedial action is not only required when average high school students join the workforce, it is even required when the best high school students enter prestigious universities. Although there has been an improvement, the report by writer and professor Gene Lyons published in *Harper's* in the 1970s, during the heyday of the ability crisis, still contains too much truth for comfort:

nearly half of the entering class at the University of California at Berkeley, a fairly selective school which takes only the top eighth of California high-school graduates, failed placement exams and had to be enrolled in remedial composition courses; . . . applicants to journalism programs at Wisconsin, Minnesota, Texas, and North Carolina flunk basic spelling, punctuation, and usage tests at rates that vary between 30 and 50 percent; a survey by the Association of American Publishers [shows] that college freshmen really do read on what used to be considered a high-school freshman level. (Lyons, 1976, p. 33)

At the Anytown High graduation ceremony, the parents listen to the resounding words. Most of them know this is a show. Most of them also wonder about the prospects of their adolescent offspring in the rapidly changing world of work. Will their child make it through a university and a professional school to become one of the elite Brahmas? Will their child be lucky and find a good vocational program and become a competent tradesman? Will their child become a docile Hereford or even an unemployed malcontent?

THE PRAGMATISM AND STRUCTUREDNESS OF THE TRAINING SYSTEM

Pragmatic Politicians, Teachers, and Students

The school is the most visible part of the American training system, a system which is characterized by its pragmatism and its structuredness. The training system is pragmatic and structured because it is a part of the techno-economic structure in the first place, but there are variations in the degree to which it is pragmatic and structured. These are a function of actual or perceived scarcity or affluence. During tough times of high trade deficits, growing national debt, and strong competition from overseas, government officials are more likely to say things like "we cannot afford the luxury of . . ." or "the costs of teaching Shakespeare exceed its benefits." During such periods dominated by economic determinism, whatever is not demanded by the techno-economic work sphere becomes a "frill," and a pragmatic style, attuned to the "new reality" of "limited resources" takes over. When times are relatively tough, pragmatism is in vogue and the training system is here to meet the collective needs of the work sphere rather than the personal needs of individual learners.

More than that: The learners suppress private needs for growth, understanding, and development and become what one widely read publication offering trenchant social criticism described as "ruthless mothers" (Katz, 1981, September). All is fair in their quest for grades and other tactical advantages in their campaign to launch and pursue a career. They have little time for the niceties of Shakespearean soliloquies and are absorbed by the acquisition of effective techniques in such "useful" areas as computer science, decision theory, and job design.

Ph.D. candidates appear for final defenses with thick stacks of computer output and little explanation of why they chose to unleash on their data every possible statistical procedure which modern software permits them to apply with a few strokes on the keyboard. Even at this highest level of the training system, the focus is less on understanding and more on techniques that work.

Exhibit 5–1
The U.S. Training System

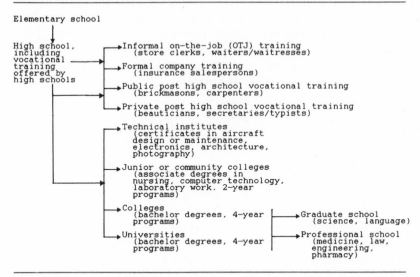

Notes:

(1) The structure is, of course, more complex than indicated. Engineers may graduate and then be subjected to formal company training programs. Also, much training is obtained by means not listed here: the armed forces, correspondence courses, from friends and relatives.

(2) The main source underlying this attempt to outline the structure of the training system is Occupational Projections and Training Data, 1986 Edition. Washington, D.C.: Department of Labor, Bureau of Labor Statistics.

This return to pragmatism has brought with it a return to structure. The "ruthless mothers" do not want to "waste time" trying to guess what is in the teacher's mind or trying to interpret a poet's vague allusions. They want to know exactly what answers to what questions will yield a high grade. In short, they want highly structured training leading to specific skills and useful knowledge, not unstructured educational groping toward something as amorphous and unsalable as mere insight.

Structured Institutions, Programs, and Objectives

The training system exudes structure wherever one looks. Its own overall structure is shown in Exhibit 5–1 which presents the types of institutions that make up the American training system. This system is designed above all to meet the needs of the techno-economic structure, although it may also attempt to meet more personal needs of its students on occasion and during periods of relative affluence. Exhibit 5–1 represents the supply side of the labor market whose demand side was earlier represented by the occupational categories based on job complexity in Exhibit 4–1.

The *Occupational Projections and Training Data* (U.S. Bureau of Labor Statistics, 1986) on which Exhibit 5–1 is based, provide information on the product of the training system and how that product was produced. It reports the percentage of all workers in an occupation who needed specific training to qualify for their jobs. Parenthetically, these percentages also provide some indication of the number of jobs and hence the demand for abilities and skills discussed in Chapter 4.

The statistics in the following apply to 1983. One is relieved to note that 100 percent of aerospace engineers and 99.2 percent of pharmacists needed specific training. Perhaps less reassuring are the percentages cited for masons (brick and stone): 69 percent; insurance salespeople, 76 percent; sales people (apparel, shoes), 22 percent, waiters and waitresses, 24 percent; childcare workers in private households, 10 percent. In other words, not every member of the workforce was deemed to require training.

Where did those who required training obtain it? Some examples may be helpful in conveying an impression of how the training system meets the demands of the production system. Of the pharmacists who needed training, 88.5 percent obtained it in what the Department of Labor inelegantly calls "4-year or longer college programs," of the aerospace engineers, 73 percent did, 18 and 14 percent of the latter obtained their training in formal company training or in the armed forces (note that one form of training does not preclude another). Most brickmasons, 43 percent of those who needed training, learned their trade on the job, 20 percent received formal company training.

Since in times of limited resources and pragmatic outlook the purpose of the training system is to supply the human resources required by the techno-economic structure of which it is a part, the demands of the latter translate into the objectives of the former. The training system is designed to produce so many plumbers, so many tool and die makers, so many airline pilots. The need for plumbers may change over time and so may the things a plumber needs to know, but on the whole there is something stable (i.e., structured) about the occupation of plumber and about the objective of training people for it.

Such structured or specific and reasonably stable objectives of the training system are met by equally structured means. In practice discipline may break down, but on the whole the schools try to impose it by enforcing regulations about punctuality, classroom behavior, restraint in linguistic expressiveness of the down-to-earth Anglo-Saxon variety, homework, and so forth. In other words, the schools teach by the mere fact that they are a restraining and structuring environment. The general emphasis on regulations teaches the students about work, scheduling, meeting deadlines, dependability, etc.

More specifically, curricula designed to meet such objectives as training tradesmen and doctors are highly structured as well. Courses of study prescribe what skills are to be mastered, what knowledge is to be acquired during each year, perhaps each month, week, and even day. This type of structure was what educational reformers revolted against with great vigor during the romantic interlude of the 1960s and early 1970s (e.g., Postman & Weingartner, 1969).

THE OUTPUT OF THE TRAINING SYSTEM

Given a structured training system, the question becomes whether it produces personnel to meet the demands of the work sphere. This industrial metaphor equating the schools with factories has something disturbing about it. Many people object to thinking of graduates as products and of people as human resources. The production metaphor does, however, bring home the fact that the training system is a part of the techno-economic structure whose main concern is production.

We can draw the distribution of workers capable of doing simple, intermediate, and complex jobs which is analogous to the distribution of jobs in Exhibit 4–2. Where the latter mainly reflects demand, this distribution of workers most directly reflects supply, that is, the human resources available. Of course, supply is generally a function of demand. For example, more people will enroll in apprenticeship programs for carpenters, and the supply of carpenters will increase, if the demand for carpenters is strong.

By comparing the distributions of workers shown in Exhibit 5–2 with the distribution of jobs in Exhibit 4–2 we can infer some answers to the question of whether the training system supplies the personnel required by the work sphere. This question boils down to two more specific issues: (1) whether the training system produces the requisite numbers of workers able to fill complex and moderately complex jobs and (2) whether it leaves enough people relatively untouched and untrained to fill the routine jobs. The latter issue makes more sense to the economist than to the educator who is concerned with the well-being of workers who are assumed to have a need to learn and develop.

As in the case of the demand curves, we can draw our supply curves reflecting different assumptions. Exhibit 5–2 shows a symmetrical and bell-shaped curve which represents the theoretical distribution of motivational dispositions and abilities. This theoretical distribution represents the outcome of chance processes, that is, it is the result of so

Exhibit 5–2
Distributions of Competence: Theoretical, Entry-Level, Mid-Career

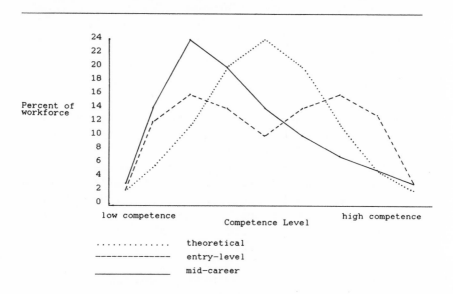

many factors that specific effects of specific factors cannot be understood and predicted. Chance produces very few extremely ambitious and intelligent people; it also produces very few individuals with no ambition and talent at all. It does produce many average individuals.

More than chance affects the actual distribution of characteristics. If the schools have a tendency to treat the children of the working and the middle class (not to mention the unemployed) differently, if they are more likely to encourage ambition and enterprise in middle class children, we expect motivation and ability levels to be distributed bimodally as shown by the second curve in Exhibit 5–2. The upper mode would represent the middle class, the lower mode the working class (at least the "working poor") and the unemployed.

The population segments represented by these modes are likely to be differentiated more sharply as their working lives progress. The routine workers receive minimal on-the-job training in work organizations whose managers think investments in technology that deskill jobs yield a better return than investments in less tangible serious training programs for their much ballyhooed "most valuable resource." The managers, professionals, and other highly trained members of the middle class, on the other hand, cannot help but acquire relevant experience and update themselves in the very process of doing their work. The result might be a positively skewed distribution as shown in Exhibit 5–2.

Fortunately, we saw earlier that while polarization is a dangerous trend, a large group of middle-level employees holding moderately complex jobs still does much of the work. We thus have to consider the production of three groups of workers: routine workers, workers qualifying for moderately complex jobs, and managers and professionals.

ROUTINE WORKERS

The reason scientific management is applied with enthusiasm to simplify and routinize work is that it increases productivity and permits the hiring of a cheap workforce which is neither ambitious nor skilled. The routine workforce which is hired to fill these jobs requires next to no training. Most of its members are drawn from always available pools of relatively disadvantaged persons. More than a few of the Anytown High graduands will at some time of their lives be part of one of these pools, this "reserve army of the underemployed" (e.g., Braverman, 1977, pp. 382–389; Marx, 1977, pp. 781–798; O'Toole, 1977, p. 55) ready to take any job.

But even routine jobs are often available only to applicants who meet certain criteria. Since they are "deskilled jobs," the criteria pertain to motivation rather than ability.

Docile Reliability and Endurance

Some critics of the training system have been particularly harsh in their condemnation of the motivating role of the schools for children of the working class. MacMichael (1974, p. 284) argues that schools promote an ethic of "obedience, conformity, and docility" among those who are not as middle class as the typical teacher and education officials, and whose parents are less likely than middle class parents to express great ambitions for them.

There is some truth to this, and obedience, conformity, and docility may certainly appear to be a desirable set of values for routine workers from the point of view of middle class employers. It is clear, however, that these values imposed by the middle class alienate rather than motivate the majority of routine workers. They may not rise in the manner of Marx's proletariat, but they murmur, and sometimes shout, in the canteens and in the bars across the street from their plants.

Fortunately, the motivating influence of the schools on the children of the working class is probably not as uniformly negative as the critics suggest. American schools constitute a heterogeneous system quite unable to uniformly impose a carefully designed set of values on any group. Within this heterogeneous system there are teachers who focus on salable skills, others who concentrate on motivation, some who try to transform their charges into disciplined characters, some who focus on the top performers and others who are more interested in the slow learners.

The On-the-Job Training of Routine Workers

Consider the following exchange which took place in the late 1970s. An Industrial Training Commission is holding hearings in a large room at the local Holiday Inn. The dozen or so distinguished gentlemen and the five alert and hawk-eyed ladies sit around a U-shaped table listening attentively to representatives of labor, management, and the local schools and colleges.

Question addressed to the representative from a large auto manufacturer: How many apprenticeships do you offer each year?

Answer: Not many. The work in the assembly plants is done by semiskilled labor, apprentices are trained as required to maintain the production lines. The training is specific, tailored to the company's needs.

Question: Is this to reduce costs and make it less likely that well-trained people will be hired away by other companies?

Answer: Yes. More or less.

Other employers appearing before the Commission make the same point. Training is costly. The idea is to make machines do the jobs requiring skill and to hire machine tenders whose jobs are as routine as possible. Besides, young men and women want to start earning wages on entering the workforce; they do not want to spend years acquiring skills at a low wage rate.

What emerges from the employers' frank presentations is that they are not inclined to produce a supply of well-trained workers, and that they are not inclined to do so because they do not perceive themselves to need such workers. On the contrary, they want employees who will do routine work and who do not require any training to speak of. By not training their workers they help assure an adequate supply of untrained workers unlikely to revolt against routine work as unworthy of their skills. The situation does not appear to have changed dramatically since the 1970s, although a more talked about feature of deskilled jobs today is the fact that they can be exported more easily to countries with cheaper labor.

WORKERS QUALIFYING FOR MODERATELY COMPLEX JOBS

As far as motivation is concerned, the techno-economic structure expects something other than docile reliability of middle-level workers holding moderately complex jobs, and with respect to ability it expects basic skills that insure trainability, and possibly some specialized skills. The training system is particularly ill-designed to meet the demand for this type of worker.

Training for Moderately Complex Jobs

What is true of the on-the-job training of routine workers generally also applies to that of workers who hold moderately complex jobs like ambulance drivers, security personnel, and insurance salespersons.

A government agency pats itself on the back for instituting a new program which extends the training of ambulance attendants to a period of several weeks. As if these attendants, who have to make life and death decisions, were less important than electricians and carpenters. This same agency supervises apprenticeship programs lasting three to four years for construction workers.

A lie detector operator is a high school graduate with a total of five days of training on his machine. This entitles him to draw conclusions about who is lying and who is not. Fortunately, he can take an advanced five-day course.

The training programs of insurance companies are primarily designed to exhort the sales staff to go out there like tigers and sell. They are about "prospecting" and "winning," they refer to Mr. and Mrs. Prospect, they feature the company's "superachievers," "champions," and "top producers." They preach a simple psychology glorifying the sales staff's desire to sell. Their attitude toward expertise is negative; experts are dawdlers who sit in armchairs talking about mere theory. In the view of W.E. McLeod (1974), "there are literally thousands of people out selling life insurance products that they do not understand. They have been given short cram courses and then let loose on the unsuspecting public. Many of these people are giving far-reaching financial advice for which they are hopelessly unqualified" (p. 52).

The "Sheepskin Psychosis"

The low achievement levels attained in schools and the unwillingness of many employers to provide solid training are not the only reasons for what probably is an inadequate supply of well-trained workers. Another reason is that the college degree has become essential to self-esteem and entry to the more demanding and challenging jobs. For most young people, there are no other ways to obtain fairly demanding training than to go to college.

The affluent 1960s and early 1970s produced the new disorder which John Keats (1963) called the "sheepskin psychosis." Mere vocational skills were valued considerably less than a college degree. Ever since, young Americans have flocked to college. No doubt, some potential first-rate short-order cooks became mediocre dietitians and some outstanding potential plumbers became mediocre engineers.

"Going to college" is to education what the private car is to transportation. It is the deluxe alternative only the rich and a rich society can afford. American society invested its dollars in colleges and universities as it has in highways. It did not put its money into meaningful large-scale apprenticeship or dual-system (part school/part work) training, in the same way as it refused to put it into public transportation systems.

Some of the results of this choice are reflected by statistics that look good on the surface. For example, in 1982, the number of third-level students (students in universities and colleges) per 100,000 inhabitants was 2030 in Japan, 2289 in the Federal Republic of Germany, and 5355 in the United States (UNESCO, 1985). Americans are proud of the high participation rate in third-level education. It may reflect, however, a lack of meaningful alternatives and low exit requirements rather than a high percentage of young people imbued by the desire to be scholars and scientists.

Some travellers try Amtrack and some Americans become apprentices, especially in times of budgetary restraint when other paths are subsidized less generously. But these are not fully developed alternatives. Somehow America's educational eggs are all in the college basket while in Japan and Germany large proportions of high school graduates enroll in challenging and carefully regulated vocational training programs.

Many of the graduates at the Anytown High ceremony will attend college in the fall. They and their parents really see no alternative to college. To them going to college is not something special. Since it is the only way to go, not going to college would mean an end of any ambitions for meaningful and challenging work. The Anytown graduates are faced by the choice the American training system forces most young people to make: to go to college or to be satisfied with rudimentary vocational training.

The Low Level of Vocational Skills

What is of immediate interest here are the range and levels of ability, skill, and knowledge actually displayed on the job. What are people at work really capable of doing? Does the insurance salesman know the advantages of term insurance over life insurance? Can the building superintendent recognize possible asbestos hazards? Can the salesperson provide the latest information from *Consumer Reports* on the products in the store and those of the competition?

If the training of workers is perfunctory, then we would expect to encounter low levels of vocational skills and knowledge in our daily association with fellow workers whose services and products we need. The following are some examples suggesting that the levels of knowledge and skill people bring to jobs of moderate complexity are indeed low.

The Toronto daily *Globe and Mail* reports that a survey of ten pharmacists yielded an average of eleven wrong answers to eighteen questions about the vitamins they were selling. The questions were of the type one might expect customers to ask, such as "Does vitamin E prevent heart trouble and keep a person young?" and "Are natural vitamins better than artificial ones?" (Roseman, 1977).

X-ray technicians and dental assistants know woefully little about the nature and dosages of the rays they work with every day. One medical doctor complained that when he called a dental office for appointments,

"I was told not to worry about . . . routine X-rays. The dentist would see me after they had been examined. And not a single dental assistant asked me when my last set of X-rays had been taken. Not one could tell me about how many milliroentgens I [would receive], or how much radiation I was allowed during my lifetime" (Gifford-Jones, 1979).

The typical life insurance agent, who may have sold lamps a few months earlier and who may sell cars next year, probably does not understand what inflation does to the value of annuity payments due sometime in the distant future; he knows little about accounting, and he does not grasp the legal issues that relate to most transactions in the life insurance field. Automobile insurance agents are no better. "Don't worry," they may say to customers who would like to know the regulations governing insurance coverage under nonroutine conditions, for example while they are selling an old car and buying a new one. To get information on insurance you may have to go to a lawyer, an accountant, or a high level insurance company manager who is not paid on the basis of sales.

When frontline employees work with computers, things can really get confusing. Most of these employees do not know what to do when faced with anything other than a strictly routine case, and very few are able to override the computer. Try to book two adjacent seats on an overseas flight for two passengers boarding at different airports! This inability to override the computer frequently manifests itself in the helplessness with which even senior employees face the problem of correcting obviously absurd errors made in computer billing.

A man we will call John works as a janitor in a school. He is not only quick to learn new procedures that are demonstrated to him, he is also reliable and proud of his work. The foreman relies heavily on him. He is in charge of the keys, passes them out at the start of the shift and accounts for them at its end. He cleans laboratories without disturbing experiments in progress. His is not a routine job. Unfortunately he runs into problems because he cannot read and write. Technology has produced a complicated world in which the broom, mop, and soap have been replaced by electrical polishers and cleaners and a variety of strong chemical cleaning solutions. There are instructions to be read and written warnings to be heeded. The ability to recognize the skull and crossbones is not enough.

There is evidence that policemen drive no better than the average citizen and that some armored trucks are guarded by overweight gentlemen who could not catch an old lady running away with a bag of banknotes.

In short, many workers in moderately complex jobs are undertrained and exhibit low levels of relevant vocational skills. The techno-economic structure gives them heavy responsibilities, but it treats their jobs as routine jobs. Although employers do not demand high levels of ability—that would force them to pay higher wages and salaries—the jobs themselves do. As a result, the lack of abilities has important consequences. For every poorly trained X-ray technician there may be future cancer patients; every ill-informed insurance salesman may be the cause of financial misery.

MANAGERS AND PROFESSIONALS

Of course, many of those participating in the rush to college do so with the realistic intention of becoming managers or professionals (doctors, engineers, etc.). The sheepskin psychosis that depletes the ranks of workers trained well for moderately complex jobs also swells the ranks of potential holders of complex jobs. Here too we have to consider the motivational and the ability-related aspects of human resources.

Aggression and Achievement

Among the graduating students of Anytown High are some imbued with the need to achieve, the drive to be successful. They have one of the ingredients that make a Brahma. Like football players they will "go for" their degrees in law or medicine. They are what J. O. Wisdom

(1966a, 1966b), in his analysis of British economic woes, called "professionals." Wisdom's analysis was based on the distinction between purposeful and expert professionals and the gentlemen and amateurs Britain is famous for and respects, but who, after World War II and until recently, have had a hard time trying to operate a competitive economy.

Professional Expertise

Professionals are not only highly motivated, they are highly trained. Americans, more pragmatic than the British, have always respected the professional who exudes "know-how." The American training system has traditionally been designed to produce a large proportion of football players trained to see life—in the laboratory, in business, in public affairs—as a game in which one is supposed to score points. Particularly in the decade after Sputnik, the universities were expected to produce football players. The unwelcome Russian technological feat in space prodded politicians, educators, and parents to do their part. No price seemed too great to produce as many scientists, engineers, and mathematicians as possible to help win the game against the USSR.

The area in which the American football player mentality has been most obvious in the decades after World War II is that of business management. There emerged the breed of the distinctly American scientific manager trained to fit into large and complex production and delivery systems and to understand how complex systems work, with some background in optimization procedures, in the evaluation of the effectiveness of systems or programs, and so forth.

In the postwar decades this football player, this professional manager, travelled all over the world extending American economic influence and control. French journalist and politician Jean-Jacques Servan-Schreiber (1968) described this influence in a book called *The American Challenge.* It was a tribute to American management expertise and it predicted that American business in Europe would emerge as the third economic superpower, after the United States itself and the USSR.

Servan-Schreiber's vision of American economic domination of Europe did not materialize. The German and French economies emerged as powerful forces of their own. While Americans grappled with the romantic counterculture of the 1960s and with the North Vietnamese, the Europeans and Japanese diligently studied American business management.

In the more sober and less affluent 1980s, the pendulum has swung back to the football player. On the campuses many students have marched purposefully to the registrar's office to enroll in courses required by the professional schools. Law, medicine, engineering, business management, computer science became the hot disciplines. Students focused on getting a good job to lay the foundation for a career. To attain these pragmatic goals they even exhibited a new willingness to go to the extreme of imposing on themselves the discipline required to master the English language and mathematics.

We have now looked at some issues pertaining to the demand and the supply of "human resources." This should make us more sensitive to the complexities of the relationships between the two. It is not just a question of whether the training system produces what the labor market demands. Perhaps the labor market should demand fewer unqualified workers for routine jobs. Perhaps all jobs should be designed so they offer opportunities and challenges.

The overview in this chapter of the output of the training system suggests that it "produces" many workers whose low qualification levels match the low ability demands of routine jobs. Whether these workers exhibit the desired endurance and docility is doubtful. Furthermore, an adequate supply of workers not overqualified or overeducated for routine work is not something to be happy about.

At the other extreme, the training system does a good job. The United States boasts many outstanding universities and programs turning out highly motivated and expert professionals and managers. However, vocational training opportunities for the sizable and important middle group are not abundant. This reduces the quality of life of many consumers of indifferent production work and services. It also reduces the quality of life, in particular the quality of work life, of these middle-level workers whose jobs offer few or no opportunities for developing a sense of competence and efficacy.

The immediate issue raised in these chapters on demand and supply is that of matching people and jobs within the techno-economic structure, that is, the work sphere on the macro-level of society. There is a basic mismatch here, although the statistics do not necessarily reveal it clearly. The mismatch is between people who have growth needs and personal concerns emanating from the life sphere, and jobs shaped by the impersonal, mechanistic, financial objectives of the work sphere. Although it is a mismatch which manifests itself within the work sphere, it transcends the work sphere and forces us to take a look at the life sphere.

6

The Life Sphere

The focus of Chapters 2 to 5 has been on the office, factory, store, and other workplaces; and on the schools and other training institutions that prepare people for work. In this chapter, the focus shifts to other aspects of society: those that constitute the life sphere, that is, a number of nonwork spheres which are primarily associated with personal and private concerns rather than the public activity comprising work. From the world of organizational rules and regulations, and of tasks and duties defined externally by supervisors and employers, we move to the world of family, leisure, politics and community affairs, education and personal growth, and even religion.

The fact that four chapters dealt with the work sphere while one will do for the life sphere is revealing: After the anti-work attitudes of the late 1960s, when young people up to the age of 50 and more wore beads and eschewed steady employment, we live again in a period that focuses on work, jobs, careers and the more affluent life styles they make possible. The book shelves fairly creak under the load of how-to books and one-minute recipes designed to make our work more tolerable and financially more rewarding.

Our first look at the life sphere focused on the material and cultural conditions listed on the level of society under life sphere in Exhibit 1–1. Here a more detailed look is required. Essentially the focus is on a number of specific cultural trends which manifest themselves in the different subspheres of the life sphere. The life sphere, in contrast to the work sphere, tends to be associated with cultural more than mate-

Exhibit 6–1
Subspheres of the Life Sphere

---

1. **Close social relationships**
Family (Burke & Greenglass, 1987; Lee & Kanungo, 1984, Part 1;
Dubin & Champoux, 1977), other social relationships (Flannagan,
1978), love (Neff, 1985).

2. **Leisure**
Leisure (Lee & Kanungo, 1984, Part 2; De Grazia, 1964),
recreation (Flannagan, 1978), play (Neff, 1985; Huizinga, 1968).

3. **Armslength social relationships**
Social, community, and civic activities (Flannagan, 1978),
community (Dubin & Champoux, 1977), political sphere (Near
et al., 1980), the polity (Bell, 1976).

4. **Education**
Unstructured self-development, personal growth
(Crandall, 1984); personal development and fulfillment
(Flanagan, 1978), art, etc. (Bell, 1976).

5. **Religion**
Religion (Crandall, 1984), church (Dubin & Champoux, 1977).

---

rial determinants. Nevertheless, these trends reflect varying degrees of
actual and perceived affluence and hence varying degrees of material
and cultural determinism. In general, they also grow out of our collective post-industrial (non-industrial!) values.

SUBSPHERES AND TRENDS

Subspheres of the Life Sphere

The life sphere is less homogeneous than the work sphere. On the
level of society it includes a range of institutions and corresponding
subspheres. Exhibit 6–1 provides some idea of these subspheres. It is
based on a survey of relevant literature. The different keywords refer-
ring to different aspects of the life sphere in this sample of the literature are listed, together with their sources. The keywords overlap, but
they convey an impression of the meaning of the subspheres identified.

These subspheres include the family and leisure, where leisure is
thought of as generally passive recreation. They also include active efforts to stimulate personal growth through such avenues as education,
art and religion. Finally, they include social, in particular community
and civic, activities. These social activities will turn out to be particularly important in changing work to bring it close to life.

Training and education were sharply distinguished in Chapter 1 and
this distinction is important to our understanding of the active efforts
made within the life sphere to develop and grow. Education, unlike
training, was defined as an end rather than a means, as activity concerned with the attainment of depth and scope. Together depth and

scope yield Peters' (1965) central outcome of education: cognitive breadth. Although it is scope that more immediately corresponds to breadth, depth is the means to attain scope. This means that education is about understanding, about seeing underlying and broad relationships involving ourselves, those around us, and the physical universe of which we are a part.

In general, the life sphere is the private sphere in which we do not pursue externally imposed objectives, such as producing sixty widgets an hour, which are merely means to our personal ends. It is about ends, ultimately about the ends of understanding and contentment.

Trends of the Life Sphere

What we consider to be objectives that are ends in themselves—objectives of our life, our life sphere—is influenced by underlying social trends: the trend toward post-industrial values, the trend of the 1960s and 1970s to reject structure and constraints, narcissistic trends, the pragmatism of the "ruthless mothers" of the 1980s, the quest for self-fulfillment.

Trends come and go; some last, perhaps assuming different forms but basically imbued by the same values. Rugged individualism was required of pioneers who opened up a new continent. Many still value this individualism; they have more confidence in the individual American, especially if he is white, with his trusty gun and his wisely cast vote than in some abstract government far beyond scrutiny. What the rice farmer working in a group is to the Japanese, the individual dirt-farmer or roaming cowboy relying on no one but himself is still to many Americans today.

In the 1950s, a dominant trend encouraged people to abandon rugged individualism and become cooperative conformists. This trend is food for thought for those who think that Americans are always individualists and the Japanese are always conformists. This was the time of Sloan Wilson's (1956) *Man in the Grey Flannel Suit*, William H. Whyte's (1956) *Organization Man*, and David Riesman's (1953) other-directed members of the *The Lonely Crowd*. Some of these adaptable types, at home in the organization and comfortable when meeting the demands of others, are also still with us.

The 1960s brought a revolt of the postwar generation. America was rich. War and destruction were taking place out of sight. President Lyndon B. Johnson promised the "Great Society" and offered "guns *and* butter." Technology was taking over production. Work seemed a thing of the past. Constraints in the work sphere and the schools seemed unnecessary and hence unjustified. It was the world of Alex Keaton's laid-back and still fairly romantic parents of the well known TV show *Family Ties*.

Then the Organization of Petroleum Producing Countries (OPEC) tripled oil prices in 1973. A "new reality" had dawned. There was recession and unemployment. The threat of scarcity brought about a rapid recovery from the romanticism of the 1960s. The new trend was the work- and career-oriented pragmatism of the yuppies scrambling for their condo in the sun. The Keaton seniors were pushed off the stage by their materialistic offspring, the "ruthless mothers."

Most recently the AIDS plague has accelerated the resurgence of conservative values, illustrating that it is not only scarcity, but material conditions in general that dominate and determine our values when they threaten our survival. Similarly, drug addiction appears to have exceeded a critical threshold and is perceived as a sufficiently severe threat to warrant putting on hold basic civil rights pertaining to privacy, the presumption of innocence until proven guilty, and so on.

The remaining sections of this chapter focus on some specific trends that have attracted attention over the last few decades. We are dealing here with values that affect and are affected by the work sphere, but which originate in and play an important role in the life sphere. No claim to comprehensiveness is made. The life sphere is the domain of the sociologists and anthropologists. The objective of this chapter is merely to provide a starting point for thinking about the nature of the life sphere on the macro-level of society.

POST-INDUSTRIAL VALUES

One of Soviet art's most representative products is the eighty-foot statue titled *Worker and Kolkhoz Woman* sculpted in stainless steel by Vera Mukhina in l937. It depicts a man and a woman who exemplify the new citizens that the Russian revolution sought to produce. The stance of the two figures is heroic. The man holds a hammer and the woman a sickle, in hands raised straight toward the sky—they look like Karate champions ready to do battle for the utopian society envisioned by Marx and Lenin. Their eyes are fixed on a distant goal. They exude strength, confidence, and determination. They reflect the ideal industrious and industrial society.

The famous hamburger sculpted by the American artist Claes Oldenburg in 1962 reflects values of a more affluent and more post-industrial society. Made of sewn canvas, stuffed with foam rubber, covered with a paint that hardened and froze the perhaps immortal form, the hamburger reflects in a witty way the fast food culture whose taste buds died some time ago, democratic impulses that selected a national food which the poor and the rich can afford equally well, which is eaten with equal pleasure by both, and which tastes exactly the same way in San Diego, California, and Bangor, Maine. It is not stone or steel that is used, but flimsy material which can be tossed together quickly in a "happening." One can almost hear the artist say: "I reflected on the human condition and this, within the limited time this issue deserves and which I am willing to put into it, is what I have come up with. Enjoy."

The serious realism of a poor society faced with the choice between dedicated labor and starvation produces different art from that of an affluent society that can afford to look beyond work to play, in fact, that can afford to do what children are admonished not to do: to play with food.

Another product of this more affluent society that in some ways is post-industrial was the alternative life style community called Sandstone. Imagine, if you will, a large mansion on a mountain top, overlooking the Pacific Ocean, surrounded by a garden sporting a swimming pool. This was the setting of Sandstone, an experimental community founded in 1969. It provided a place for a "I wanna feel good now" and "letting go" life style familiar to Californians then and now and introduced to millions by Hugh Hefner, the bon-vivant and publisher of *Playboy*.

Twice weekly the Sandstone community organized party nights at which the participants did what they felt like doing, from playing chess, to frolicking in the pool, to cleaning and maintaining the premises, to private and public sexual intercourse. Some accounts suggest that the emphasis was on intercourse, that neither the chess sets nor the brooms and dust cloths suffered excessive wear.

Like Hefner's glossy displays of the good, that is, hedonistic life, Sandstone operated on the principle that only those acts are immoral which hurt someone else.

But while the guests let go at the Sandstone parties, the organizers of this community put a lot of thought and effort into their work. Sandstone was part of broad cultural developments such as the emergence of the hippies and flower power, psychotherapy as means to a fulfilling life and a higher consciousness, and eastern mysticism. It was not by accident that Bell (1976) formulated the distinction between the techno-economic structure and his culture during this period of upheaval. At no time was the gap between work and life spheres greater. At no time did the life sphere so completely overshadow the work sphere. Sandstone was dedicated to life, and the neglect by many of its participants of the mundane world of work eventually was its downfall.

The gap between tedious work and exciting personal life widened in the United States at that time because of a high level of affluence which permitted people to pursue personal concerns, confident that the techno-economic structure would provide whatever they needed without a real contribution of time and effort from them. Such affluence made it easy for substantial segments of the population, in particular the young, to reject the techno-economic structure. It was an easy target in the first place. It demanded subjugation of personal needs to those of employers and society, it was greedy and accepted no limits, it bulldozed ravines and transformed agricultural land into plastic suburbs and parking lots, it tempted politicians and generals to fight a war in Vietnam, and it polluted land, water, and air.

Chapter 1 referred to Trist's (1973) hypothesis that the reaction to the work ethic of the industrial age is a shift of values along four different dimensions: Achievement becomes self-actualization, self-control becomes self-expression, independence becomes interdependence, and endurance of distress becomes capacity for joy. Among these emerging post-industrial values, self-expression is of particular interest. According to Bell (1976), the "axial principle [of the American culture of the 1960s] is the expression and remaking of the 'self' in order to achieve "self-realization and self-fulfillment" (p. 13).

Trist's four transitions become more concrete when expressed in terms of the more specific values defined by social psychologist Milton Rokeach (1973). Rokeach constructed a measure of values that requires test-takers to order eighteen instrumental values and eighteen terminal values in terms of their importance. The instrumental values are attributes which serve as means to a person's goals. Examples of instrumental values include the values placed on achieving one's ends by being *ambitious* and *capable*. The terminal values are the goals themselves. These include *freedom* and *a comfortable life*.

Trist's and Rokeach's values differ, but certain relationships can plausibly be inferred. Ron Frisch, William Libby, and the present author suggest, for example, that Trist's transition from achievement to self-actualization is, in terms of Rokeach's terminal values, a shift from seeking a comfortable life and social recognition to seeking a sense of accomplishment, self-respect and wisdom (Frisch, Morf, & Libby, 1975/1976).

Given Trist's paradigm and Rokeach's specific lists of terminal and instrumental values it is possible to study experimental communities, such as Sandstone, which sought to anticipate future post-industrial life styles in a world perhaps liberated from routine production of life's necessities. In an analysis of data obtained from a sample of Sandstone regulars and visitors and data, made available by Rokeach and the National Opinion Research Center, of a comparison sample drawn from the population at large, Frisch et al. found some reasons that help explain the community's demise.

In accordance with Trist's paradigm, Sandstone participants did value self-expression more highly than self-control, and capacity for joy more than endurance of such distress as is involved in cleaning up after the party. However, too many of the participants did not value self-actualization and interdependence. Too many were individualists thirsting for the freedom to do what they felt like doing. Increasingly it became difficult to organize and execute the housekeeping chores, and the community folded by 1972. Its place was later taken by a second community, also called Sandstone, which had quite a different character.

It seems clear that the freedom from the constraints imposed by the necessity to produce essentials does not by itself bring about utopia. For example, some basic unpleasant work always remains to be done if a community is to survive and whatever post-industrial values emerge must form a coherent set of values that take this fact into account. They must fill the vacuum left by the abandonment of the industrial values that promoted self-control and social control. Trist's post-industrial value of interdependence, not widely adopted by the visitors to Sandstone, may play a crucial role in filling this vacuum.

If interdependence is valued, the quality of production and service should rise, since the doctor who perfunctorily glances into the butcher's throat instead of performing the required physical examination will be more aware that the butcher may reach perfunctorily for the poorest cuts the next time he sees the good doctor or his wife on the other side of the counter. Sandstone and other post-industrial pioneer communities failed not only because they neglected the work sphere, but also because they were absorbed by the leisure subsphere and neglected the community and civic aspects of the life sphere.

THE REVOLT AGAINST STRUCTURE

Pendulums always swing. In the 1930s, the state was worshipped and the individual was deemed to be dispensible. The post-World War I chaos had produced a veritable veneration of structure and order. As Erich Fromm (1941) pointed out in *Escape from Freedom,* the citizens of Germany and Italy, the very countries in which affluent young anarchists of the Baader-Meinhof group and the Red Brigades more recently wreaked considerable havoc, were at that time willing to give up their democratic rights and let the *Fuehrer* or *duce,* the party, and the state make the decisions.

The American counterculture, on the other hand, rejected the state, put the FBI and CIA under great clouds of suspicion, and regarded policemen as crypto-Nazis. Its denizens exhibited a thirst for untrammeled freedom to do their thing and to express themselves. Everyone became a Patrick Henry shouting "give me liberty or give me death."

Fromm's escape from freedom turned into a clamor for freedom from all constraints, whether they were justified or not.

The revolt against structure was especially strong among educators, an occupational group which, paid by the public, is fairly quick to follow its lead. Of course, educators are usually trainers, but in the context of this revolt we encounter social critics who run the gamut from trainers on the front line to philosophers of education.

Among the anti-structure advocates in education or training, Neil Postman and Charles Weingartner stand out. In the view of these two authors (Postman & Weingartner, 1969), there was no such thing as a fundamental concept. There were only teachers who believed that what they happened to know must be fundamental. True romantics, the Postmans and the Weingartners fought to the death the brutal constraints implied by words like *linear, sequential, plan, curriculum, syllabus,* and *prerequisite.*[1]

The romantic gurus of education who emerged in the wake of the counterculture had no use for structured training programs producing competent tool and die makers. They espoused values quite the opposite of those of the work sphere, a sphere they thought was on its last legs in a society moving away from the "wasteland" (Roszak, 1973) toward "a greening of America" (Reich, 1970). They refocused attention on the centrality of the life sphere in which we pursue the personal ends that ultimately matter to us. But they also helped to bring about a decline of ability which made it difficult for the United States to compete with better trained workforces in Japan and Germany.

The counterculture abhorred structure and the restraints and differentiations it implied. It bade goodbye to mathematics, spelling, and grammar; it welcomed communication and relevance. Schools, though more progressive than ever, were not progressive enough to escape charges of brutalizing and enslaving young minds. One of the most widely acclaimed documents of the 1960s was Jerry Farber's (1969) expressively titled book *The Student as Nigger.*

This revolt against structure in education was part of the conflict between industrial parents and post-industrial children. Every child has ample opportunity to feel oppressed by its physically overpowering parents, and rebellion is likely to erupt when the parents seem unsure of themselves. Parents did feel unsure of themselves as they read Benjamin Spock and listened to the education gurus of the 1960s, to the Neil Postmans and the Charles Weingartners, to the John Holts who scornfully rejected tests and examinations, and to the George Leonards who offered to replace the tedium of traditional learning with nothing less than ecstasy (Holt, 1970; Leonard, 1968).

Educators became more concerned with letting the child grow freely and unencumbered, and less with providing the child with the structured opportunities to acquire knowledge and skills that could lead to informed choices and the ability to solve problems independently at some later point in time. Students were encouraged to engage in social criticism before they had learned to read the cogent criticisms made by thoughtful thinkers since Plato and Aristotle or earlier. The illiterate, inorate, and inumerate were given videotape portapacks to produce instant statements. Learners were expected to grow on their own, there was little help from the gardeners, there were few stakes to facilitate straight growth. The negative freedom from constraints was emphasized at the expense of the positive freedom made possible by understanding and ability.

Rebellion did erupt. It was directed against the past and against the idea of permanence. History was declared to be irrelevant and the meticulous acquisition of skills that might lead to mastery and competence was regarded as a waste of time. Immediate rewards, relevance, and style were, and remain to a large extent, the watchwords of youth. Competence and substance were not in vogue.

Two more specific trends which in some ways appear to be part of the revolt against structure are the environmental monism and the equalitarianism of the life sphere. Both reject structure and level it like bulldozers.

Environmental Monism

The belief that human beings are shaped by their environment is referred to here as *environmental monism*. Exhibit 6–2 lists strong expressions of environmental monism which, with one exception, have been uttered during the romantic 1960s and in their immediate aftermath. They are reactions to the traditional overemphasis on genes and reflect the important fact that we are indeed largely shaped by the environment. But they also show that the pendulum once again had swung from one extreme, the hereditarian position of the first half of the twentieth century, to another extreme that is equally unprofitable.

Environmental monism is a comforting belief because it is simple and because it suggests that by arranging the environment properly, we can assure the human behavior we want. Like most monistic beliefs it is also wrong since the world is a complex entity in which ultimately everything affects everything else.

Environmental monism is simple because it dismisses classes of determinants of the person other than the environmental ones. Biological determinants are dismissed as having little significance, at least by the dominant social sciences. Let the biologists mutter under their breath about complex interactions between genes and environmental factors,

Exhibit 6–2
Expressions of Environmental Monism

...a person does not act upon the world, the world acts upon him.
B. F. Skinner (1971, p. 211)

We keep trying to find something wrong inside people. It's the culture that's wrong, not the people.
B.F. Skinner. Quoted in Hall, E. (1972, Nov., p. 72)

...give me...infants...and my own specified world to bring them up in and I'll...take any one at random and train him to become any type of specialist I might select--doctor, lawyer, artist, merchant-chief and, yes, even beggar-man and thief, regardless of his talents, penchants, tendencies, abilities...and race.
J. B. Watson (1930, p. 104)

If an environment fails...to educate, it is the environment's, not the learner's, fault.
G. B. Leonard (1968, p. 154)

If at the end of a year he [the student] has truly learned nothing,...then I am the one who should be failed...It is terrible [that students can't read], and all the more so because the fault is not theirs but the school's.
J. Holt (1970, pp. 253–254)

I think the idea that people have something like free will is obscene and disgusting.
M. Minsky. Quoted in Brown (1984, Oct. 6, p. 10)

With the possible exception of intelligence, highly generalized behavioral consistencies have not been demonstrated, and the concept of personality traits as broad predispositions is thus untenable.
W. Mischel (1968, p. 146)

Behavior depends on stimulus situations and is specific to the situation.
W. Mischel (1968, p. 177)

Note. The other side of the coin:

The fault, dear Brutus, lies not in our stars, but in ourselves.
Shakespeare, Julius Caesar

---

the media rarely interview them. The public wants to hear from the more relevant and vocal social scientists!

There are also personal determinants, that is, putative causes of our behavior and personality development which are said to be reflected by our own "freely-made" decisions. Humanists are ready to consider these personal determinants, which we experience as emanating from within ourselves when we talk about responsibility, guilt, freedom, and choice. Scientists reject them, however, because the evidence for them is introspective, that is, subjective and nonreplicable. The nature of such complicating and difficult determinants, both biological and personal, need not worry the environmental monists.

It thus appears that behavior can be manipulated fairly easily. After all, environmental determinants are not as final as biological ones. We can change the environment more easily than biological determinants. Molecular biology and surgical sophistication are progressing by leaps and bounds, but in the backs of our minds we are aware that we are not yet very good at using these tools for change and may end up with new and dangerous forms of man-made life.

Environmental monism is something Americans share with the

Marxists. In both cases, it not only serves the purpose of simplifying the world one is looking at, but also of supporting hopes of overcoming acute social problems. But the reasons for the need to simplify and the social problems faced are different in the United States and the Soviet Union. Levelling and simplifying in America serve the purpose of untrammeled post-industrial self-expression and they promise a solution to the problem of racial and other discrimination. In the still very industrial USSR they may serve the purpose of instilling hope that it is possible by human effort to change everything, to create the new Soviet man or woman. This hope must be fanned because the ideal is very different from the reality of the average Russian, who is not very different from his or her prerevolutionary grandparents and who grumbles and probably entertains reactionary thoughts while standing in line at the butcher shop.

Equalitarian Excesses

This brings us to the uncompromising equalitarianism of the romantic culture. Equalitarianism, as opposed to the egalitarianism discussed later in Chapter 8, is based on the belief that essentially everyone is the same as everyone else. This second simplifying and levelling belief, expressed in the silly dictum "I can do anything I want," grows directly out of environmental monism. If the only thing that matters is the environment, be it the oppressive school or the wise guru, then any important differences between individuals are the result of the different environments they have experienced. That means you cannot blame the criminal, the lazy student, the egocentric bore. We are all essentially the same. Whatever differences there are were produced by accidental past environments and can be corrected by cleverly engineered future environments. We can all benefit from the same schooling. We should all go to a university and take a stab at being a nuclear physicist or a psychoanalyst.

The equalitarianism of the education gurus of the 1960s and later is illustrated by educator Herbert London's description of a credit-review session

in which a young man who claimed to be teaching swimming in a community club was granted six credits of advanced standing in physical education. He presented no corroboration, took no swimming test, and was asked only one serious question ("How long have you been doing it?"). In another case a student received advanced standing in sociology for having lived in a ghetto all her life. No paper describing her experiences was submitted and no examination was required. "My experience is worth more than all the theories in those textbooks," she said, and she was granted eight credits. (London, 1972, p. 63)

One reason equalitarians refuse to make distinctions among individuals is their *nonegalitarian* belief that to say "A is different from B" is to imply that one is better than the other. With egalitarians they share the conviction that there is no justification for structuring society in hierarchical fashion with superior or upper classes or castes lording it over inferior or lower ones. But their premise that there cannot be diversity without hierarchy forces them to conclude that everyone must be essentially the same as everyone else.

With this well-meaning but not entirely accurate conclusion one is well launched on the path of uniformity that makes one accept a society that offers record stores and radio stations for rock fans, but not (with very few exceptions) for Mozart or Bach fans; TV stations broadcasting news, weather, and sports at exactly the same time of the day; supermarkets that supply a dozen essentially identical detergents or toothpastes. All of this is apparently meant to fulfill the needs of the consumers out there who are all perceived to be equal in the strong sense of identical.

Of course, even the most rabid equalitarians have to admit once in a while that people do differ in a variety of respects. But they are quick to qualify such differences as "so-called," "apparent," and "trivial" differences due to environmental factors whose influence can and must be counteracted. Equalitarianism and environmental monism are clearly compatible sets of beliefs. Equalitarians tend to be environment-oriented and to assign at best a very minor role to heredity, and they tend to see their fellow citizens, though not necessarily themselves, as externally controlled. They are likely to endorse vigorously the environment-oriented assertions presented in Exhibit 6–2. Some probably believe that the devil makes us do things or that murder should be blamed on the full moon.

THE "CULTURE OF NARCISSISM"

A number of social commentators, in particular historian Christopher Lasch (1978), have invoked the so-called "new narcissism" to describe the life sphere of the 1960s and 1970s that clashed so discordantly with the techno-economic structure. By this they meant that the life sphere fostered individuals resembling Narcissus who, according to Greek mythology, saw himself reflected on the surface of a pond and promptly fell in love with the handsome physique and beautiful visage he saw there. This narcissism appears to be a substrate of both some of the romantic excesses of the 1960s and early 1970s and the new pragmatism and search for self-fulfillment more characteristic of the life sphere today. It warrants closer scrutiny.

Narcissism, the infatuation with one's self, is related to both the romantic orientation of the counterculture in general and its more specific post-industrial values in particular. If our true selves are admirable, then we are justified in lavishing lots of attention on them. Since it was Jean Jacques Rousseau's basic tenet that man is naturally good, it is not surprising that Bell (1976, p. 132) already detects a certain narcissism in Rousseau's *Confessions*. In addition, the post-industrial value of self-expression, central to Bell's culture, is both romantic in nature and likely to foster narcissism.

The term *narcissism* was popularized by Sigmund Freud (1957). He used it to refer to a stage of development of infants after they have learned to distinguish between themselves and the external world, and before they care, love, or are at least interested in salient features of the world around them, such as their mothers or their bunny rabbits. According to Freud, the infant's energy or "libido" is at that point not directed toward things in the environment. As a result, the infant's little ego is oozing with energy and is inflated, and we find "an over-estimation of the power of [the child's] wishes and mental acts . . . and a technique for dealing with the external world— 'magic'—which appears to be a logical application of these grandiose premisses" (1957, p. 75). Freud saw this narcissism of the child as primary and normal.

What the social critics have in mind when they refer to the "new narcissism" is secondary narcissism, a loss of interest on the part of adults in others and in external things generally. This secondary narcissism is pathological. According to Freud, if one no longer cares much about the things "out there," one must care more about the self, since motivational energy has to be directed and discharged toward something.

Examples of secondary narcissism given by Freud include the schizophrenic's dramatic withdrawal from the world. They also include reactions of the physically ill and the deprived. Freud (1957, p. 82) cites Wilhelm Busch's famous line describing a poet suffering from a toothache who finds it impossible to direct his thoughts to the creative task at hand: "Concentrated is his soul in his molar's narrow hole."

Freud interprets the myth of Narcissus broadly: The attention and interest of narcissists are directed toward themselves, rather than to their environment, in particular their social environment. He further argues that narcissistic parents regard their children as perfect, as incapable of doing wrong, and as deserving a better life than their own often humdrum existence. Unconsciously they regard their children as extensions of themselves, and these beliefs are actually beliefs about what they, the parents, are really like and really deserve. This may be one reason for the enthusiastic acceptance and frequent misinterpretation of the progressive childrearing theories of Benjamin Spock, and it is certainly a factor that has produced a generation somewhat naive about the realities of adult life in a world in which, alas, manna does not daily fall from heaven.

The narcissistic personality that emerged in the golden 1960s and somewhat more introverted 1970s concentrated its efforts on developing the self and on striving for higher levels of consciousness elevating it above the rabble. It was not content with being part of the herd. Elitist in nature, it sought to acquire esoteric and mysterious knowledge and insight. The narcissists felt destined to be superstars. They were imbued with the belief that their admirable selves had the potential to be and do anything they wanted.

The narcissists attributed the same potential to everyone else. This allowed them to entertain some bizarre beliefs. For example, if everyone can do what they want to do, then the peasants of Bangladesh must be starving because they *want* to starve. Some people want to attain self-fulfillment, others want to starve, but all are doing what they want. A belief system of this kind allowed the narcissists to ignore the misery around them, perhaps even to travel through India in search of fulfillment while stepping over the skinny limbs of beggars. In short, it allowed them to pursue their quest of self without qualms.

The narcissists were typically well-off products of the affluent society, able to affect disdain for merely material objectives. Their concerns related to the life sphere, in particular to the task of developing that most precious and astonishing of all resources, their own selves. With condescending smiles they moved through everyday life, occasionally pointing out modestly that insight and understanding of the mysterious essence of being a person did not escape them entirely. They flocked around high-living gurus who exhorted them to be ascetic and they followed esoteric intellectual ants while remaining untainted by any knowledge of Socrates or Kant.

THE REVIVAL OF PRAGMATISM

Narcissism characterized not only the romantics of the 1960s and the introspective searchers of the wonderful significance of their own selves of the 1970s, but also the more pragmatic generation of the 1980s. Pragmatism is a philosophy which holds that one should do what works. We have encountered it as the philosophy of Benjamin Franklin in Chapter 2. By itself, it is clearly neither good nor bad. It has done wonders for the United States in the past, but it was carried to extremes in the 1980s.

The new generation of the 1980s rediscovered the work sphere, and its narcissism and pragmatism manifested themselves not only in the life sphere, but also in the work sphere. The work sphere became the realm in which one acquires the expensive house and the BMW which are the visible signs of having made it, of being on the fast track, of being among the fittest who come out on top in the competitive jungle. There are echoes of the Calvinist ethic here: You work hard for visible signs of your status as one of the selected ones.

We have clearly reached the post-1973, post-OPEC oil-price blow, reality of Alex Keaton Jr., the career and money oriented preppie and eventual yuppie. The counterculture once embraced by the senior Keatons of *Family Ties*, alternative life style communities like Sandstone, the revolt against structure, and the environmental monism and equalitarianism associated with that revolt—all have a somewhat frivolous component. They are removed from the serious business of making a living. They are aspects of a life sphere which had moved far from the work sphere.

Thus it is not surprising that the American life sphere changed markedly when recession and unemployment, overseas competition, demographic changes resulting from an aging population, and a mounting national debt put limits on the size of the economic pie. Suddenly it became important to scramble for one's slice. The new generation of "ruthless mothers" crowded the colleges and universities, demanding admission to professional schools and training concentrating on clearly salable skills. Businessmen and managers—yes, even they had been seduced by the counterculture—once again strove to make their organizations lean and mean. Personal growth was postponed.

Appearances changed. The long-haired hippie wearing beads made way for well-coiffed future organization men wearing ties. The radical leader Jerry Rubin shaved his beard and became a Wall Street broker. Research funds were channelled to applied and practical projects; basic research merely trying to further understanding of the world no longer elicited the old enthusiasm from funding agencies. Social Darwinism replaced the luxury of equalitarianism. *Accountability* and *the new reality* became the expressions summing up the public mood. The question "what is the right thing to do?" changed to "what do the lawyers say about how much we can get away with?" Achievement was once again in vogue.

As the life sphere in general moved away from the concerns of the romantic counterculture and toward the concerns of the new pragmatists facing a pie of limited size, the romantic gurus of education made way for the high priests of specialist expertise, the new pragmatic professionals of the 1980s. The radical sociologists and prophetic poets disappeared and the tanned business professors and engineers carrying laptop computers proliferated. The new pragmatism made it sometimes difficult to draw the line between work and life. In general, the work sphere dominated, such life concerns as grappling with questions asked by the Greeks two and a half millennia ago were put on the back burner.

This chapter's overview of trends of the life sphere has covered the romanticism of the 1960s, the more subdued and introspective narcissism of the 1970s, and the unabashed pragmatism of the 1980s. Trends obviously come and go. This makes it necessary to cast the net somewhat into the past, in the hope of detecting patterns and underlying similarities beneath the rapidly changing surface. Such hope is not unwarranted, there are stable patterns as well as change.

Underneath both the romanticism of the 1960s and the pragmatism of the 1980s one can detect a need to focus on the immediately relevant and a need to simplify the world which threatens to overwhelm one with its complexity. Wearing a tie, obtaining a business degree, acquiring useful and practical skills are things that generally work, which are immediately relevant. They get one the job. The pragmatist's tactics are not only relevant, they are simple and easily understood and they simplify the world in the way the rejection of structure, equalitarianism, and environmental monism did in the 1960s.

Narcissism did not suddenly flower in the 1970s, it has long roots and is quite visible among the exponents of the counterculture and again among the pragmatists of the 1980s. Its more solid cousin, the quest for self-fulfillment also links the world of the two Keaton generations. Yankelovich (1981) has probed the changing values of Americans over time by means of survey questionnaires. He reported that the thirst for self-fulfillment which developed in the affluent 1960s did not weaken markedly when inflation and unemployment threatened jobs and financial security. It did, however, express itself in different forms.

Yankelovich distinguished between three segments of the population. The first consists of the 20 percent espousing the traditional values of "familial success," that is, focusing on the raising, maintaining, and financial improvement of the old-fashioned, nuclear family. The second segment is the 17 percent of the population engaged in "strong form" quests for self-fulfillment. These he presents as relics of the 1960s and early 1970s, the pre-scarcity era. In the age of the new reality of scarcity, this segment finds that its inward-orientedness, and its inability to deal with external economic matters, lead to less than satisfactory adjustment. The third segment is the majority 63 percent who pragmatically try to combine both the older economic goals and objectives with the newer concerns for self-fulfillment. In the 1980s, few wore flowers and burned incense, but self-expression, self-fulfillment, and self-development continued to be important.

This chapter thus leaves us with a framework within which we can analyze more closely various aspects of the life sphere. One can think of this framework as a 5×3 contingency table, whose five rows represent the five subspheres of the life sphere represented in Exhibit 6–1 and whose three columns represent trends affecting these subspheres and rooted in the past three decades. To provide some kind of framework suggesting a way for developing the concept of life sphere has been the modest aim of this chapter.

The particular trends identified here have a somewhat hedonistic and selfish flavor, and other observers would doubtlessly be struck by different influences and patterns. It seems likely, however, that any trends identified as characteristic of the life sphere in America today will reflect the marked differences between it and the structured, organized, and orderly work sphere.

NOTE

1. Postman and Weingartner's contribution to the battle against structure was titled *Teaching as a subversive activity*. As the 1960s receded and as the 1980s arrived, Postman (1980) rethought his position considerably and produced a follow-up volume titled *Teaching as a conserving activity*.

7

Redefined Work

In the industrial society, the work and life spheres have become separated. In the present transition to a post-industrial society high expectations have evolved that technology will somehow assume the burden of much of the work done by humans up to now. This has led to a rejection of work as unnecessary drudgery in some quarters and has made the gap between work and life even greater. Other factors at work in this transition have raised at least possibilities for narrowing the gap between them. For example, there are ways in which technology can be used to upgrade jobs, to make them more challenging and more like the tasks we face in personal life.

The question that now arises is how satisfaction with work and life can be raised by working toward a reintegration of work and life. Clearly on the macro-level it cannot be a question of discovering steps that will change American society in some dramatic fashion. Conditions are far from sufficiently grim for revolution, and revolution seldom has only the intended effects. Actual and planned change usually occurs on the micro-level, consists of modest steps affecting individuals and specific jobs, and produces small, gradual, though hopefully incremental and hence non-negligible, effects.

What we can do on this level is consider possibilities which might at least encourage actual change. If the climate is right on the macro-level, action is more likely on the micro-level.

The preceding chapters constitute an initial, modest, but essential step in the analysis of the relationship between work and life and of the prospects for their reintegration. They are descriptive chapters. On the basis of the description of the work and life spheres it is possible, first, to isolate critical aspects and, second, to consider possibilities for changing these critical features.

Three features of the work sphere have emerged. There is its actual structure, a structure of jobs, occupations, work organizations, and so forth. Then there are its demands for workers or for certain abilities and motivational dispositions. These demands are shaped by the structure of the work sphere, in particular the jobs in this structure. Finally, there is the training system designed to meet the demands of the work sphere for human resources. The schools are the most important part of this training system.

It is the first two of these aspects, the jobs of the work sphere and the demands for human resources that spring from them that are the most likely loci of intervention, action, and change. Changing them would create new conditions to which the training system might adapt, since its purpose is to meet the demands for personnel within the work sphere. In the work sphere of society change means creating a climate that encourages the upgrading of jobs. This is the subject of the present chapter.

The thesis of this chapter is that by being open to ideas of other cultures, we can redefine work and take steps toward a climate that encourages actions to upgrade jobs. This involves primarily a shift of emphasis from productivity to the neglected aspect of maintenance, from basic industrial values and their implications of high achievement levels, hierarchical structures, and strong leadership to post-industrial values and resulting emphases on self-actualization, worker participation, and a maintenance-oriented management style. In terms of Exhibit 1–1, interest here thus focuses on collective industrial and post-industrial values.

Another likely locus of intervention is the person who holds the job, in particular, the upgraded job. As noted in Chapter 1 and reflected in Exhibit 1–1, the person, individual, or worker is to the life sphere what the job is to the work sphere. Just as we may be able to change the climate of the work sphere in ways that encourage the upgrading of jobs, so we may be able to change the subspheres and trends of the life sphere to create a climate that encourages people to upgrade themselves. It seems likely that the subsphere of education, concerned with personal growth and development, will play a crucial role. This also implies a role for the trend to focus on self-fulfillment, which is part of the tendencies of the past three decades discussed in Chapter 6. Chapter 8 will pursue possibilities along this line.

The particular focus of this chapter is thus on the larger social context of upgrading jobs to produce a better fit between job and worker.

Efforts to improve jobs by means of job design and quality of work life programs have not been very successful in North America. They seem to be half-hearted and to have minor effects on the quality of work life or work satisfaction, and none to speak of on productivity. Managements think they should directly and immediately impact on the bottom line. Unions view them with suspicion as attempts to get more out of the workers for less. The social context or climate does not encourage efforts to upgrade jobs in a sustained and serious way.

Japanese and European efforts, on the other hand, appear to be more successful. Here is a key: We can look more closely at other societies, particularly at societies in which the gap between work and life is less marked and in which the social climate encourages, even demands, challenging work done by workers who are partners, not subordinates, or even chimpanzees.

Ironically, in both Japan and West Germany, democratic ideals encouraging worker participation were introduced and revivified during American occupations after World War II. In combination with the Japanese collectivism focused on family, clan, and nation, and with the European collectivism of the socialist state, these ideals grew into fairly sturdy plants. In both Japan and Western Europe, worker participation in decision making, particularly as it concerns the design and execution of jobs, is generally taken for granted.

COLLECTIVISM IN JAPAN

The Japanese are no strangers to conflict. Their native equivalents of the movies of the Wild West feature sword-wielding and eye-gouging samurai that make American outlaws look like well-bred matrons meeting over a cup of tea. Ketchup (or something) flies in buckets when the Japanese imitate American wrestling matches. The confrontations between employers and unions were violent and paralyzed the country during the American occupation. No one can mistake for love-ins the protests of the radical Japanese student organization, *zengakuren*.

However, the Japanese are primarily noted for their preoccupation with preserving harmony and avoiding conflict. This emphasis is deeply rooted in their culture, it pervades both their life and work spheres, and it appears for many Japanese to fuse work and life into a coherent whole. While western and industrial values have made inroads in Japan since Commodore Perry's 1854 arrival in the harbor of Yokohama, older cultural values have remained strong and have counteracted the tendency of industrialization to separate work and life.

Among these older cultural values two stand out. The first is the idea that Japan is still basically a nation of hard-working and cooperative rice farmers. Many Japanese see themselves as exponents of the Japa-

nese rice culture, of *yamato gokoro*. The second is the emphasis on harmony (*wa*) which partly springs from the collectivist nature of the rice-
farming tradition and partly from the influences of Confucianism
stressing social harmony between people, and Zen Buddhism and its
ideal of ultimate and cosmic harmony.

The "Japanese Rice Culture"—Yamato Gokoro

It is 1982. The hills and mountains of Kyushu appear red in the sun-
set as the electric train rattles through valleys and around a lake or
two. The young Japanese employee on the opposite bench smiles when
asked how he accounts for the economic success story of Japan. "We
are a rice culture," he says. He explains that the model Japanese worker
is still imbued with the spirit of the rice farmer who as part of a group,
not as an individual, had to grow enough rice to survive on limited
and not always cooperative land.

A tough population used to hard work evolved here, somewhat similar to that other nation of workaholics, the Swiss. Where the latter had
to contend with avalanches and rock slides, the Japanese were threatened by typhoons and earthquakes. Again and again the terraces holding their rice paddies, and the irrigation systems, had to be rebuilt.

That Japan was indeed a rice culture is suggested by the most common names of its citizens, by names like *Yamada* and *Tanaka*. The syl-
lable *ta* or *da* means rice paddy. It is possible that Messrs. Tanaka and
Yamada in the modern auto plants of today work in the same way their
ancestors did in the rice fields, imbued by *yamato gokoro*, the "Japanese
spirit" of their ancient, patient, accepting, terrace-rebuilding rice culture.

Yamato gokoro appears to refer to a national consciousness which
emerged in the eighth century A.D. and earlier, when indigenous values encountered the spirit of the Chinese from the mainland. This was
the time in which Japanese prehistory made way for history, in which
Japan's oldest annals or records, the *kojiki* and the *nihongi*, were re-
corded.

The Japanese became aware of their indigenous values as a larger
collectivity when these values were challenged by imports from the
much more advanced Chinese civilization. From about 400 A.D. on,
travellers, explorers, and early merchants brought horses, metal objects
and the art of metallurgy, and above all word of Confucianism and
Buddhism. *Yamato gokoro* may have been the spirit of those who resisted these new influences from China, the centralized hydraulic state
(Wittfogel, 1957. See also M. Harris, 1977) concerned with organizing
masses of laborers to construct public works like the Great Wall, the

palaces of its emperors, and above all the giant dams and channels to redistribute and control the water of its great rivers.

For some hundreds of years the Japanese had grown wet rice, a crop and technology probably imported from the south, perhaps from the lower Yangtze River valley. The Japanese had adopted wet rice farming and made it their own way of taking care of the primary need to feed oneself and one's family or clan. *Yamato gokoro* was shaped by economic necessity and then became one of the cultural determinants of Japanese work behavior (Ishida, 1974, p. 92).[1] When the young man in the train resorts to the term *yamato gokoro* to explain Japanese economic success, he implies that the Japanese workforce today works hard and as a team because its ancestors have worked hard as sedentary and cooperative rice farmers for two thousand years or more.

But having said that the Japanese were and are different from the Chinese, it must also be said that the spectacular civilization of the latter could not be resisted for long or completely. For example, the Chinese script of thousands of characters was adopted and the Confucian and Buddhist traditions flourished in Japan.

The idea of the "Japanese spirit" has intuitive appeal, but no one really knows when the Japanese nation emerged and where the populations that made it up came from. The Japanese are probably not quite the homogeneous, hard-working, rice-growing subjects of a god-like emperor that they sometimes thought they were.

Two things seem clear, however. First, the Japanese are similar to the Chinese in appearance and hence, presumably, in genetic makeup. Second, the Japanese are different from the Chinese in the language they speak; they are said to speak an Altaic rather than a Sinitic language, a Central Asian language like that of the Turks and Mongols rather than one belonging to the same group as Mandarin or Cantonese (Miller, 1980).

It has been suggested that for many thousands of years Japan was inhabited by people who belonged to different groups of migrants from the Rijuku Islands in the south, Southeast China, North China, Mongolia, and Siberia, and that these migrants had to settle down for the extremely good reason that the Pacific Ocean stopped them from going further.

These groups must have included the population of the Jomon period, named after the Japanese word for the type of decoration on the vessels or pots it produced, of the Late Paleolithic (late stone age). The Jomon people were probably descendants of *proto-Mongoloid* southern immigrants who came by the sea perhaps sometime between 20,000 to 30,000 B.C. (Turner, 1985). They appear in turn to have been the ancestors of the puzzling Ainu (Hanihara, 1985). Different *Mongoloid* groups must later, sometime between 5000 and 3500 B.C. (Rouse, 1986) have immigrated from Northeast Asia and Central Asia, via Korea, and brought with them the Altaic elements of the Japanese language.

A time of major change was the Yayoi period from about 200 B.C. to about 300 A.D. It is named after a district of Tokyo in which its archeological traces were first found. It is in this period that new migrants, traders, and/or curious travellers brought wet-rice agriculture, horses, metal, and four-post rectangular housing to Japan, presumably from regions part of the then already 1500 year old Chinese civilization. It is also in this period that the immediate roots of *yamato gokoro* presumably lie.

To those who believe that the Japanese are rice farmers at heart, it will come as no surprise that they are generally a patient people. Rice grows, it is not discovered like gold nuggets that make the finder rich overnight. It grows particularly slowly when typhoons and earthquakes destroy carefully nurtured terraces and irrigation canals. The patience of the Japanese manifests itself in their expression "sonouchi ni"—"in the course of time." Expressions like this reflect an underlying attitude which still pervades both the work and life spheres of many older and traditional Japanese workers.

Harmony—Wa

That the notion of harmony, what the Japanese call *wa*, is deeply embedded in Japanese culture is shown by the Chinese character which represents it: It combines pictorial representations of *grain* and *mouth*. A long time ago, in both China and Japan, this character apparently meant "one's spirit softening after a meal" (Yoshida et al., 1969). We have encountered already the sensible belief that to think we must eat. It is only a small step from that belief to the belief that the fundamental requirement for harmony is having a full stomach.

Disharmony, on the other hand, seems to give the Japanese acute indigestion. If you speak in a manner designed to get a point across, that is, loudly and unambiguously, in a Japanese store, office, or restaurant, looks of surprise and downright alarm will focus on you from all directions. The Japanese, at least in formal interchanges, speak in a low voice, resort to the many higher levels of politeness for which their language is famous, and instead of "no" they will say things like "it is inconvenient," "you are right, however . . . ," and "later." Their concern is to avoid unpredictable situations, confrontation, and argument.

Why this obsession with *wa* or harmony, this tense anxiety when harmony is threatened? As noted earlier, when the Japanese are not restrained, things tend to get out of hand. The aficionado of samurai epics knows that the Japanese were quick to get on each others' nerves and to do away with each other in imaginative ways when the threshold of irritability was passed. Japan also offers limited natural resources forcing its people to pull together in order to survive. Finally, Japan is a crowded country and its traditional houses—to reduce the effects of earthquakes and possibly because of the southern origins of ancestral populations—have been flimsy constructions with paper room partitions. Such living conditions require politeness and sensitivity to others.

These requirements of Japanese social life meshed with Confucian and Buddhist ideas from China. Confucian ethics stress harmony in social relationships, between husband and wife, emperor and subject, etc. The Buddhist seeks a state of desirelessness, calm, and balance. Japanese life thus alternated between violence and serenity, and every effort had to be made to let the latter prevail. Visions of a sword-swinging attacker may cross a Japanese executive's mind when an American descendant of individualistic cowboys and lone rangers rides into town and starts banging on the table to get some action.

Hence the Japanese politeness, the ever-present smile, the polite forms of speech, the bowing. Hence also the emphasis in Japanese management on the maintenance functions in addition to the performance functions of the leader, the growing into positions of authority rather than striving for power, the stress on what Richard Pascale and Anthony Athos (1981) call the soft S's of management: staff relations, skills development, style, and superordinate goals beyond the quarterly bottom line.

It would be wrong to think that Japanese corporations are all managed the same way, but Japanese managers are different from the archetypal American machomanager whom Pascale and Athos describe as "full of go," "hard ball," "never say no," "can do," and "black belt" types who complain about "goddamn award dinners" and "hand holding."

More than Americans, Japanese managers are expected to have social skills that go far beyond a friendly demeanor. They need complex skills to promote and maintain harmony and are expected to exercise thoughtful and patient authority rather than brute, swift, and decisive power. Their job is to assure smooth functioning and harmony, a state of affairs seen as important in its own right and as a precondition of long-term productivity.

The clan-oriented rice culture and the Buddhist interest in harmony imported from China may once have been perceived as incompatible native and foreign influences, but both represent values conducive to cooperative and harmonious relationships in the workplace. At least to the older Japanese workers, the work sphere is not something dominated by a different set of values from those of the life sphere, by

Exhibit 7-1
Participation in Europe and America

	Europe	United States
Basic Trends	Bass et al. (1978), Bass et al. (1979): Industrial democracy Buchanan (1979): Organizational restructuring [sociotechnical systems analysis, autonomous groups]	Participative management, participative decision making Job restructuring
Theoretical Bases	Participation as general social phenomenon (a) Socialist collectivism (b) Democratic self-determination (See Bass et al., 1979; Dachler, 1978; Dachler & Wilpert, 1978; Greenberg, 1975; Locke & Schweiger, 1979; Locke, 1982)	Participation as organizational treatment strategy (a) Productivity and efficiency orientation (b) Human resources theory
Types of Participation	Formal (statutory, "forced") Indirect (representative participation) High intensity and wide scope (See Bass et al., 1978; Bass et al., 1979; Dachler, 1978; Dachler & Wilpert, 1978; Greenberg, 1975; Locke & Schweiger, 1979)	Informal ("voluntary") Direct Productivity and efficiency orientation: low intensity and narrow scope. Human resources theory: high intensity and narrow scope

authoritarian managers who impose restraints that conflict with vigorously individualistic personal values. These workers appear to be a part of a culture that stresses cooperation and harmony and which pervades both the life sphere and the work sphere.

WORKER PARTICIPATION IN EUROPE

A promising phenomenon in the West that appears to be designed to decrease the gap between work and life is the trend toward participation by workers in the decisions that affect their work. This trend has assumed a variety of forms referred to by many different labels such as industrial democracy, worker self-management, power equalization, autonomous work groups, and democratic leadership (Dachler & Wilpert, 1978). Specifically, it has assumed quite distinct forms in North America and in Europe. Some of these differences are shown in Exhibit 7-1.

In West European countries like Norway, Sweden, and Germany, participation has generally assumed the forms of industrial democracy (Bass & Rosenstein, 1978; Bass, Shackleton, & Rosenstein, 1979) and organizational restructuring (Buchanan, 1979). David Buchanan points out that both of these foci of the European approach to worker participation have roots in the Tavistock Institute of Human Relations in London. Such advocates of the serious and committed European style of worker participation as Fred Emery, Einar Thorsrud, and Eric Trist have been associated with this institute.

Industrial Democracy

Industrial democracy refers to participation of workers on the highest levels of policy making within the work organization and the industry. Among the earliest efforts to introduce industrial democracy was the Norwegian Industrial Democracy Project carried out by Einar Thorsrud and his colleagues. The report on this large scale project studying employee representation on company boards was published in English in 1976 (Emery & Thorsrud, 1976). The project was initiated because of national concerns about work morale following World War II, but its overall effect as a morale booster was less than startling.

In Germany, industrial democracy also evolved soon after World War II; it did so in the vital steel and coal industries. Since then it has become the norm in all industrial sectors of the German economy. The Co-determination Law of 1976 required enterprises with more than 2000 workers to establish supervisory boards of directors, responsible for company policy, on which workers and shareholders have equal representation. The day-to-day execution of policy was left to the management board of the companies.

Sociotechnical Systems

Organizational restructuring as Buchanan (1979) defines it centers around sociotechnical systems analysis and the formation of semi-autonomous work groups. The two go hand-in-hand as the early study by Trist and K. W. Bamforth (1951) in Britain's Durham coal mines illustrates. Trist and Bamforth examined the gradual evolution of the composite longwall method of coal-getting in mines in which the conventional longwall method had been introduced. The latter required workers to specialize and it produced unintended effects on the social relations among them. It had been introduced from the top down, without adequate consultation with the workers.

Informally the workers changed the officially adopted and conventional longwall method. The resulting composite longwall method managed to combine both the technological advantages of the conventional longwall method and the socially and psychologically more satisfactory old-fashioned "hand-got" and composite shortwall methods. It relied on miners with a wider array of skills, able to do a wider range of jobs, and able to function in semi-autonomous groups.

Participation as a "General Social Phenomenon"

Peter Dachler (1978) and Dachler and Bernhard Wilpert (1978) point out that worker participation is a heterogeneous concept meaning a number of different things. They distinguish between two fundamentally different interpretations: participation as a "general social phenomenon" or a "central concept of organizing," and participation as an "organizational treatment strategy." Exhibit 7-1 reflects this broad dichotomy.

Each of these interpretations is put forward by two different camps (Dachler, 1978). In the case of participation as a general social phenomenon, it is seen from the socialist perspective as part of a workplace which, in contrast to the capitalist workplace described by Marx and Engels, offers the opportunity to play a meaningful part in maintaining society and which does so in a way that permits personal development. Others approach it on the basis of the democratic assumptions that people have a need for freedom and autonomy, and that they are not only capable of making decisions but also need opportunities to do so and develop their decision-making skills. Dachler (1978) and also Dachler and Wilpert (1978) derived these two orientations from Edward Greenberg's (1975) "participatory left" and "democratic theory" schools of thought on worker participation.

On the whole, these approaches to worker participation are more characteristic of Europeans than of Americans. The former tend to be favorably disposed toward socialism (Bass et al., 1978); the latter tend to reject it (e.g., Locke & Schweiger, 1979). One might also expect the fundamental assumptions about the nature of human beings of democratic theory to manifest themselves in broad democratic policies, of the type more clearly reflected by industrial democracy than by circumscribed participatory management schemes used as tools to change specific organizations.

Exhibit 7-1 also reflects the differentiation, made by a number of authors, between participation which is formal and informal (Bass & Rosenstein, 1978), "forced" and "voluntary" (Locke & Schweiger, 1979), indirect and direct (Bass & Rosenstein, 1978), high intensity and low intensity (Greenberg, 1975), and wide scope and narrow scope (Greenberg, 1975). Industrial democracy is usually regulated by statutes, that is, it is formal. It is also indirect, since the rank-and-file workers cannot vote on small policy-making bodies but have to be content with electing representatives to them (Bass et al., 1979; Dachler, 1978). Edwin Locke and David Schweiger (1979) also consider it to be forced rather than voluntary. In addition, Greenberg (1975) links high intensity and wide scope to both the socialist and democratic positions which, as suggested above, are more characteristic of Western Europe than the United States.

It is somewhat puzzling that worker participation European style is regarded as "forced" participation by Locke and Schweiger (1979). These American authors appear to believe in untrammeled individualism and they espouse a competitiveness which is in the best tradition of Social Darwinism and ideologically antithetical to cooperation and worker participation. It is difficult to reconcile this antipathy toward participation with the democratic ideals Americans regard as more characteristic of their society than any other, even that of the Swiss who met on an Alpine meadow to form a democratic union and throw off the yoke of tyrants in 1291, two centuries before Columbus reached the Caribbean.

WORKER PARTICIPATION IN THE UNITED STATES

As the Locke and Schweiger article suggests, Americans are more circumspect in their approach to worker participation than Europeans. Their variant of participation is participative management (Bass & Rosenstein, 1978). They tend to avoid the sweeping reforms and long-term commitments implied by industrial democracy and sociotechnical systems.

The type of participation characteristic of the American work organization is described as informal, voluntary, and direct. It also differs from European style participation in that it must take place and evolve in the context of generally adversarial relationships between managers and workers. Finally, Americans evaluate the prospects of participation less in terms of what it does for workers and for the organization in the long run, and more in terms of short term profitability. They see it as a means rather than as an end. One would expect them to see participation as an "organizational treatment variable," to be applied when worker dissatisfaction reaches the point at which it impairs productivity, rather than as a "general social phenomenon."

According to Dachler (1978) and Dachler and Wilpert (1978) there are also two theoretical or ideological orientations underlying participation in the sense of an organizational treatment variable: the *productivity and efficiency* orientation and *human growth and development* orientation. These orientations are opposite poles of a single dimension; maximizing the objectives of one usually involves neglecting those of the other. For example, if company policy is to increase productivity in the short run by deskilling all jobs as much as possible, to automate operations, and to fire workers made redundant as a result, opportunities for human growth and development will not exactly be boosted. On the other hand, a company cannot suddenly provide the latest in New Age growth training for all of its employees without risk to productivity and profit, the goose that lays the golden eggs of pay and pension checks.

These opposite poles of productivity and efficiency versus human growth and development represent two important and conflicting positions Americans assume on the subject of worker participation.

The Productivity and Efficiency Orientation

Of the two, the dominant orientation is the productivity and efficiency orientation of classical organization theory generally associated with Frederick Taylor. This typically American efficiency orientation corresponds to Greenberg's (1975) "management school" of thought leading to participation which is low in intensity and narrow in scope. It has been endorsed vigorously by Locke and Schweiger (1979). After a thorough review of the literature these authors conclude that the "research findings yield equivocal support for the thesis that PDM [participatory decision making] necessarily leads to increased satisfaction and productivity, although the evidence for the former is stronger than the evidence for the latter" and that "the effectiveness of PDM depends upon numerous contextual factors" (p. 325).

Unfortunately, much of the article is controversial. The authors allege that the real motive of the New Left and others was to establish a dictatorship, not to promote social welfare. "The rights of . . . owners . . . to use their property as they see fit" (p. 270) is taken for granted. The authors define egoism benignly as "the freedom to . . . reap the consequences of one's individual choices" (p. 271). Egalitarianism, on the other hand, is the root of much evil and reflects "hatred of the good" (p. 329) and competent. Egalitarians are alleged to harbor resentment against mental effort and to suffer, as a result, from "arrested cognitive development" (p. 329).

The authors manifest a strong ideological commitment to Ayn Rand's ethical egoism extolling the strong and wealthy and denigrating the liberal state which gives to the poor and, especially, the socialist state which not only gives to the poor but also takes just about everything from the rich! Ayn Rand and even the Founding Fathers are invoked to battle the forces of evil—mysticism, collectivism, stagnation, dictatorship, and so forth—arrayed against good old scientific management.

From the perspective of Locke and Schweiger, Rand, and perhaps the Founding Fathers, the successful businessperson is seen as wise and efficient, an altogether admirable individual who is wealthy because of productive decisions and who rightly is unwilling to share the decision making with those evidently less successful in the Social Darwinist struggle for survival and hence clearly less qualified as decision makers. It is a view of internally controlled people whose environment has reinforced their efforts and who, therefore, see themselves as the originators of the good things that happened to them. It is also a view that shows little understanding of the less successful, usually externally controlled person, whose environment did not stand by with rewards for effort to the same degree, and who thus tends to attribute good and bad outcomes to a capricious fate or system (Morf, 1986).

Worker participation clearly plays a limited role in this worldview. But Locke and Schweiger (1979) and Locke, Schweiger, and Gary Latham (1986) do not entirely rule it out. They assign it a possible role, particularly when the workforce exhibits dissatisfaction. They see it as a tool of management, something which might sometimes be "used"; they do not see it as an end that could make organizations more compatible with the basic needs of those who work for them.

Human Growth and Development Theory

Fortunately, the human growth and development orientation is more congenial toward participation. It corresponds to Greenberg's (1975) "humanistic psychology school" of thought associated with participation of high intensity, albeit narrow scope. It focuses on human needs, in particular growth needs, rather than on the needs of the organization. It is based on the work of Abraham Maslow, Chris Argyris, Douglas McGregor, and others, and it plays a role in a variety of positive assessments of worker participation.

Viewing the world from this humanistic perspective, Lee Preston and James Post (1974) see participation as the third managerial revolution after the invention of hierarchy and the separation of management from ownership. In the same spirit, Marshall Sashkin (1984, 1986) argues that worker participation is an "ethical imperative" and that "the evidence of 50 years of action research clearly, consistently, and strongly demonstrates the effectiveness of participative management" (p. 7).

The climate in the United States may be changing, competition from abroad may cause American managers to look beyond immediate efficiency and productivity and to take more seriously what they have claimed for years to be their most important resource: their people. Foreign competition is already causing them to look at what the Germans and Japanese are doing right. Efforts will certainly continue to increase the quality of work life, to attain better matches between people and jobs, and to reintegrate work and life by detaylorizing jobs and giving the worker greater responsibilities and more opportunities to grow and develop on the job. The success of these efforts to date may have been limited, but they clearly are modest steps in the right direction toward reducing the gap between the generally authoritarian work

sphere and the life sphere in which we are expected to act as autonomous, decision-making, participating, and democratic individuals.

NOTE

1. See also Boye DeMente (1981) for a succinct reference of the related concept of *yamato damashii*—"the heart and soul of the great peace." Things are
obviously more complex than the present discussion might suggest. A kind
Japanese mentor pointed out to me that foreigners cannot understand his culture. But: The western mind needs explanations. The discussions of things
Japanese in Chapter 7 and 11 are admittedly nothing more than one foreigner's
attempts to reduce the tension of unanswered questions with some potentially
explanatory concepts.

8

Equal Opportunities

Just as it is important to have a climate within the work sphere that encourages the upgrading of jobs or humanization of work, so it is important to have a climate—not only in the work sphere but pervading especially the larger life sphere—that enables people to upgrade themselves as persons and as workers. No doubt many conditions must exist before such a climate prevails, but an important set of conditions that can serve as examples are *egalitarian* ones.

Egalitarianism is like air: You don't notice it when it is there, but you suffer acute distress when it is not. The pain of nonegalitarian relations usually affects markedly how people perceive themselves, how they function psychologically, their level of self-esteem and confidence. It is within the work sphere that egalitarianism has become a familiar issue to most Americans in the form of restraints placed—by equal employment opportunity and civil rights legislation—on managers and owners deciding whom to hire, promote, or fire. However, it clearly goes far beyond the work sphere and relates to the very core of our personal and life sphere concerns.

Much of the preceding chapter was about the important dimension that pits productivity against personal development in North America: the dimension that encompasses the exponents of the productivity and efficiency orientation at one pole and those of the human growth and development orientation at the other. In this chapter, the focus is on another important dimension: that which pits merit against equality. This dimension also emerges from a larger model involving four orientations, the question is also how to balance two opposite and equally legitimate interests, and this attempt to balance extremes may also call for corrective emphasis on a neglected pole of the dimension.

The thesis of this chapter is that any step which brings the egalitarian society closer is also a step which makes it easier for people to upgrade themselves. This process of people upgrading themselves is what we usually mean by education. In terms of Exhibit 1–1, interest here focuses on the cultural conditions of the life sphere on the level of society, in particular, on the cultural conditions conducive to educational activity.

EGALITARIANISM AND POWER

Americans are proud of their democratic tradition and they have little use for aristocrats. The Declaration of Independence states flatly: "All men are created equal." In World War II the United States emerged as the white knight rescuing democracy in Europe and imposing it, with great success, in Japan.

But there is a paradox here: In the work sphere, Germany and Japan are today more democratic than the United States. American business leaders can ignore their workers and unions with impunity unless there is a collective agreement. They can award themselves salaries and benefits that are a large multiple of that of their workers, sometimes while insisting that the frontline workers take a cut in wages or salary. Special parking spaces, corporate dining rooms, executive washrooms and other signs of privilege are common.

In Germany, as we saw in Chapter 7, workers and shareholders have equal representation on boards of directors. In Japan the salary differences between the highest level managers and the frontline workers are much smaller than in the United States and bottom-up management is the rule.

Thus Americans are distinctly nonegalitarian in the work sphere, while their culture and polity in Bell's (1976) sense value egalitarianism. This contributes to the gap between the work sphere, where authoritarian relations prevail, and the life sphere, of which the at least theoretically egalitarian culture and polity are a part.

Of course, just because egalitarian values are supposed to reign supreme in the life sphere does not mean that they actually do. Egalitarianism is often confused with equalitarianism, the view that all people are essentially the same. This unrealistic view is in fact based on nonegalitarian beliefs, as discussed in Chapter 6. One such belief might be, for example, that a nuclear physicist necessarily is a more valuable individual than a caretaker. If this is true, and if all people are essentially the same, then everyone can and should be a nuclear physicist, or at least a university graduate.

But progress has been made in curbing discrimination against blacks, women, Hispanics and other groups. In fact, equalitarians have contributed greatly to efforts in this direction. The effort to make American society more egalitarian has been a macro-level effort, like the efforts to redefine work described in the preceding chapter. However, unlike the latter, making America more egalitarian implies activities that are person-oriented rather than task- or job-oriented and that originate in the life sphere rather than as a direct result of concerns of the work sphere.

Efforts toward egalitarianism originate in the political subsphere of the life sphere, the subsphere concerned with the distribution of power within society and its various groups. In Chapter 1 we encountered Bell's (1976) polity whose "axial principle" in the United States is the legitimacy conferred by "governance exercised only with the consent of the governed" (p. 11), whose "axial structure" is characterized by representation and participation, and in which decisions are arrived at by bargaining and negotiation.

O'Toole (1979, 1985) notes that in the political sphere there are four generally conflicting objectives on the agenda: efficiency, equality, the quality of life, and liberty. There are parallels between some of these objectives and the Greenberg (1975), Dachler (1978), and Dachler and Wilpert (1978) orientations toward worker participation. Quality of life is a central concern to those who espouse the humanistic growth and development point of view, while equality is prized above all by socialists. On the other hand, O'Toole associates liberty and libertarianism with American managers arguing that governments should get off their backs, and efficiency with European business leaders fashioning ties to governments and forging ahead with industrial policies.

O'Toole's framework originates in the political subsphere of the life sphere. It has a different origin and serves different purposes from that of Greenberg and of Dachler and Wilpert. That is why the overlap between them is limited and why the dimension of libertarian versus egalitarian values, of merit versus equality, emerges far more clearly from the O'Toole model than the Dachler and Wilpert model.

In the developed and reasonably affluent societies in which cultural determinants are perceived to play a more important day-to-day role than purely material or economic ones, all four principles or values of the political subsphere determine the decisions made within the work sphere. O'Toole (1985) distinguishes between four types of managers, organization theorists, social critics, and so forth: the corporatists living for performance, productivity, efficiency, and effectiveness; the egalitarians proposing reforms to equalize rewards; the humanists concerned about the quality of life offered by the work place and the environment in general; and the libertarians seeking to allow expression of merit unhampered by government and by external regulations.

O'Toole maintains that all four orientations are legitimate and in potential conflict with each other, and that progressive "vanguard corporations" are characterized by their ability to jointly maximize the objectives of all four.

The merit versus equality dimension is almost as important to the issue of integrating work and life as is the dimension ranging from efficiency to personal growth and development. It pits two sets of values dear to Americans against each other. Interludes of equalitarian frenzy notwithstanding, the libertarians and their merit principle have generally prevailed in this contest. While "all men are created equal," Americans are quick to note that some are created more equal than others. Furthermore, Americans abhor Marxism or socialism, the ideology most often associated with the ideal of egalitarianism. They do so because they are pragmatic and tend to distrust ideologues, because Marxism has been the enemy for decades, and because at heart Americans are individualists.

CASTE AND CLASS

The meritocracy may appear to us to be the opposite pole of the egalitarian society, but it is a dramatic improvement over societies based on caste and class.

Castes Based on Birth

In *Brave New World,* novelist and social critic Aldous Huxley (1946) depicts a society in which eggs and sperm with known genetic potential are combined to produce test tube babies destined to be cultivated into different castes ranging from "alpha plus" intellectuals, to "gamma minus" machine minders, and to retarded "epsilons." The maturation process is controlled. The future alphas are stimulated; the epsilons are deprived of oxygen to ensure they will be sufficiently retarded not to be bored by the routine and mind-numbing work for which they are being engineered. Appropriate conditioning is administered so that each caste acquires its required repertoire of skills and attitudes.

Huxley's futuristic world depicts an old and familiar way in which societies have structured themselves: by assigning people to different groups on the basis of birth. Individuals have no control over the family, race, or caste to which they belong by birth. The boundaries between the different groups based on birth are impermeable. No matter what she did or how much Lady Luck beamed upon her, the medieval peasant woman could not become a blue-blooded aristocrat. No matter what he does or how lucky he is, the Indian untouchable can never become a Brahman.

Classification on the basis of birth was based on the belief that birth is closely related to the type of person one is. The aquiline-nosed aristocrats were seen to have aquiline-nosed offspring. It was only a small step to assume that parents and their children also share nonphysical characteristics, that the aristocrat's son was destined to exhibit his father's leadership qualities.

There is a grain of truth in the belief that "like father like son," but the genetic diversity within large social categories formed on the basis of birth is usually almost as great as that within society in general. There are exceptions, of course, mainly pertaining to physical characteristics. Black parents are likely to have black children. But physical characteristics are usually irrelevant to effective functioning in modern society. What matters are differences in motivational disposition, ability, and hence behavior.

By itself, assignment by birth need not be a problem. What makes it a problem is that the groups to which different infants are assigned differ in status and power. There are more privileged groups that tend to exploit and oppress less privileged ones. This is particularly galling since the reasons for the privileges associated with membership in one group as opposed to another are always more clear to the dominant than to the oppressed group. The aristocrats of medieval Europe—the ancestral Tudors, Bourbons, Hapsburgs, Hohenzollerns, etc.,—may initially have been selected because they were great warriors or possibly because they were wise leaders. However, in the course of centuries these qualities certainly did get watered down to the point of invisibility.

Groups differing in power and privilege and separated by impermeable boundaries are castes, and classification by birth alone thus can produce caste societies. Castes have played, and do play, an important and not admirable role in social organization. In the work sphere we see remnants of it in the low proportions of blacks, members of other minority groups, and women who hold complex and challenging jobs. In the life sphere the role of castes is both more subtle and more pervasive and important. It manifests itself, for example, in white neighborhoods that keep out blacks by subtle or brutal means and that psychologically scar the rejected in either case; in the way parents and teachers foster scientific interests more intensively in boys than in girls; in the rewards society offers for evidence of independence and aggressiveness in men but not in women.

Classes Based on Wealth

The television series *Upstairs, Downstairs* of the British Broadcasting Corporation (see Hawkesworth, 1973), shown on the Public Broadcasting System in the United States, depicts a typical class society. Social classes differ from castes in that the boundaries between them are not completely impermeable. In the Victorian world of *Upstairs, Downstairs* class membership depended to some extent on aristocratic roots, but money and perhaps even merit also played a role. In the United States today class membership typically depends on wealth, which is, something that can be acquired by luck, ingenuity, or ruthlessness.

Upstairs, Downstairs chronicles the life "upstairs" of an aristocratic British family during the first decades of this century. It depicts the degree to which the family of the fictitious Sir Richard Bellamy depends almost entirely on the work of the servants "downstairs."

It would not strike anyone as fair today to be assigned to the downstairs world, and the BBC series' depiction of the relations between the two classes of the Bellamy household has aptly been described as a "trifle idealized" (Hardwick, 1976). However, each servant has a meaningful role as cook, chamber maid, porter, and so forth, and the boundaries separating the two worlds are occasionally crossed. The servants perceive the possibility of a better life, perhaps even the possibility of one day joining the world upstairs as a result of luck, heroism in the war raging on the continent, or merit finally recognized. The character exuding the most irresistible competence is not one of the relatively idle and fairly helpless upstairs people, but Mr. Hudson, the butler.

Whatever else it may have been, the Victorian downstairs world was not a faceless and hopeless mob of epsilons far removed from contact with intelligent, skillful, and knowledgeable human beings from whom they could learn to improve their lot. Within their own social class there were role models, teachers, and exemplars of talent and motivation besides which many of the elite faded into ineffectual obscurity. Thus even the traditional class society can offer some opportunities to upgrade, that is, educate, oneself. The people cleaning the toilets are at least not necessarily condemned to cleaning toilets all their lives.

THE RISE OF THE MERITOCRACY

In Victorian Britain, class membership depended on birth and wealth, and wealth could often compensate for being born in the cottage instead of the manor. In many ways, the United States is a class society in which class membership is assigned almost exclusively on the basis of wealth. Sometimes wealth is inherited and sometimes it is acquired. Old families value the former, the *nouveaux riches* value the latter. George Gilder (1981), for example, comes out in favor of the *nouveaux riches* who are "wealthy" rather than "merely rich." Those who place acquired wealth above inherited wealth presumably think that acquired wealth reflects recently demonstrated merit. This brings us to the third fundamental criterion people use to structure their society: merit.

Recently demonstrated merit is obviously more deserving of rewards than being born into the right family or being in possession of sizable assets. It is clearly more impressive than the merit of having a distant progenitor of an aristocratic line or that of being a descendant of a robber baron who struck it rich.

Merit is usually confounded with wealth, however. The best educational opportunities are usually the most expensive. As a result many attempts have been made to separate the two. There is affirmative action, there are quotas imposed by the state, there are scholarships. Measures like these are designed to level the playing field so that all can develop their talents and then exhibit their merits in high, and highly rewarded, levels of achievement.

These solutions are only part of the answer. In fact, if merit is defined in a narrow and traditional way, they can even make matters worse. In recent years a number of psychologists have argued that social status depends on one's occupation, and that performance in one's occupation depends on one's intelligence (e.g., Hunter & Hunter, 1984; Hunter, 1986). Thus merit becomes deployed intelligence, and a lack of intelligence means that there is no possibility of merit and hence upward mobility in the social structure.

A number of writers have depicted the bleak future of the meritocracy when merit is defined as a function of intelligence. In his futurist novel *The Rise of the Meritocracy*, Michael Young (1958) foresaw the possibility of new castes determined by the capacity to benefit from education. The degree to which students can exploit traditional educational opportunities depends largely on their intelligence. Differences in intelligence, defined as the capacity to acquire a wide range of skills, depends on biological factors under any circumstances, but biological factors account for a particularly large proportion of the differences in intelligence between individuals when the environment is held relatively constant; for example, when every child has the same opportunity to attend good schools.

Young depicts a Britain of the future characterized by a large caste of the uneducable which has emerged as a result of genetic differences among individuals. The members of this caste are sullen, frustrated, and angry because they know that the system gave them their chance and that they have only their irreversible genetic makeup to blame, and because the caste to which they belong is a homogeneous and boring group offering no hope of learning and of upward mobility.

John Wain (1973), another British writer, describes an evening out during which he felt he faced Young's two castes in present day England. He started out at a party given by some friends against a background of classical music and poetry readings. He ended up in an all-night diner frequented primarily by "gamma men" with "low foreheads, small eyes, potato noses." Making liberal use of hyperbole, he notes that "Neanderthal man seems . . . to have had a dignity and a repose in his features that were wanting in those [members of the lower caste] I saw [that night]" (p. 4).

Young and Wain expand or describe a situation they saw developing in Britain, but shortly after the war novelist Kurt Vonnegut (1952) also projected a version of the future two-caste society of the United States in the novel *Player Piano*. In this society, a small proportion of the population has Ph.D.s, runs the complex technological systems, and lives on snob hill. The rest of the population keeps busy, either as members of the comical armed forces or of the reclamation and reconstruction crews (the "Reeks and Wrecks" as they are called) who dig ditches and fill them up again.

In all three of these depictions of society we run into the Brahma versus Hereford dichotomy mentioned in Chapter 3. There the root cause of this polarization was seen to be scientific management, that is, managers trying to reduce costs and to increase efficiency by deskilling as many jobs as possible, so that mere Hereford type workers who are cheap could do them. Here we encounter another determinant: individual differences in intelligence which are, to some degree, the result of genetic constraints.

The meritocracy does not seem to be the answer, at least not as long as merit is regarded as a manifestation of intelligence. It simply fits too well for comfort the relatively dichotomous occupational structure. If technology is used to routinize many hitherto moderately complex jobs of secretaries, supervisors, lower-level managers, etc., the resulting dichotomy of simple and complex jobs would match perfectly the castes produced by the meritocracy.

Birth once again might determine who gets the complex and challenging elite jobs and who gets to do the dirty and the routine work. True, in the meritocracy it is no longer a matter of birth into the right family. But it is a matter of birth with the right complement of genes assuring an adequate level of "g," Charles Spearman's (1927) general intelligence, said to be the ultimate predictor of work performance in any job (Hunter, 1986).

THE EGALITARIAN SOCIETY

This brings us to the egalitarian society, the macro-level environment which meets important, largely cultural, conditions that must prevail if people are to upgrade themselves.

Differences Between Egalitarians and Equalitarians

It is easy to confuse egalitarian beliefs with the equalitarian beliefs to which Chapter 6 alluded. Egalitarians are defined here in such a way that they differ from equalitarians in three fundamental respects.

1. Egalitarians take it for granted that human beings differ from each other in many ways. Unlike the equalitarians, they can accept individual differences because they do not link differences in human characteristics to differences in worth. They argue that while apples and oranges differ, it would be silly to argue that one is intrinsically better than the other.

2. Egalitarians believe in "equality of opportunity," not in "equality of results." As far as the egalitarians are concerned, quantitatively equal efforts deserve quantitatively equal outcomes. A should be paid as much as B if they invest the same energy and time (including the energy and time required to develop the knowledge and skills the job demands) in their work. The equalitarians, on the other hand, go further and are quick to award university degrees and other qualitatively different rewards indiscriminately. The egalitarians believe in a level playing field but not necessarily in tied scores at the end of the game.

3. Egalitarians would like to see a society in which the different occupations essential to its functioning are all considered to be of equal worth or value. Equalitarians arrange the occupations hierarchically, the college-educated accountant is more important than the tradesman, hence in order to be equal, everyone must go to college or everyone must be a tradesman. Egalitarians on the other hand are likely to argue that while we speak of "elite jobs" and "routine jobs," this distinction does not refer to the contribution of these jobs to the quality of life offered by society.

Their conception of a hierarchy of occupations causes the equalitarians to advocate "equalizing treatment" rather than "equal treatment." Like the egalitarians, they are willing to assist the weak, but unlike them, they are also quick to curb the swift. Like Procrustes, the highwayman of Greek mythology, the equalitarian cuts a piece off those who are too big for the standard length bed and stretches those who are too short. While the egalitarian is likely to sow wheat on fertile land and build houses on the firm foundation of rocky terrain, the equali-

tarian is inclined to expend great energy and other resources trying to
make swamps fit for building houses and rocky terrain fit for growing
wheat.

The American equalitarian's response to the problem of "undesirable" occupations is to send everyone to college. This solution requires
a sophisticated technology that can produce the machinery and the robots required to replace the workers in the "demeaning" occupations.
It also requires large expenditures on the universities. In other words,
only an affluent society can contemplate this policy.

Other societies have toyed with the less expensive idea of job rotation. Some have sent their academics and bureaucrats to the rice paddies or into the sugar cane fields. Unfortunately job rotation tends to
be used as a method of keeping certain segments of the population in
line, particularly those inclined to dissent, and while the surgeon may
end up with the farmer's shovel in his hand, the farmer had better not
end up with the surgeon's scalpel. Besides, this second kind of equalizing treatment is also quite costly. Less developed countries in particular can ill afford to train academics and professionals only to have
them spend part of their time ineptly doing other work for which they
were not trained.

A distinction must be made between taking one's turn at cleaning
the corridors and even the toilets, and dropping the coding sheets to
work on a farm for two years. An egalitarian might go along with the
first, an equalitarian with the second. In the first case, but not in the
second, the loss in productivity is probably outweighed by the educational effects of getting a taste of basic work tasks we tend to take for
granted, and by a healthy reduction in social status differences.

The Ways of Diversity and of Uniformity

All three ways that distinguish the egalitarian from the equalitarian
individual can be summed up by saying that the former follows a path
of diversity while the latter follows one of uniformity. What makes the
egalitarian path the path of diversity is its basic assumption that it is
possible to recognize that people have different talents and assets which
are of equal worth. Some people may be intelligent, others may be
patient, others may be good Samaritans, still others may have the talent to keep a dozen unruly six-year-olds enthralled. In the egalitarian
view, people may be different in the type of talents they have and even
in the degree to which they are talented, but they are all considered to
be of equal worth regardless of these differences.

In her book *Individuality*, psychologist Leona Tyler (1978) asks questions which touch the core of egalitarianism. Should we think of people
as having a set of abilities whose levels range from "low" to "high"

and which are relatively unchangeable? In other words, should we concentrate, as we have in the past, on the question "How much?", for example, "how much numerical ability does Johnny have?" Or is it more helpful to think of a person as having a "repertoire of competencies," where competency is defined as a "particular skill"? Should we ask the question "which?"

"How much" questions imply value judgements and a competitive philosophy, but when we ask "Can Johnny cook a Chinese dinner?", or "Can he repair the fuel system of a Volkswagen Rabbit?", we focus on differences among people without implying that one is somehow more capable than the other in an overall sense. In other words, "which" questions focus on unique individuals who can complement each other in a cooperative rather than competitive way.

Since egalitarians accept the idea that people differ markedly from each other, they are not upset by the suggestion that these differences may in part be due to heredity. They are not too interested in the great debate on the role of genetic factors in shaping personality and intelligence, and in the degree to which these factors account for the differences between people.

What is of great concern to the egalitarians, however, is to spread the doctrine that different occupations contribute equally to the quality of life offered by a society; that the elevator operator who spends much of the day riding up and down in order to be available when needed by a handicapped passenger, or the cleaner who sweeps the floors littered with the debris left by a thoughtless public should not necessarily be paid less than the carpenter or the manager. It is also apparent to egalitarians that the conscientious garbage collector may do as much for public health as some doctors; and that the hospital cook who prepares decent meals—meals which do not cause the surgeon's stomach to convulse during a delicate operation—plays a crucial role in the hospital.

Egalitarians also believe that everyone is entitled to the same treatment unless one of many possible good reasons for different treatment prevails. For example, they are likely to favor special services for the handicapped. They would probably encourage the mathematically adept with considerably greater vigor than the mathematically inept to enter a program in computer science.

However, in the egalitarian view, nothing justifies an income that is not enough to live on, or different treatment by the legal and medical systems. Income is of particular importance because it enables people to participate in training programs offered within the work sphere and to educate themselves in the life sphere. In short, the egalitarian society makes it possible for people to upgrade themselves.

One of the best known analyses of social inequality in America is that of Christopher Jencks and his colleagues at the Center for Educational Policy Research at Harvard. "Economic success," Jencks et al. (1972) write, "seems to depend on varieties of luck and on-the-job competence that are only moderately related to family background, schooling, or scores on standardized tests" (p. 8). On-the-job competence in turn is seen by Jencks et al. as primarily a function of personality: The person high on traits like endurance and eagerness to learn and do a good job is most likely to acquire the technical skills required to do the job well.

This implies that the answer to inequality is not to concentrate on equalizing family, school, or level of cognitive skill measured by standardized tests. If anything, it is luck and competence that would have to be equalized. But that is not possible. Thus what we need are " 'insurance systems' which neutralize the effects of luck, and income sharing systems which break the link between vocational success and living standards" (Jencks et al., 1972, pp. 8–9).

Jencks et al. admit that some financial incentives are essential to motivate people. They argue, however, that "even if we assume, for example, that the most productive fifth of all workers accounts for half the Gross National Product, it does not follow that they need receive half the income. A third or a quarter might well suffice to keep both them and others productive" (Jencks et al., 1972, p. 10).

The conclusions of Jencks et al. differ markedly from those of John and Rhonda Hunter (1984) and John Hunter (1986) to the effect that job competence is largely a function of cognitive skills, that is, intelligence. It is likely that the discrepancy of views between the two camps on this issue is attributable to different basic assumptions they make. Hunter and Hunter (1984) espouse a traditional view of merit as manifested intelligence. Jencks et al. and other egalitarians have broader definitions of human capacity and are less worried about paying the price of reduced efficiency for more equal opportunities to develop a wide range of talents other than general intelligence (e.g., Tyler, 1986; Gottfredson 1986).

Egalitarian Education and Training

The egalitarian society clearly provides material and cultural conditions conducive to educational activity. It offers a climate that facilitates the process by which people upgrade themselves. This person-focused educational process takes place primarily within the life sphere. It is concerned with fundamental issues, usually far more important than those we encounter in the work sphere, although we are often so absorbed by the latter that we do not get around to the former. Nevertheless, questions about the meaning of one's life are more important than questions about how to beat a competitor for a job on the next rung of the hierarchical ladder.

In practice, however, education and training are often confounded. The training system portrayed in Chapter 5 can provide for some of its students opportunities to increase their cognitive breadth. In fact, although its relationship to education is generally incidental, the training system is the institution which most directly bears on how the egalitarian society enables people to upgrade themselves.

Egalitarians are likely to insist on "difficult exit" programs, that is, programs which require that certain criteria be met to obtain a certificate. A school's decision to fail a student is not seen as a crushing value judgement; it is seen as the result of the incompatibility of a set of aptitudes on one hand, and a set of demands of one of many different programs on the other.

As far as the input side of education systems is concerned, an egalitarian outlook is compatible with either "difficult entry" or "easy entry" systems.

Difficult entry systems. As "the way of diversity," egalitarianism can be expected to generate a training/education system offering a variety of equally valued programs. The diversity of programs should match the diversity of talents and the majority of young people should be able to meet high admission standards of at least one program of interest to them. Hence "difficult entry" is not incompatible with egalitarian values.

It makes economic sense to develop the entire range of available talent, and to do that a training/education system obviously must offer a diversity of paths to develop a variety of complementary skills. European training/education systems appear to offer a wider range of respectable alternatives than that of the United States. Secondary school graduates in France or Germany do not have to go to college in order to be able to show their faces in the neighborhood. The German word for occupation is *Beruf*, and literally translated that word means "calling." Although their numbers are dwindling, some European apprentices pursue the knowledge and skills required by their calling with a thoroughness that is not dramatically different from that of the medical student in the United States. Partly as a result of the wider range of options for high school graduates, most European university systems are "difficult entry" systems.

Easy entry systems. Of course, "easy entry" systems are preferable in a society that can afford them. While they usually involve expenditures of resources in fruitless attempts to train the inept, and while students who fail to graduate from them may wish they had not been granted the freedom to devote one or more years to what in the end turned out to be a vain effort, it seems only fair to let the students themselves

122 The Work/Life Dichotomy

decide whether they want to take the risk. It also seems only fair to provide them with the opportunity to demonstrate aptitudes and abilities that are not easily assessed by admission tests, interviews, or past scholastic performance.

One of the best examples in the anglophone world of an egalitarian easy entry/difficult exit system may be Britain's Open University, an institution addressing itself to students learning at home and noted for carefully designed courses. Easy entry/difficult exit systems offer as much hope as any system can for facilitating the process of people upgrading themselves to become competent workers for whom work and life are one sphere.

WORK AND LIFE ON THE LEVEL OF THE INDIVIDUAL

9

The Interaction Between the Work and Life Spheres of Individuals

Part 1 has considered the work and life spheres on the macro-level. Certain suggestions designed to reduce the gap between them were made. These suggestions were general and centered around the ideas of upgrading the work sphere by redefining work and of increasing the opportunities—by working toward more egalitarian conditions—available to people for upgrading themselves. So far the emphasis has been on the climate within the work and life spheres, the participation-oriented work organization and the egalitarian society, which would facilitate actual change.

Changing social conditions is a cumbersome process. The proposed changes should be based on an accurate diagnosis of problems to be remedied. Such diagnosis is likely to involve macro-level considerations since the problems have to affect many individuals before the effort is generated to change things.

However, the implementation or action part of changing social conditions is likely to begin with small changes on the micro-level of particular individuals. To actually do something about the gap between work and life we have to understand better what form it takes on the level of the individual and then, based on this understanding, make small changes that will affect increasing numbers of individuals until broad social conditions are changed. The object in this part of the book is thus to obtain a high resolution view of the gap between work and life on the level of the individual, and to suggest more concrete changes based on this more detailed understanding.

This chapter provides an overview of the relationships between the work and life spheres of the individual. In terms of Exhibit 1–1, the focus is on the level of the individual and on the material and cultural or psychological conditions of both the work and life spheres. The conditions of the work sphere of the organization are the subject of Chapter 10, but they will also be relevant here since they impinge on the work spheres of individual workers.

ENVIRONMENT, PERSON, AND BEHAVIOR

On the macro-level of society the question of the relationship between the work sphere and the life sphere boils down to the relationship between two sets of environmental conditions. The conditions characterizing either set may be material or cultural.

On the micro-level of the individual we no longer deal only with the environment, but with something more complex, best called *situation*, which includes both the person, represented by the cultural or psychological conditions on the micro-level of the individual in Exhibit 1–1, and the environment within which the person functions. On this level the problem of the relationship between work and life touches on the broader issue of how person and environment interact.

Complicating matters further, a third element enters the picture as well: the person's behavior, which is both determined by and which determines personality. The context of the relationship between work and life spheres on the level of the individual is thus ultimately provided by a model that considers the interactions between three sets of variables: those pertaining to the person, those pertaining to the environment, and those pertaining to the person's behavior.

Albert Bandura's (1977, 1986) model of *triadic reciprocality* is a straightforward representation of the theoretically possible cause and effect relationships between the environment, person, and behavior. The three entities E, P, and B are the corners of an equilateral triangle whose sides represent the reciprocal effects between any pair of them.

The interaction between environment, person, and behavior is important at this point for two specific reasons. First, the way workers perceive the relationship between their work and life spheres constitutes behavior, albeit cognitive and hence covert rather than overt behavior. As behavior, the worker's perception of this relationship is influenced not only by conditions which actually prevail, but it is also influenced by—and influences—his or her personality. As we will see later in this chapter, Rotter's (1966) ubiquitous personality characteristic of locus of control is of particular interest in this context.

Second, the focus of study in the United States has been the question of what determines work behavior. After all, managers are interested in manipulating behavior, to make it as productive as possible. The reverse possibility, that behavior shapes personality, has not received much attention. The one exception to this rule is the area of work-related stress. It is easy to see why: Stress interferes with productivity in a fairly direct way. In general, however, the long-term negative and positive effects of work on workers have been neglected. Perhaps we have to wait until workers sue their employer for subjecting them to mind-numbing working conditions which irreparably dulled their intellect.

Determinants of Behavior and of Personality

The insight that the environment, person, and behavior are all reciprocally related has taken some time to become generally accepted. Until recently, interest focused on two distinct issues pertaining to their relationship. It is out of these specific issues that the model of triadic reciprocality has evolved.

One of these issues is how biological and environmental factors shape personality. Heredity-oriented investigators saw personality as the result of genetic dispositions which, to varying degrees, manage to develop and to express themselves in different environments. Environment-oriented scientists, in particular the radically behaviorist psychologists, assigned the primary roles to the environment and the learning processes which it instigates through eliciting stimuli, and which it controls through reinforcers. At issue between the two camps is the relative importance of biology and the environment, nature and nurture. Everyone agrees that both play some role and that personality is the result of interaction between them.

The other issue is how the person characteristics which resulted from past interaction between environmental and biological factors and the stimuli currently impinging on the person, the present environment, determine behavior. One camp is again the environment-oriented scientists, but the other is a group not involved in the nature versus nurture debate: the personalists. The latter see behavior as largely determined by personality characteristics or dispositions: People act aggressively because of an aggressive disposition, not primarily because someone stepped on their toes or ego. It is important to note that the personalists could take a nature- or nurture-oriented view on the question of how personality dispositions develop in the first place.

RELATIONSHIPS BETWEEN THE WORK AND LIFE SPHERES OF INDIVIDUALS

Before proceeding it may be wise to define more precisely the work and life spheres of individuals. The work sphere of an individual has

at least three components. There are its material conditions: the work
environment and tasks impinging on the individual. These are environmental factors. They include the authoritarian or democratic supervisor and the production quotas set by management.

Then there are the psychological conditions of the work sphere of
the individual: the cognitive reflections within the individual of the work
sphere on the levels of society and the organization, and of the material (i.e., external) conditions of the work sphere on the level of the
individual. These are aspects of the work sphere of the individual which
pertain to the person rather than the environment. They include an
individual's perception of the supervisor as cold autocrat or friendly
fellow human being, and of the quotas as reasonable or exploitative.

Finally, there is the work-related behavior of the person which affects the material conditions under which work is done as well as certain personal characteristics. Enthusiastic work may produce conces-
sions regarding vacation periods; conscientious work may lead to a
sharpening of skills and a rise of competence levels.

Similarly, the life sphere consists of environmental factors, personal
characteristics, and some aspects of the person's behavior, all of which
interact as suggested by the model of triadic reciprocality.

The next step is to look more closely at possible relationships between the work and life spheres of individuals within the general context provided by the model of triadic reciprocality. The specific models
of use here can be classified as noncausal and causal models, and the
latter are likely to be either generalization or compensation models.

Noncausal Models

Models of the relationship between work and life must either be causal
or noncausal. The former rest on strong statements about what causes
what, that is, on how the life sphere affects the work sphere and/or
vice versa. Noncausal models may also have something to say about
cause and effect, but such causal statements are not central to them.

Three noncausal models or patterns of relationship which have received some attention are the segmentation, congruence, and identity
models.

The segmentation model. In a nutshell, the segmentation model postulates two spheres between which there are no relationships. Of course,
this is quite theoretical; in the real world just about everything is related to everything else. For example, the life sphere may be kept apart
from the work sphere because the work sphere produces stress which
the worker seeks to avoid, or, probably less often, because the life sphere
generates stress which must be kept out of the work sphere. Millions
of workers drag themselves to work, perform their tasks, and rigidly

refuse to let the demands of work impinge on their jealously defended "own time" because they don't like their work and want to forget it.

The model is useful because in some circumstances there are forces and trends that work toward segregation. For example, in Dubin's (1973) society characterized by multi-equal institutions, in which work and life are separated spatially, temporally, functionally and organizationally, it is quite possible for some workers to keep the two spheres distinct in order to prevent the frustration, hostility, and anger generated in one from spilling over into the other. Such separation would play a role similar to that of Freudian compartmentalization which causes thoughts that belong together, such as anxiety-generating thoughts about a parent and that parent's birthdays, to be separated by an impenetrable wall.

There is a difference between thinking that the work sphere and the institutions comprising the life sphere are independent, that is, segmented, domains and believing that they should be segmented. This is the difference between Mankin's (1978) "theoretical/empirical" (essentially explanatory and descriptive) perspective and his normative one. The issue of whether work and life should be reintegrated is important, and it is clearly the holistic rather than segmentalist position of this book that, in general, they should.

The congruence model. A second noncausal model postulates a relationship between the work and life spheres accounted for by a third factor or cluster of variables which affects both in similar ways. For example, on the micro-level this third factor could be a basic personality disposition (e.g., Ulich & Ulich, 1977). A person characterized by a happy-go-lucky temperament may experience little stress and much enjoyment both on the job and at home.

The identity model. This model postulates that the work and life spheres are indistinguishable. They could constitute a single system consisting of variables pertaining to work and life which are so closely and *causally* related that it is impossible to cluster them into two subsets.

However, one can also envisage a *noncausal* identity model in which the two spheres merge into one because of underlying common determinants. For example, and again on the micro-level, personal dispositions and the nature of the job may interact and generate total commitment to activities that cannot be clearly separated into work and life activities. Such a relationship may prevail in the case of many writers, artists and researchers (P. Groskurth, cited from Ulich & Ulich, 1977). The noncausal identity model is an extreme form of the congruence model. Both generally assume a positive correlation between work and life variables such as work and life satisfaction. In this sense they are also the opposite of the segmentation model which postulates correlations of zero between work and life variables.

Causal Models: Generalization and Compensation

This brings us to the causal models postulating definite cause and effect relationships between the work and life spheres on the macro-level of society and on the micro-level of the personalities of individuals. Dominant among these models are two identified by Harold Wilensky (1960) in Engels' (1892) famous depiction of *The Condition of the Working Class in England in 1844*. The two models are *spillover* from the work sphere to the life sphere, and *compensation* for mind-numbing routine and exploitation in the work sphere by means of excesses and outbursts within the life sphere. Today we tend to talk about generalization rather than spillover, and we consider both generalization and compensation to describe not only effects of work on the life sphere, but also effects of the life sphere on the work sphere.

We have a case of generalization when the satisfaction or dissatisfaction experienced in one sphere extends into the other sphere and produces within it corresponding satisfaction or dissatisfaction. Compensation involves either the search in one sphere for what the other is lacking, or for what will compensate for actual frustrations and hardships the other imposes.

Generalization produces positive, and compensation produces negative correlations between corresponding characteristics, aspects, or variables of the work and life spheres. An exciting and demanding home life could foster the skills and competencies required to do well on the job through generalization, while a bored housewife could make the most out of her job, changing it to be more challenging and more of a growth opportunity through the mechanism of compensation (Lehr, 1974).

The next two sections look at how generalization and compensation account for effects of work on the life sphere, and how they account for effects of the life sphere on the work sphere. It should be noted that concentrating on the effects of work on life implies, in general, both materialistic determinism and environment-orientedness, while concentrating on the effects of life on work implies, again in general, both cultural determinism and person-orientedness. Paid work in the industrial society satisfies material, physiological, or deficit needs and is imposed by the environment which says: Do this or starve. Life implies freedom from necessity and it is about personal and private goals and concerns.

EFFECTS OF WORK ON LIFE

The nature of a person's work experience is shaped by numerous influences. It varies across occupations: Successful businessmen, doctors, and teachers are more likely to report high levels of job satisfaction than unskilled manual workers, miners, and oil rig workers (Parker & Smith, 1976). It depends on various characteristics of the organization. Chris Argyris (1964, Ch. 3) notes, for example, "the organizational dilemma" of pyramidal and authoritarian structure on one hand, and the need of workers and managers to experience success. A person's work experience also depends on characteristics of the particular job: Does it offer autonomy; are the tasks done complete entities with a certain significance visible to the worker? Ultimately, the work experience depends on the work process itself: Are skills utilized (O'Brien, 1986)? Does the work consist of actions which form personality, or reflexes which do not (Hacker, 1986; Leontiev, 1981; Rubinstein, 1977).

The effect of work on the worker is a general topic, however, within which certain issues have arisen on which there is less agreement. Two issues are of particular interest in the present context:

Does work affect the worker's personality? No one doubts that the nature of the work they do, and the work experiences they accumulate as a result, can affect workers in many ways. Stressors on the job have been a favorite subject of investigation for decades because their effects are uncontested and often dramatically impair productivity. Contradicting Freud, the Jesuits, and others who held that personality is shaped completely in early childhood, the current consensus is that personality is shaped throughout the course of life-span development. This means that the large proportion of time spent working is likely to have major effects on the relatively enduring traits of a person. Work on the assembly line might make workers intellectually rigid; other jobs could raise self-confidence and aspiration levels.

Does work have positive as well as negative effects? The Reverend Kingsley's uplifting thoughts on the beneficial effects of work on character certainly suggest that work affects the worker's personality (see Chapter 2). North American industrial and organizational psychology, however, has focused on the negative effects of job-related stress. It has viewed work as a necessary evil and has sought to reduce its negative effects and the dissatisfaction of workers which lead to unproductive behavior ranging from working slowly to strikes and sabotage (see O'Brien, 1986). Russian psychologists, in sharp contrast, have focused on the positive pedagogical effects of work in shaping the character of the new socialist man or woman. American culture produces books on the joy of sex, the Russian culture produces books on the joy of work. The needs of a less-than-affluent society, and propaganda objectives explain this Russian attitude toward work only in part.

The two issues overlap, since what would be of greatest interest are positive effects on the personality. That a person's experiences on the job affect his or her personality in positive ways has, of course, been suspected for a long time. The seventeenth-century philosopher G. W. F. Hegel uttered the famous thought, echoed by Marx, that man makes himself through his work. Adam Smith and Emil Durkheim were convinced that increasing specialization, the division of labor, affected the personality of workers in both positive and negative ways.[1] The next section focuses on studies which have recently provided convincing evidence supporting these earlier surmises.

Generalization from Work Experience to the Individual's Life Sphere

Sociological and psychological studies. Melvin Kohn and Carmie Schooler (1983) presented a series of studies on the reciprocal effects of job conditions and indices of psychological functioning. Critical among their findings are those on the effects of the job conditions of substantive complexity, control of supervision, and routinization (three indices of occupational self-direction) on ideational flexibility. Their (Kohn & Schooler, 1973) causal analyses show that while ideationally flexible individuals are selected for, or choose, jobs offering opportunities for self-direction, the effects of such selection on ideational flexibility are less important than those of the jobs themselves. It seems conceivable that job design which keeps this and related findings in mind could help make an organization's workforce happier, more committed to the organization, and more capable.

A similarly ambitious series of cross-sectional and longitudinal studies reported by Jeylan Mortimer, Jon Lorence, and Donald Kumka (1986) examines three stages of psychological development: first, the effects of the family of origin on work related values and career choice; second, the effects of work experience on personality development and psychological functioning; and third, the interaction between work experience and family, both the family of origin and the "family of procreation."

It is the second of these three stages, the stage of young adulthood preoccupied with work, job, and career that is of interest in the context of the effects of work on life. Mortimer et al. conclude, along the lines of Kohn and Schooler (1983), that jobs offering the opportunity for self-direction, or work autonomy (Hackman & Oldham, 1980), markedly and positively affect personality functioning and development, and that they do so independently and beyond positive effects of opportunities for social interaction on the job.

The sociological evidence is clearcut: Jobs characterized by autonomy, opportunities to participate in decision making, and opportunities to apply skills and develop new ones have powerful positive effects on the personality of workers.

What the sociologists describe on the basis of field studies involving large samples and many variables, psychologists can explain in terms of more specific processes which raise the confidence and competency levels of individuals off and on the job. Bandura (e.g., 1986) discusses the processes which foster self-efficacy, the expectation that one is capable of attaining specified standards of performance. His focus is on personality development in general, but the processes have specific implications for development within the work sphere, the occupation, the job.

The data of interest here are quite basic, "pure" research data from learning and cognition. While Bandura's self-efficacy overlaps mainly with effort-performance expectancy, attention has also been paid to the other aspect of personal control: the performance-outcome expectancy of interest to Rotter (1966. See also O'Brien, 1986).

Self-efficacy depends on ability. A number of case studies published by researchers at the Swiss Federal Technical Institute have focused on the effects produced by increasing the workers' control of the work process on what the researchers call the workers' "Qualifikationen." This term is difficult to translate. The English term "qualifications" certainly does not do it justice. The German term does, however, appear to overlap with both objective ability and subjective self-efficacy (Baitsch & Frei, 1980; Baitsch et al., 1986).

Generalization of learning and spillover. The sociological and psychological data on the effects of work on behavior and especially on personality suggest that focusing on the macro-level effects of job conditions and the micro-level effects of work processes is justifiable on social grounds. Anything that permits people at work to grow and develop rather than atrophy cannot be all bad.

However, there may also be direct economic payoffs. A number of studies show that self-efficacy increases performance levels, including performance in the context of work (Barling & Abel, 1983; Barling & Beattie, 1983; Locke et al., 1984). Julian Barling and M. Abel (1983) note that self-efficacy is consistently related to performance while performance-outcome expectancy is not. The implications of these findings for personnel selection, training and other organizational concerns have been pointed out by Marilyn Gist (1987).

Both the sociological and basic psychological evidence support the view that there is generalization from the work sphere to the life sphere, and that the results can be positive and can pertain not only to behavior, but to personality as well. It must be noted, however, that two variants of generalization are involved here. The first is the generalization of learning in which new responses acquired in one context, for example, on the job, are later elicited or produced in another, for example in the process of living one's nonwork life. Both Kohn and Schooler and Mortimer et al. indicate clearly that this is what they mean by generalization. The second variant is the more global notion of Wilensky's spillover. It is too early to tell exactly how they are related or whether or how the second is reducible to the first.

Further clarification is required. One study which analyzes Wilensky's concept in an early step toward such clarification was done by Thomas Kando and Worth Summers (1971). These sociologists have distinguished between two kinds of generalization. They call generalization of the type Wilensky had in mind, in which low quality work leads to a low quality of life, passive generalization. This they distinguish from active generalization in which high quality work has beneficial effects in the life sphere.

Marxist writings abound not only with excellent examples of passive generalization in their depiction of the working class in nineteenth-century Britain, they also provide the best examples of active generalization when they describe the ideal worker of the socialist future. Two types have to be distinguished among the latter depictions. The first is the propagandistic type focusing on ideal workers performing meaningful work with and for comrades and for the socialist fatherland. The second is the type of depiction based on scientific analysis, exemplified by the work of psychologists Sergei Rubinstein (1977) and Alexei Leontiev (1981), which focuses on the productive as well as the "personality-promoting" (Frei, 1986) and occupationally socializing (Frese, 1982) aspects of work.

Compensation for What Work Inflicts or Fails to Offer

Work experience generalizes to the life sphere, but earlier in the chapter the possibility of compensatory relationships was raised. Examples are the person with the boring job who buys a boat and seeks excitement on the nearby lake, or the repressed and placid accountant known as a "party animal" off the job.

Kando and Summers (1971) distinguish between supplemental compensation in which the worker strives to obtain in the life sphere rewards which are not available in the work sphere, and reactive compensation in which the worker compensates for undesirable characteristics which are present in the work sphere by seeking their opposites in the life sphere. The distinction is helpful, although in practice it is probably not always easy to specify which of the two mechanisms is at work. We would need, for example, more information to make the distinction in the cases of the motor boat owner and the party animal above.

EFFECTS OF LIFE ON WORK

The focus now switches from work to life, from materialistic determinism to cultural and psychological determinism, from the environment to the person. The life sphere, cultural and psychological determinants, and the person are seen by some people as more important, or primary causal agents, than the work sphere, material conditions, and the environment.

The example cited from Lehr (1974) earlier illustrates on the level of the individual the effect of the life sphere on aspects of the work sphere: The dissatisfied housewife may go out and actively arrange her work to be demanding and fulfilling in response to the emptiness of her existence in a less-than-fulfilling home. Another example might be the tendency of the members of a work group involved in an organizational development or quality of work life project to carry over from their life sphere certain expectations about being able to make decisions on their own rather than have them made by autocratic or paternalistic superiors. In both cases the life sphere, comprising primarily cultural determinants, produces effects on people's approach to the generally material or economic concerns of the work sphere.

A cultural determinist stance is assumed by Edgar Schein (1981) in a discussion of work organizations. His analysis is as relevant to the macro-level as it is to the micro-level since the organization often forms the interface of society and the individual. It is reported here because it throws light on the nature of the organization without which it is difficult to imagine the changes required for reintegrating work and life on the level of the individual.

Schein argues that the root and ultimate set of determinants of an organization's culture are its basic unformulated, and preconscious assumptions that pervade it because it is a part of the larger social culture. These assumptions pertain to fundamental questions concerning time, space, and the relationships between human beings and between human beings and nature. They are a part of Bell's culture and of the religious subsphere of the life sphere. Work organizations may not spend much time on trying to integrate work and life, but they are subject to the broad values which dominate their society's life sphere.

Schein cites two key assumptions of U.S. society which are reflected by its work organizations: "Where there's a will there's a way" (p. 64) and "maximizing one's opportunities, and fully utilizing one's capacities [are] moral imperatives" (p. 66). These assumptions reflect, in Schein's words, a "proactive optimism" about " 'man's' relationship to nature" (p. 65) and an "individualistic egalitarianism" regarding " 'man's' relationship to 'man' " (p. 65). To firstline workers, these key assumptions may not be immediately apparent. But, according to Schein, from them derive specific ideals, as well as goals and ideas about how to attain them. For example, proactive optimism explains "the most notable characteristic of U.S. managerial practice [which is] that we are never satisfied and are forever tinkering to find a better way" (p. 65).

RECIPROCAL RELATIONSHIPS BETWEEN WORK AND LIFE

The Work and Life Spheres as Interacting Subsystems

One can entertain three causal hypotheses about the relationships between the work and life sphere: that work influences personal or nonwork life, that life influences work, and that the two are reciprocally related.

Like the noncausal models, the first two of these hypotheses, discussed in the previous sections, fall into the category of useful fictions. We all know that the two spheres always interact. However, situations in which one-way effect causal models and the noncausal models apply are special and instructive cases. These simpler models have heuristic value. By exploring the simpler world they postulate we can develop a basis from which to launch more ambitious campaigns to understand the larger picture.

In the real world with which we must eventually deal the two spheres have to be viewed simultaneously in all their complexity. For example, objective conditions of the life sphere generate values and expectations about one's individual rights. Friends, teachers, family, and the media may tell us that we have the right to be ourselves, to express ourselves, to develop and use our talents. Such expectations often conflict with the proscriptions and prescriptions of the work sphere, ranging from the demand for punctuality to sudden "requests" to submit to a drug test. On the other hand, exposure to stressors such as intrusive drug testers in the work sphere can cause tension which carries over into the life sphere. In this daily interaction of work and life, one would expect generalization and compensation, as well as segmentation and other mechanisms, to play a role.

We have to look at the work sphere and life sphere of the individual as two subsystems which constantly interact, thus constituting a larger system. In the study of this interaction we have to identify and measure specific variables, the variables in the work and life spheres studied must correspond to each other in some meaningful way, and variables such as personality traits, sex, and education level which affect the relationships under investigation have to be considered (Kabanoff & O'Brien, 1980).

A study by Janet Near and her colleagues (1980) offers some hints on how one might define more precisely the variables of the two spheres. Near et al. distinguish between objective conditions and subjective experience variables. These correspond, or at least overlap, with the material and psychological conditions referred to in Exhibit 1–1 and elsewhere. Near et al. (1980) identify the six possible relationships between four sets of variables: the objective conditions and subjective experience variables of the work and life spheres. They then review the empirical evidence on the strengths of these relationships. The results appear to suggest that objective conditions, such as the degree of autonomy permitted by one's work, tend to affect particularly strongly subjective experience variables such as various indices of satisfaction within the life sphere.

Locus of Control as Moderator of the Work/Life Relationship

The personality variable of locus of control exemplifies the role of variables which affect the relationship between the work and life sphere.

Objective data. Kabanoff and O'Brien (Near, Rice, & Hunt, 1980) suggest that externally controlled individuals are doomed to a lower quality of life, regardless of whether they hold routine or complex jobs. If their jobs are demanding, they exhibit reactive compensation, that is, they look for rest, peace, and quiet because their demanding jobs constitute too much stress for them. On the other hand, if their jobs are routine, they exhibit passive generalization and do nothing to make the life sphere more satisfactory than the work sphere. The external assembly line worker may go home, open a six-pack, and watch TV. The external professional may find the challenges of the demanding job too much; he may burn out and seek nothing but rest in the life sphere.

According to Kabanoff and O'Brien, the opposite is true of internally controlled individuals: Regardless of whether they hold routine or complex jobs, they are likely to undertake efforts to make the life sphere interesting, by supplemental compensation if the job is routine, by active generalization if it is complex. The internal assembly line worker as well as the internal surgeon would be expected to create challenges and variety in the life sphere by means of activities ranging from raising a family to hunting in the northern woods.

Subjective perceptions. Ernst-H. Hoff (1986) carries this analysis further by distinguishing between objective data and subjective perceptions. He focuses on the latter. Internals perceive themselves as masters of their destiny. Externals believe it is in the hands of fate or the system whether their work and life spheres form, or fail to form, a harmonious whole. Hoff notes that internals are person-oriented, externals are environment-oriented, and that either point of view may not be realistic. Individuals usually have to adopt a position between extreme internality and externality if they wish their worldview to reflect something resembling reality.

This means that being internal is not always an advantage and that being external is not always a disadvantage. A realistic view of the world is what matters. Under some conditions individuals can exercise control over the relationship between their work and life spheres. Under others, for example in routine jobs, they cannot.

The basic models or patterns of the relationship between work and life which have been identified in this chapter constitute an important first step. Kabanoff and O'Brien (1980) point out that they permit us to go beyond questions like "how does work determine leisure?" and to address the more complex interactions between work and life raised by questions of the type: "Which factors, personal and situational, are associated with or cause people to have different work/leisure patterns?" (p. 607). This more sophisticated perspective brings us closer to the identification of optimal work/life patterns for different individuals in different situations, and to the devising of ways to bring such optimal patterns about.

NOTE

1. See Frese (1982), Hacker (1986), Mortimer et al., (1986), O'Brien (1986), and Ulich (1974) for examples of awareness of these long roots of the belief that work shapes personality.

10

Redesigned Jobs

This chapter returns to the dimension of efficiency and productivity versus human growth and development which was central to Chapter 7. We saw how its poles determine the climate or context within which work organizations approach the person/job fit problem. The present chapter deals with actual techniques used in organizational development and job design, two clusters of techniques that overlap and offer means for reintegrating work and life by upgrading jobs and people.

ORGANIZATION THEORY: FROM STRUCTURE TO PEOPLE

In a way, organizational development still concentrates on climate, except here it is the climate within a particular work organization that is of interest. This organizational climate directly influences the perception of specific jobs, that is, the perception of what they should entail and whether and how they should be changed. It is a more specific entity than the general social climate of Chapter 7.

Like any other body of techniques, those of organizational development should have a theoretical basis that specifies and accounts for the relationships among the variables of interest. This allows one to predict, or at least make educated guesses about, the effects of planned interventions. An organization theory is a set of concepts and statements that introduce some order to, and sometimes account for, observations made about organizations. These observations may be about organizations in general, groups of organizations (industrial plants, insurance companies), or particular organizations.

For example, we might observe that organizations tend to become more bureaucratic as they get older, that organizations with few hierarchical levels respond more slowly to unexpected changes, or that a particular factory produced 10,000 widgets last month but only 5000 this month. Organization theory may tell us why the observed phenomena occurred, whether we should do something in response to them, and perhaps even what it is we should do.

Organization theory is like personality theory: It is really a host of theories reflecting the different interests and perspectives of the theorists and the wide range of organizations coping with different sets of circumstances. This multitude of theories is difficult to classify, but one recent and promising way is that of Lee Bolman and Terrence Deal (1984) who distinguish between structural, human resource, political, and symbolic theories. Each of these fits best a particular set of conditions and makes different prescriptions.

Organization theorists also emphasize systems theory (e.g., Bolman & Deal, 1984; Certo & Applebaum, 1983; Katz & Kahn, 1978). Obviously, every organization is a system, that is, a set of entities interrelated to such a degree that they can be considered as constituting a whole, a configuration, some larger entity. Systems theory applies to organizations and to any other such whole, and it applies to organizations whether the problems of interest are structural, personnel-related, political, or symbolic. It is an underlying metatheoretical approach rather than a substantive theory like Bolman and Deal's four other types.

According to Bolman and Deal, structural theories take for granted a certain stability, while human resource theories may be useful during times of rapid change when employees at all levels have to adjust in major ways. Political theories usually fit the bill when resources are scarce and when different interest groups struggle mightily to get their famous "fair share." Symbolic theories, stressing organization culture and climate, and symbols of that culture ranging from new logos to expressive company T-shirts for the annual company picnic, are usually invoked when a company consists of diverse elements, for example, after a merger.

The different prescriptions made by these four types of theories can be illustrated by how they handle the central (Tausky, 1978) problem of motivation. Still according to Bolman and Deal, structural theory recommends monetary rewards; human resource theory relies on higher level needs for growth and self-actualization; political theories concentrate on coercion, manipulation, and seduction; the symbolic theories would rely on employee-of-the-month plaques, rugs on the office floor, company cars with or without chauffeurs.

Of the four types of theories, the structural and the human resource theories are the best established and most important. They reflect the productivity and the human growth orientations of Chapter 7, respectively, and they both contradict and complement each other.

Structural Organization Theory

We saw that the term *structure* connotes a stable framework and that, for example, the training ("education") system is highly structured in terms of its institutions, programs, and the means it uses to attain training goals. The structure of an organization refers primarily to the hierarchy of its positions, the interlocking roles the occupants of these positions are expected to play, the available communication channels, both formal and informal, and so forth. The structure of an organization is part of the larger techno-economic structure. This means, as Exhibit 1–1 suggested, that structural organization theory is the organization theory most compatible with the productivity and efficiency concerns of the work sphere.

Bolman and Deal's structural theories include both classic and contingency theories. Curt Tausky (1978) points out that the former are based on the model of *economic man*, man who is motivated by profit, while the latter are based on the model of *instrumental man*, man who does things which will allow him to attain his objectives under specific circumstances or conditions.

Classic organization theory. Classic organization theory, in turn, consists of two variants. One focuses on the "physiology and organization of work" (Tausky, 1978, p. 24) providing the basis of what came to be called *scientific management.* The other focuses on organizational structure.

In 1898, Frederick Taylor studied how workers at the Midvale plant of the Bethlehem Steel Company loaded ninety-two-pound "pigs"— iron castings from the smelting furnace—on railroad cars. They loaded 12.5 tons per man per day. Taylor, an engineer by profession, studied the time and motions involved in the loading activity and the amounts of fatigue generated or reported. He calculated that a suitable worker performing the job in the one best way could load forty seven tons per day.

Taylor trained a worker by the name of Schmidt and offered him a substantial pay incentive. As a result, Schmidt consistently exceeded even the forty seven-ton target. This is one of the earliest examples of scientific management. Controversy soon erupted around this approach because it reduced work to simple operations and made what once required decisions and complex skills into a routine that was mind-numbing for many. But it has been and probably still is the dominant approach to organizing work. It received a particularly strong boost when, in 1913, Henry Ford set up assembly line production of the Model A and then the Model T in Dearborn, Michigan. Both Taylor and Ford argued that they were not demeaning work and workers, that the price of routine and specialization was more than outweighed by the more efficient generation of wealth of which the workers would receive their share.

Classic theory associated with organizational structure is primarily the contribution of Weber (1947) and Henri Fayol (1949). Like that of Taylor and his American colleagues, it evolved around the turn of the century. What the *work tasks* (and the "one best way" to do them) was to the proponents of scientific management—to Taylor, Frank and Lilian Gilbreth, Henry Gantt and others—the *position* was to Weber and Fayol.

Together the positions of an organization constitute its hierarchical structure, its skeleton. Frank Landy (1985) notes that according to classic organization theory it is "important to build the skeleton of the organization carefully since the behavior of the people in the organization would be a *product* (original italics) of this skeleton" (p. 470). One of Weber's specific interests was how positions are filled, either through the hiring or the promotion process. He saw the newly emerging bureaucracies at the turn of the century as a major improvement over nepotism, as replacing the whims of the powerful with objective, rational, and fair rules.

The rules and forms (in triplicate) of bureaucracy may be cumbersome and time-consuming, but as sociologist David Riesman (1978) points out: "red tape is the only substitute for red blood" (p. 53). The emerging organization which replaced personal fiefs reduced the control superiors can exercise over their subordinates. This is no small accomplishment. The modern organization, like Hobbes' king, restrains and, in the view of classic organization theory, civilizes. It substitutes impersonal justice for personal whim and power. Although bureaucracy is often bloodless and inhuman, the trend toward impersonal regulation and away from powerful superiors restricting the personal control of subordinates is among the positive developments within the techno-economic structure.

At first sight it may not be clear what Taylor and Weber have in common, what puts their theories into the same category of classic organization theory. Of course, both theories have been influential since the beginning of the century. More important is the fact that both are derived from the assumption that the world is an orderly and rational

place in which careful planning based on sound principles will be rewarded. One focuses on organizing the tasks constituting individual
jobs, the other on the organization or structure of the positions which
constitute a work organization. Both strive to improve production and
reflect Greenberg's (1975) management school of thought and Dachler
and Wilpert's (1978) productivity and efficiency orientation.

Contingency theory. This brings us to contingency theory, the current
incarnation of structural theory. It reflects a more complex world of
organizations and a more sophisticated understanding of them. More
specifically, it assumes that the best way or the best structure is dependent on, contingent on, prevailing conditions. For example, different
circumstances dictate smaller or larger spans of control. This aspect of
organizational structure is defined as the number of people for which
the first-level supervisors are responsible. A small span of control implies a highly hierarchized organization, a large span of control implies
a flat one.

In an early study, Joan Woodward (1958) found that in mass production organizations like auto assembly plants, the span of control was
between forty and fifty, while in process production plants, like an oil
refinery, it was between ten and twenty. Process production requires
more supervisors because mistakes are more costly (Dubin, 1965).

Humanistic Theory

Structural theory is rational theory. But human beings are not rational and logical creatures, they are psychological ones. They are not
automatons loading pig iron or checking forms all day without a murmur. They have needs, perhaps even quirks, and they behave in unexpected and "irrational" ways.

This became obvious in a series of studies conducted between 1924
and 1932 at the Hawthorne plant of Western Electric in Cicero, Illinois.
The object of the first of these studies was to look at the effect of illumination on productivity. The surprising result was that groups under
investigation produced more, whether illumination was increased, decreased, or held constant. Subsequent studies looked more closely at
the role of the people constituting various work groups at the Hawthorne plant and at the social interactions between them. One study
found, for example, that people do not necessarily respond to incentives by working harder. Instead, the members of the work group may
establish norms so that slower workers are not penalized (see Roethlisberger & Dickson, 1939). These studies led to a break with classical
theory and toward what Tausky (1978) calls *humanistic theory* and what
Bolman and Deal (1984) call *human resources theory*.

Humanistic theory is to the life sphere what structural theory is to the work sphere. Just as the latter reflects the productivity concerns of the work sphere, humanistic theory reflects the growth and development concerns of individuals operating in their life or personal spheres. As noted in Chapter 1, it asserts that organizations are here for people, not people for the organization (Bolman & Deal, 1984, p. 65).

Like structural theory, humanistic theory has two strands. The earlier strand coming out of the Hawthorne studies was human relations theory. It is based on what Tausky (1978) identified as the *social man* model. The more recent strand is called human resources theory, where the term is used in a more specific sense than that of Bolman and Deal. This second variant is based on what Tausky (1978) calls the *self-actualizing man* model.

The difference between the two is that human resources theory, like contingency theory in the context of structural organization theory, is a current and more comprehensive incarnation of humanistic theory. It is not just people-centered, but it also takes into account the possibility of task or job design as a means to provide opportunities for workers to raise their expectancies of success (self-efficacy) on work-related tasks and, more generally, to become better qualified and to learn, to draw on more deeply-rooted and stronger motivational dispositions.

The Hawthorne studies have generated considerable controversy over the years (e.g., Bramel & Friend, 1981). However, they pushed organization theory in the direction of people and away from the impersonal efficiency experts and organizational structures. Today humanistic theory originating in the Hawthorne studies and joined by Maslowian growth need theories and awareness of the interaction between human needs and characteristics of organizations and jobs, constitutes the theoretical basis for efforts which try to reduce the gap between work and life through organizational development and job design.

ORGANIZATIONAL DEVELOPMENT: THE EXAMPLE OF SUBJECTIVE ACTIVITY ANALYSIS

Let's assume we have a work organization that we can productively examine from the point of view of humanistic theory. Let's further assume that our first objective is to create an organizational or departmental microclimate that will facilitate concrete steps designed to increase worker participation and learning opportunities.

Psychologists (e.g., Landy, 1985) distinguish between three types of organizational development techniques. There is *survey feedback* which establishes discrepancies in the perceptions of different groups, such as supervisors and their subordinates, as well as discrepancies between people's perceptions of actual and ideal conditions or situations. There is *laboratory training*, both unstructured and structured, which focuses

Exhibit 10–1
Hypothetical Ratings for Five Work Activities of Cafeteria Work Group

Criteria	Work Activities				
	Dish-washing	Cleaning	Keeping inventory	Cooking hot food	Serving customers
Decision making	6	6	2	7	4
Task variety	2	3	2	8	8
Learning opportunities	1	1	4	9	8
Mutual support and respect	0	3	5	4	5
Meaningfulness of work	3	3	6	7	8
Desirable future	1	0	8	10	2

on such objectives as bringing to the surface and changing attitudes of participants toward each other and the organization. Finally, there is *process consultation* or process intervention. An example of this third technique is team-building. In contrast to laboratory training, process consultation concentrates on changing behavior, in the belief that when behavior is changed, new attitudes will follow.

In the real world, the different organizational development techniques are difficult to keep apart. One way to illustrate what actually happens in practice is to look closely at a typical approach applied to a concrete, albeit hypothetical situation.

Let's assume that the workers of a small cafeteria exhibit sufficient dissatisfaction with their jobs that it seems advisable to do something. Let's say there are twelve cafeteria workers and they constitute a single work group. An industrial/organizational psychologist is called in who decides to apply the Subjective Activity Analysis procedure (*subjektive Tatigkeitsanalyse*) based on F. E. Emery and M. Emery (1974) and on work done by Eberhard Ulich (1981) and his co-workers (e.g., Alioth, 1980). We can break down what the psychologist and the work group might do into a series of steps.

1. *A set of criteria is adopted which, according to the workers and their supervisor(s), the work ought to meet.* The criteria developed by Emery and Emery (1974) are listed in the left-hand column of Exhibit 10–1. They reflect the person-oriented view of humanistic theory that a job should, wherever possible, provide opportunities for practicing a variety of skills, for learning in general, to experience and provide support and respect in social relationships, to experience one's work as meaningful and as contributing to a better future.

2. The specific work activities of the members of the work group are identified. This step could take the form of either a formal and quantitative job analysis or of an informal one. In the cafeteria example we might find that the workers themselves report activities like the following:

Dishwashing: emptying dishes, cleaning pans, loading dishwasher, stacking dishes in appropriate cupboards.

Cleaning: sweeping and mopping the cafeteria, kitchen, toilets, hallways; cleaning the stoves and the food service counter.

Keeping inventory: monitoring available supplies of staples, ingredients, and perishable foods; accounting for dishes and cutlery. Planning ahead to maintain supplies, ordering supplies as needed.

Preparing food: washing, peeling, and cutting vegetables.

Cooking: boiling potatoes, simmering soup, frying steaks.

Serving customers: taking and filling orders for hot main courses at the food service counter.

Handling cash: operating a cash register: adding charges, collecting money, making change.

3. Ratings of the degree to which each activity meets the criteria are obtained from the work group. The ratings are obtained from the group as a whole, in the course of a group discussion, and they reflect a consensus. Hypothetical ratings that might be obtained from a typical cafeteria work group, including its supervisor(s) are also shown in Exhibit 10–1. They range from 0 to 10, where 10 indicates the conviction that a particular activity meets a particular criterion extremely well.

4. The cells containing low ratings are identified. A low score reflects a discrepancy between the desirable and the actual state. Such discrepancies, which have been arrived at with the participation of the whole group, focus attention on specific activities that call for action and change. Ulich (1974) points out that it is often not clear what conditions lie at the root of discontented and vague mumblings and of low work morale. Low ratings break the impasse and pinpoint problems. Exhibit 10–1 shows, for example, that dishwashing is perceived as offering little opportunity to learn and even less opportunity to experience the support and respect from fellow workers and to extend such support and respect to them in turn.

5. Changes in the work activities are considered with a view to raising the ratings of low cells without lowering those of high cells. To Ulich and others, a job which does not offer opportunities to learn new skills and/or acquire new knowledge is a particularly troublesome sight. The work group is probably more motivated to do something about such jobs than is management. It might suggest some form of job rotation. This raises some interesting problems in the North American context in which the tiniest duties of workers are fought over bitterly when collective agreements are worked out. Cumbersome and antiquated job classifications could turn out to be a stumbling block at this point, since each classification is associated with a particular set of meticulously defined activities which particular workers have the right to do, or, more to the point, the right to refuse to do. Fortunately, Japanese and other competitors are forcing American unions and managers to reevaluate their position on this matter.

6. *The skills, the abilities, and knowledge available to the work group are assessed to determine the training required by the proposed changes.* Given the proposed changes, what skills must the different members of the work group have? For example, if job rotation is considered, each worker must have all skills required by all jobs. Which of the required skills are already available? It is probably unrealistic to consider changes which require considerable and expensive training.

7. *The ways and means in which the new skills can be acquired at minimal cost to the organization are identified.* It could very well be that members of the group with certain skills can teach them to others, until every member can fill a wide range of the work group's jobs. Union feelings on the matter of who is entitled to exercise what skills on what tasks again can interfere here.

8. *The proposed changes are implemented.* This is the critical phase. Presumably the changes proposed are quite small and can be made by the members of the work group without undue friction. In practice, the group will probably hold further meetings to iron out problems as they arise.

9. *The effects of the implemented changes are evaluated.* How do the workers feel about their work three months later? Does the group give higher ratings to their various tasks, thus reducing the gap between the actual and the desirable state of affairs? There are likely to be effects on the attitudes of the participating workers toward the work tasks, the work organization, the supervisor(s) and higher level management. There may also be effects on productivity levels. Work satisfaction or the quality of work life are likely to increase. There will certainly be effects on the range of competencies developed by the workers.

A complex process like Subjective Activity Analysis usually includes variants of several or all of the basic organizational development techniques. It seeks and acts on the input provided by workers. It is likely to sensitize members of a work group to the needs of fellow members. It could involve retraining of workers and different kinds of process intervention. Subjective Activity Analysis and related methods also assume a climate that values worker participation and bottom-up management styles characteristic of Japanese work organizations. They are sensible approaches to bridging the gap between the work sphere and the life sphere by encouraging workers to act on the job as they usually do in their personal lives: as decision-making, autonomous, mature adults.

JOB DESIGN

Of course, organizational development is not enough. It raises questions and leads to broader awareness of the processes underlying organizational behavior and problem situations. It does not necessarily lead to specific action, to concrete changes in jobs. Such action, however, is the proof of the pudding, and this section looks at the types of action that can be taken to change not only jobs, but the motivation, abilities, and expectations of the people who hold them. Job design efforts can change both the jobs of the work sphere and people whose basic concerns belong to the life sphere. In the process, job design can cause jobs and people, work sphere and life sphere, to mesh more harmoniously.

The Spectrum of Job Design

Job design can be defined broadly to include any deliberate actions taken to design or change a job. Both changes of the job itself and aspects of the work environment, such as illumination level and style of supervision, may be involved. Job design can be pursued following two strategies which lead to quite opposite results and which are based on quite different orientations: job design that reduces job scope and job design that increases it. These two strategies are contrasted in Exhibit 10–2.

Charles Darwin is said to have distinguished between two kinds of scientists, the lumpers and the splitters. Exhibit 10–2 is clearly more palatable to lumpers. It represents a broad dichotomy whose two sides, representing basically once again the concerns of the work sphere and the life sphere, reflect the implications in many areas of the two basic job design strategies. This dichotomy bears looking at in the context of the dichotomy of American and European perceptions of worker participation reviewed in Chapter 7. In general, American managers and unions favor reducing job scope while Europeans often seek to increase it.

Job design that reduces job scope appears to be based on a pessimistic model of man, such as that which emerges from the writings of the eighteenth-century British philosopher Thomas Hobbes who argued that, left to their own devices and in the absence of the civilizing effect of a king or of enforced laws, human beings will be inclined to destroy each

Exhibit 10–2
The Two Job Design Strategies

Feature	Job Design Strategy	
	Reducing Job Scope	Increasing Job Scope
Focus	Work sphere	Life sphere
Philosophical antecedents	Hobbes' model of man	Rousseau's model of man
Theoretical context	Structural organization theory (scientific management)	Humanistic organization theory
Disciplines and methods	Engineering (methods analysis, human factors methods and techniques)	Psychology (job enrichment, flextime, flexplace)
Model of worker	Deskilled and easily replaced unit	Motivated and able member of a team
Primary output variables	Work performance (productivity and efficiency)	Work satisfaction (quality of work life), often also maintenance of the organization and larger systems in which it is embedded

Note: This is an extension of Exhibit 10-1 in Morf (1986).

other. One does not have to be a Hobbesian pessimist to want to decrease job scope, but it helps to have a model of human beings that does not assign to them unique patterns of needs and abilities which job designers must consider.

Structural organization theory, particularly of the classic variety, tends to be Hobbesian at least in the latter and weaker sense. It holds that managers must prescribe to the worker what to do; it constrains the worker by assigning simple tasks or by setting up rigid rules. In general, this approach is characteristic of engineers and of human engineering or ergonomics whose objective is man-machine systems that maximize productivity and efficiency.

In the context of structural organization theory the worker is often, though not always, seen as an interchangeable and easily replaced entity which can be plugged into the man-machine production system the way a new transistor or memory chip is plugged into electronic machinery. The primary output, given the production and efficiency orientation, is work performance.

Job design that increases job scope, on the other hand, reflects a positive view of human nature. This is job design in the sense of upgrading jobs and increasing the quality of work life. It reflects more the optimistic conception of human beings as basically good, constructive, motivated, and ready to learn. This second of two fundamentally different models of man was propagated by Hobbes' contemporary Jean

Jacques Rousseau. It underlies humanistic organization theory which regards the worker, generally speaking, as bringing to the job constructive motives and complex capabilities that enable him or her to produce in the absence of tight managerial control.

Job design that increases job scope tends to be the province of industrial/organizational psychologists rather than that of industrial engineers. The techniques used include horizontal and especially vertical job enlargement. The former involves increasing the range of tasks constituting a job, the latter involves redesigning and redefining the job so that it includes making decisions about what to do and when.

Decreasing and increasing job scope are markedly different activities with different goals. Only job design that increases job scope can be regarded as a form of upgrading jobs. Decreasing job scope focuses on the job; increasing it focuses on both the job and the job holder who is expected to change, learn and develop. Incidental and unintended results of decreasing job scope may be deskilled and unmotivated workers, while increasing job scope almost inevitably means upgrading people. In some ways, job design to increase job scope is a reaction to taylorization, an attempt to undo some of the damage it can inflict.

However, the two basic job design strategies are not always as contradictory as they appear to be. Both seek to reduce stress-producing aspects of work, one by engineering the job in such a fashion that the burden of physical labor falls on machines rather than their operators, the other by taking into account human needs for development, variety, challenge, and even self-actualization. In short, from a sufficiently large distance, both appear to be concerned with the same broad problem of matching people and jobs. Also, both appear to have the potential for increasing productivity, one by making the work less stressful and fatiguing, the other by raising self-efficacy (Bandura, 1986; Barling & Abel, 1983; Locke et al., 1984). The basic difference is that one takes a short-term view and is not concerned about worker satisfaction, while the other looks into the future and aims for a satisfied and capable workforce.

Increasing the Scope of Jobs

Probably the two best known American efforts to design or redesign jobs are those of Herzberg (Herzberg, Mausner, & Snyderman, 1959) and of Hackman and Oldham (1975, 1980).

Two-factor theory. Herzberg's two-factor theory maintained that work performance and work satisfaction are affected by two types of factors: factors intrinsic in the work, such as the opportunity it offers to achieve worthwhile goals, and factors extrinsic to the work, such as salary which is paid regardless of performance level. According to Herzberg et al., factors intrinsic in the work happen to meet growth needs, such as the need to achieve, while factors extrinsic to it address deficit needs, such as the needs for food and housing. As noted in Chapter 1, Herzberg's theory further maintained that all the extrinsic factors can do is reduce dissatisfaction and that only intrinsic factors can generate satisfaction.

While this theory has served the purpose of generating further research efforts, attempts to define its terms and to formulate its postulates explicitly have generally led to difficulties and the empirical evidence for it has not been encouraging.

Job characteristics theory. Thus psychologists were ready to embrace the job characteristics theory of Hackman and Oldham when it was formulated in 1975. Hackman and Oldham concentrated on five job characteristics: *skill variety*, the range of skills required by the work; *task identity*, the degree to which the job involves the completion of a self-contained set of tasks (such as assembling an engine); *task significance*, a job's consequences for others; *autonomy*, the freedom to choose among different ways to do the job; and *feedback*, the degree to which workers can tell whether they are doing the job well.

Hackman and Oldham postulated effects of these job characteristics on three psychological states of the worker. Skill variety, task identity, and task significance were thought to affect *experienced meaningfulness of the work*; autonomy was thought to affect *experienced responsibility for outcomes of the work*; and feedback was obviously a determinant of *knowledge of the actual results of the work activities*. Hackman and Oldham further postulated that these three psychological states in turn act jointly on the outcomes of work: That they raise internal work motivation, quality of the work performance, and job satisfaction, and that they lower absenteeism and turnover.

Finally, Hackman and Oldham saw the strength of growth needs as a variable moderating the relationship between their five job characteristics and their three psychological states, and between the three psychological states and work outcomes. These relationships were expected to be stronger for workers with high growth needs than for workers with low growth needs.

This model is not unequivocally supported by the empirical evidence. For example, the moderating effect of growth needs is not as great as predicted and the correlations between job characteristics, psychological states, and outcomes tend to be low. Gordon O'Brien (1986) notes, however, that both Herzberg's and Hackman and Oldham's models have generated a considerable amount of research on job design which increases job scope.

The action latitude model. In an interesting approach to job design which increases job scope, Ulich (e.g., 1981) and Alioth (1980) have formulated the concept of action latitude (*Handlungsspielraum*), a term which refers to the amount of latitude, freedom, or slack a worker has on different dimensions of his or her work. The action latitude model underlies not only much of what Ulich and his colleagues do with Subjective Activity Analysis, it also provides a useful definition of job design which increases job scope.

Ulich and his colleagues make the point that such job design means that the job must in the end be high on three dimensions. The first is the *range of work activities* and it comes close to Hackman and Oldham's (1975, 1980) job characteristic of skill variety. A job's position on this dimension is usually increased by horizontal job enlargement, for example, by adding the responsibility for scheduling rooms to a secretary's typing duties. It would, of course be advisable to simultaneously reduce the latter. The introduction of job rotation generally changes a range of jobs by increasing skill variety for most or all of them. Such rotation often reduces the productivity of workers in the short term, but the benefits of more motivated and more highly qualified workers who can do many different jobs has been brought home to those studying Japanese management techniques.

The second dimension is *decision and control autonomy* and it appears to come close to Hackman and Oldham's (1980) job characteristic of autonomy. A job's position on this dimension can be changed by vertical job enlargement, the technique usually called job enrichment. It is a more difficult undertaking than horizontal job enlargement. The worker has to be given responsibility to make decisions which in the typical American work organization are assigned to supervisors and middle-level management.

The third dimension is one added by Alioth (1980) to the original Ulich model: *social interaction.* The typical Detroit assembly line job is low on this dimension. The opposite is true of the job of a worker in the Kalmar Volvo plant in Sweden, involving the assembly of an entire car by a group of workers accompanying it as it moves through the factory on its mobile platform. The standard job design intervention of forming autonomous or semi-autonomous work groups was mentioned in Chapter 7 in the context of the British and European emphasis on the sociotechnical systems approach.

Models like Ulich's are the stimulus for more specific ideas on how to increase the scope of jobs. They suggest the questions summarized in Exhibit 10–3: What should the job include? With whom should the job be done? When and where should the job be done?[1]

1. *What should the job include?* This is the most important question which gives direction to job design efforts meant to increase job scope. From the point of view of humanistic theory, jobs should encompass a variety of tasks, including the making of decisions about which tasks they should encompass. As noted in Chapter 9, upgraded jobs, chal-

Exhibit 10–3
Increasing the Scope of Jobs

What should the job include?

The substantive aspects of work. Conditions intrinsic in the work.

Job enlargement increasing the range of work activities (the number of different activities encompassed by a job).

Job enrichment increasing the decision and control range (the level of responsibility involved in making the decisions required by a job).

With whom should the job be done?

The social aspects of work. Agents extrinsic to the work.

Semi-autonomous work groups increasing the social interaction range (the number of different types of social interaction required by a job).

When should the job be done?

The temporal aspects of work. Conditions extrinsic to the work.

Flextime

Job sharing

Where should the job be done?

The spatial aspects of work. Conditions extrinsic to the work.

Flexplace

Work decentralization

---

lenging work, and occupational self-determination promote positive changes in the personality of the worker. Among these changes are increased ideational flexibility (Kohn & Schooler, 1973), high expectations of success (self-efficacy, Bandura, 1986), and generally higher qualifications or abilities of workers (Baitsch & Frei, 1980).

What is at issue in the context of this question are the substantive aspects of work, the conditions intrinsic in the work (Schneider & Locke, 1971). The job design techniques which Buchanan (1979) considers to be typically American and which he calls "job restructuring" are relevant here: Horizontal job enlargement increases the range of activities encompassed by a job and raises its position on Ulich's range of work activities; and vertical job enlargement or job enrichment increases the level of responsibility involved in holding the job and raises the job's position on Ulich's decision and control autonomy. In some respects, the familiar technique of job rotation falls into either of these categories.

2. With whom should the job be done? This question addresses some of the social aspects of work. These tend to be neglected in North America, land of individualists, while the European socialist tradition and Japanese cultural values assign them an important place. This question concerns the agents extrinsic to the worker (Schneider & Locke, 1971) and Alioth's (1980) dimension of social interaction. Among the specific approaches to job design relevant here are those which Buchanan (1979) puts under the rubric "organizational restructuring" and which he regards as largely European.

Here the differences between job design on one hand, and organizational development and worker participation on the other, become blurred. Out of the sociotechnical approach grows the development of autonomous or semi-autonomous groups, and this is the approach Alioth had specifically in mind when he added the social interaction dimension to the action latitude model. Such groups increase action latitude by increasing the possibilities of social interaction on the job, including various forms of participation in decision making.

3. When and where should the job be done? Where there is the will to do so, technology makes it increasingly possible to let workers choose when and where they will do their work. As a result, alternative work schedules have been introduced under labels like flextime, job sharing, and flexplace. What is changed here are conditions extrinsic to the work (Schneider & Locke, 1971). By giving workers options about when and where they will work, obviously within the basic constraints dictated by the job, the position of jobs on Ulich's decision and control range is raised.

Chapter 2 and Exhibit 2–1 reflect the trend toward decentralization of the workplace. Office work is of paramount importance in the "service society" and it is increasingly automated. At the extreme end of possibilities, computers and telecommunication systems make possible the electronic cottage, an arrangement which raises the prospect of optimizing the advantages of flextime, flexplace, and perhaps job-sharing.

Not that the electronic cottage is an unmixed blessing. Labor spokesmen see it as the "electronic sweatshop" whose occupants are engaged in monotonous keyboarding and monitored by relentless computers. It also may bring work and life too close. At work one sits behind a desk in an environment consisting of stimuli closely associated with work behavior. At home one may be too close to the kitchen, and the conditioned response to make another sandwich may be stronger than conditioned responses to work. Besides, some people need to keep work and life separate, to keep the dissatisfaction generated in one sphere from generalizing too easily into the other.

As noted in Chapter 2, work decentralization does not have to assume the extreme form of electronic cottagers laboring away in their own homes. In the early 1970s, Jack Nilles and his colleagues (1976) studied what happens when large corporations establish satellite work centers in the suburbs of large metropolitan areas. They noted that on the level of the society at large, satellite work centers reduce fuel consumption, the need for ever bigger freeways that are optimally used only during rush hour, and air pollution generated by auto traffic. As Nilles and others point out, work decentralization also offers advantages on the level of the work organization: There is less need for centrally located and expensive land for head offices and parking spaces. From the perspective of this book, obliterating the spatial and, to some degree, the temporal gap between work and life also raises dramatic new possibilities for reintegrating them on the level of the individual worker.

Thus electronic home work and other forms of work decentralization open the possibility of leaving it to the worker to decide when, and also where, to do the work. These possibilities look much more promising at this time for managerial and professional workers than for clerical workers who, for example, update insurance records. Nevertheless, technology is in a place which should cause us to take a close look at where and when much of our work really needs to be done, and who really should decide where and when it will be done.

NOTE

1. The contributions to the formulation of these questions made by graduate students in my Psychology of Work course at the University of Windsor are gratefully acknowledged.

11

Competent Workers

The crucial feature of the egalitarian society is its belief that people can be different and still have the same worth. It does not insist on equal treatment. A diversity of ways of doing things is tolerated, as are different ways of attaining competence. This chapter looks at some different, albeit related, ways in which one can execute work competently. In particular, four types of workers that have served as role models in different cultures and over the centuries are examined: workers who play the role of craftsman, warrior, monk, and citizen. Reliance on such role models is ultimately a personal, micro-level activity. Each individual has to make choices: Are any of these models useful? If so, which one meets one's needs most effectively? Reliance on these or other models pertains to the upgrading of people rather than the upgrading of jobs and to the personal life sphere rather than the work sphere.

THE WORKER AS CRAFTSMAN

An excellent characterization of the modern craftsman is provided by Pirsig (1975) for whom the symbol of classical competence is the motorcycle mechanic who meets exacting standards and who works with precision and with precision tools because "the enormous forces of heat and explosive pressure inside [the] engine can only be controlled through . . . precision" (p. 91). This need for precision makes good mechanics "modest and quiet." There definitely is a right way and a wrong way, and "there's no way to bullshit your way into looking good on a mechanical repair job" (p. 308). The work of mechanics is "careful observation and precise thinking." That is why mechanics sometimes seem so "taciturn and withdrawn when performing tests. They don't like it when you talk to them because they are concentrating on mental images, hierarchies . . . using the experiment as part of a program to expand their hierarchy of knowledge of the faulty motorcycle and compare it to the correct hierarchy in their mind. They are looking at underlying form" (p. 103).

We can imagine such mechanics, although they are rare and usually work in small and hard-to-find garages. Today the idea of craftsmanship has something quaint and old-fashioned about it. The pace of the work sphere has quickened. People are concerned about careers and about being on the fast track. Craftsmanship is characterized by taking one's time to develop, in the course of years, complex competencies and to produce the goods, advice, decisions, etc., which constitute the craftsman's output. Work has also become the output of systems (i.e., of interrelated sets of entities like firstline workers, managers, resources, equipment) rather than of individuals.

In the history of Europe, the ideal of craftsmanship emerged with particular strength in the Middle Ages. The feudal society of powerful barons, national kings, and sought-after military leaders gradually made way for successful merchants, tradesmen, and artisans. Goods of high quality were produced and sold profitably. Wealth accumulated in the hands of a rising class of entrepreneurs and highly qualified workers. The guilds became powerful corporate bodies and demanded high standards of training and workmanship. In such countries as Germany and Switzerland, the apprenticeship tradition with clear links to the Middle Ages, still survives today.

Of course, Europe has no monopoly on craftsmanship. Prehistorians admire the quality of the work of early Indians who fashioned the elegant Clovis point which, tied to wooden shafts, epitomized early hunting cultures of North America (Michener, 1974). Early bronze artifacts, the results of a complex metal-using technology dating to perhaps 2000 B.C., have survived as examples of outstanding workmanship. Anthropologists tell us that not only in Europe, but also in China, Japan, the Middle East, and many other parts of the world, craftsmen acquired a high status. Their expertise was sought eagerly by the ruling class.

Fortunately at least the ideal of craftsmanship has remained alive. Our quality of life is raised by people who do their work carefully and who are proud of what they do, as anyone who has taken a car to a garage repeatedly for repairs done in a haphazard manner will know. From the point of view of this book, the tradition of craftsmanship is particularly important because it links the work and the life spheres. This bridging potential is obvious in polarized societies, such as the

hydraulic societies like early China in which the elite planned the critical irrigation projects and the drudges labored to build them (e.g., M.
Harris, 1977), and in modern American society in which technology
routinizes much of the work while making some of it, that of the tech-
nocratic elite, more complex. The craftsmanship tradition does not distinguish between work and life, between behavior executed because it
is demanded and paid for by others on one hand, and personal decision making and pride in what one is doing on the other.

THE WORKER AS WARRIOR

In an important way, workers and warriors are opposites. One creates (the Old English word *weorc* means "creation"), the other de-
stroys. The craftsmanship tradition notwithstanding, workers tend to
be ruled while warriors tend to do the ruling.

Such distinctions between workers and warriors have long historical
roots. Europe had been settled for several thousand years by generally
peaceful farmers when, according to many historians, the pastoral, mobile, and aggressive Indo-Europeans migrated from the steppes of
southern Russia and imposed themselves on the European populations
sometime between 4000 and 3000 B.C (e.g., Gimbutas, 1977). They also
made themselves at home in Asia Minor, the Middle East and India.

Distinct soldier and worker classes and even castes have characterized the societies of Indo-European speakers since their earliest migrations (Dumezil, 1973). The oldest of these that we know of are the
ksatriyas (soldiers) and *vaisyas* (producers) of India. Perhaps the warriors were the descendants of the conquering invaders while the workers were the descendants of the original population.

Japanese Perceptions of Work

However, from Japan we get the idea of a close link between workers and warriors. This link evolved after the sixteenth century, in times
of relative peace when many samurai could no longer make a living by
swordplay and had to get used to constructive work. They maintained
old ideals in this new role. Today we can speak of the worker as warrior in the sense that he or she stresses training to perfection, tools that
are in excellent shape, loyalty to the leader and the organization, and
even the Japanese variant of the work ethic.

The Japanese language offers some clues about the meaning of work
to the Japanese and, in particular, its relationship to the activities of
the much admired samurai or bushi. The basic interpretations of terms
and characters which follow have been taken from an introduction to
Japanese by Yasuo Yoshida, Keizo Saji, and Ikuyo Nishide (1969).

Ku and *ko, shi, yaku* and *eki* are some of the syllables and words used to refer to work, typically as something worthwhile and honorable. Each is represented in writing by a Chinese character which tells much about the development of its meaning.

Ku and *ko* are two syllables representing a character which is said to be a stylized version of the carpenter's square. It stands for work, primarily manufacturing work. The Japanese have a long tradition of emphasis on the similarities between a competent carpenter, a competent samurai or bushi, and a (by definition competent) Zen master (see Musashi, 1982).

Shigoto means work in the sense of "serving as an officer" and "doing things." The character *shi* represents a "person sitting in the proper position," an official. It appears in *bushi* ("military man") and *shinshi* ("gentleman") and suggests a link between work and man of distinction.

The syllables *yaku* and *eki* also denote work and are represented by a character which represents *going, weapon,* and *hand.* It means "to go out with weapon in hand" and, more generally, to work (the weapon presumably turned into an instrument or tool). Thus, *yakume* means duty, and *heieki* means military service. Again there seems to be a link between work and a highly regarded social class, that of the samurai.

These terms give only an inkling of how the Japanese express the idea of work. One gets the feeling that historically they have regarded it as anything but demeaning, quite in contrast to the West, in which the Graeco-Roman tradition assigned work to slaves until the Benedictine monks, perhaps not unlike the Zen Buddhists, decided to closely tie together prayer and work, and until Calvin and Luther linked work with salvation.

Bushido—The Way of the Warrior

The particular Japanese tradition of relevance here is that of *bushido.* The three syllables of the word mean *martial, man,* and *way,* respectively. The term stands for a complex ethic originally characteristic of the *bushi* or *samurai* who emerged in the twelfth century as a class of warriors in the service of the emperor or some lesser lord (*daimyo*). They were a disciplined, austere, and fanatical lot.

As a warrior, the bushi faced essentially two kinds of situations. There were the ritual or formal situations involving important others, especially the leader toward whom the samurai had obligations and duties. Then there were unstructured situations involving unimportant strangers and actual enemies. Toward his superior the bushi was circumspect and obedient; toward strangers and enemies he was ruthless and bent on dispatching actual or potential opposition as rapidly as possible to a final resting place.

Bushido is an ethic or *way* of loyalty to one's superior and of mental and physical readiness to do battle. The latter requires constant effort. Indeed, the samurai had to be a superb swordsman in order to survive, and his swords (he usually wore two) had to be made of the finest steel. The Japanese did not build huge Gothic cathedrals, but their swords are said to be achievements of a similar level of craftsmanship.

The samurai class was receptive to the ideas of Zen Buddhism and adopted them as its more or less official creed. The samurai was expected to perform perfectly, with, as the phrase goes, "the concentration of a Zen master." The rules of fighting were not exactly chivalrous and the samurai had to sense enemies hiding in the trees behind him. He had to frighten these enemies sufficiently so that they would attack him reluctantly and one at a time. If he was killed by opponents jumping on him from behind, it was his own fault, the result of his own lamentable imperfection.

A good example of what a samurai was expected to do is provided by Eiji Yoshikawa's (1981) novel *Musashi* about the seventeenth-century samurai Miyamoto Musashi. In a confrontation which pits him alone against a band led by his rival Denshichiro, Musashi kills Otagura Hyosuke (whose head or part of it flies past him like a "monstrous red cherry") and Denshichiro with two perfectly executed blows of a perfectly made sword.

Bushido, the unforgiving way of the samurai, affected the Japanese in many ways. On the social level, it evolved into a set of values appropriate to the new and less martial times. Edwin Reischauer (1981) points out in his introduction to Yoshikawa's novel that "disciplined self-control and education in a society at peace was becoming more important than skill in warfare" (p. xi) and that "Yoshikawa portrays Musashi as consciously turning his martial skills from service in warfare to a means of character building for a time of peace" (p. xii).

Yoshikawa's biographical novel details how the young Musashi, as a quasi prisoner under the influence of the Buddhist monk Takuan, begins to learn his martial craft in a cell in Himeji. But learning is a lifelong process for him; for example, he takes another step forward in a monastery in which he is told that he is too strong, that he must learn to be weak (Yoshikawa, 1981, pp. 161, 162, 167).

The training Musashi receives in the monastery is dangerous; he must sign a waiver of a type familiar to many in modern and litigious America, stating that he discharges the temple of all responsibility in the case that he is wounded or killed during training. We see variants of such rigorous training in Japanese corporations whose flag-waving employees run in tight formations up steep mountain sides or twenty miles across rugged terrain, and perhaps in the phenomenon of *shiken jigoku* or "exam hell" which Japanese students go through in their quest to be admitted to good schools and universities and to avoid disgracing themselves and their families.

Also, as the values of bushido spread from the declining samurai class to the population at large, in particular to the administrators and merchants who took the samurai's place, its values of loyalty and perfection began to play a role somewhat similar to that of the Protestant ethic in Europe and the United States.

Bushido is embraced in a very specific way by many, perhaps somewhat nationalistic, Japanese managers who are a little tired of being dismissed as imitators and who feel that Westerners tend to take advantage of the Japanese concern to maintain harmony and to avoid embarrassing or offending others. Musashi's (1982) own book, *The Book of Five Rings*, has become a bible for many of these managers. He has many things to say about means and a few things about the end. The end is to survive the most dramatic situation of all: when faced by a horde of enemies trying to transform you into minced meat. The means are mental discipline and martial competence, both attained through constant practice and vigilance. As readers of James Clavell's (1976) *Shogun* will know: Only the most paranoid warriors survived in those days, and even they had to be lucky.

When dealing with a Japanese businessman, one must consider the possibility that he sees himself as a samurai. On this point, Reischauer (1981) notes that "many Japanese prefer to see themselves as fiercely individualistic, high-principled, self-disciplined and aesthetically sensitive modern-day Musashis" (p. xii). A Japanese manager is likely to follow Musashi's advice: "Never show your *honne* (real intention)" and "know your enemy." This twentieth-century samurai operates according to a code that demands he diligently prepare himself and that he do his best. Like a sumo wrestler, he may wait, ready and watchful, until the opponent makes the first move, loses his cool, and reveals a vulnerable spot.

THE WORKER AS MONK

From Japan comes a second model of the worker that sounds at first surprising to western ears: the worker as monk. In the combative turmoil of Japan's past, the Buddhist monks and priests played an important role. Frank Gibney notes that, in Japan,

Warriors, farmers, or artists were encouraged to pursue excellence in whatever they did. By following a discipline well, whether they were learning swordsmanship or painting black-and-white landscapes, believers, the Zen masters argued, could find enlightenment as readily as through prayer or reading the sutras. (Gibney, 1982, p. 23)

The influence of the Buddhist monks and priests still seems pervasive in Japan today. It manifests itself in assertions like the following by the Japanese author Shichihei Yamamoto:

We [the Japanese] work hard because we believe in it. To do a good job and help one's company grow and prosper—that for so many of us in Japan is our *ikigai*—what makes life worth living. Our worldly activity and achievement become part of a religious exercise. (Cited from Gibney, 1982, p. 34)

Is Zen a Joke?

When Buddhism emerged in India in the sixth century B.C., it absorbed many elements of the prevailing Indian religious practices, including the Yoga practice of meditation. In the sixth century A.D. a particular variant of Buddhism arrived in China. The Chinese called it *Ch'an* Buddhism. Ch'an and its Japanese equivalent Zen are derived from the Sanskrit word *dhyana* for "meditation." In the twelfth century, Ch'an arrived in Japan where it flourished and rose to its greatest height or sank to its lowest depth of absurdity, depending on one's viewpoint.

Arthur Koestler (1960) raises the question whether Zen is a joke and he points out that Zen is a paradox in a society that observes elaborate and rigid codes of social interaction in order to avoid unexpected situations or disturbances of the all important harmony within the group. He describes Zen as "rude, abrupt, direct, and sarcastic" (p. 234), that is, as exhibiting just about all those characteristics the polite Japanese ordinarily abhor. Zen masters, for example, appear to have regularly answered their disciples' questions by hitting them on the head with the nearest available stick. Western style minds asking the question *why* have suggested that this may have been done to knock budding monks out of their rational thinking and into the world of "im-mediate" experience, or to illustrate the importance of spontaneous action.

Koestler surmises that the "rude" and "abrupt" Zen masters serve the "therapeutic function" of breaking up the rigid constraints and social obligations that hold the Japanese in their tight grip. Zen may provide relief not only with succinct actions, but also with comical anecdotes (*mondo*) and peculiar puzzles (*koan*, e.g., the famous "What is the sound of one hand clapping?"). Both force listeners to drop what they are doing.

Is Zen a practical joke? Are the Westerners who spend their lives pouring over endless and obscure Zen aphorisms and commentaries gullible victims of a hoax? Are the peculiar practices of Zen (such as shooting an arrow without shooting it) taken seriously by the apparent eccentrics who teach them? Or is Zen a serious set of insights which allow its adepts to circumvent the rules of Aristotelian logic and of Japanese social ritual in order to make it possible to experience the world and one's self without the distortions produced by cognitive schemata and social pressures?

Zen and Routine Work

There may be jocular aspects to Zen, but it is central and primary. It leaves no room for a gap, let alone conflict and disharmony, between the work sphere and the life sphere. It leads to the quest for competence which is an end in itself, rather than a means judged by its effects in the work sphere. If Zen had objectives, one could say that its ultimate objective is long-term harmony and balance, including harmony and balance between work and personal life. But it does not have objectives, so we can't say it. At least not for the record.

Few things are probably farther away from the life sphere than the routine work on the assembly line of an autoworker in Detroit who practically has to suspend normal thought activity until the weekend, when he or she can drive the Winnebago to northern Michigan to go fishing.

Routine work may look exactly the same to a young worker in the Honda plant of Sayama City as it does to one in Detroit, but for many of the older Japanese it is vitalizing and meaningful activity. The Zen monks spent hours sweeping floors and boiling rice. They thought of such activities as exercises in the quest of self-discipline and enlightenment. Given this tradition, many workers in Sayama do not understand why their counterparts in Detroit consider routine work to be stupefying and mind-boggling. To them this important problem in the American factory does not seem to be a problem at all.

According to Jyuji Misumi (1982), Zen is even more important than yamato gokoro and bushido in explaining the centrality of work in the life of the Japanese. He argues that it is particularly as Buddhists that the Japanese seek to attain harmony. On a relatively concrete level it is the harmony between self and others that must be promoted and maintained. This is one factor, apparently Confucianist as well as Buddhist in nature, causing the Japanese to stress teamwork. On a deeper level the Buddhists' concern is to attain harmony between the self and the environment and ultimately the cosmos.

For centuries, the Buddhist monks have seen repetitive work as a strangely powerful means to the end of attaining harmony. The Japanese workers may not be monks, but they belong to a culture which has admired monks for hundreds of years, a culture which values work— both repetitive and intellectually demanding—as a means to the end of becoming a better person more aware of, and attuned to, reality.

Zen and Competence

Zen has much to say on the subject of competence. The Zen master who teaches archery is not satisfied until the pupil stops shooting the arrow and lets *it* shoot the arrow instead, in an automatic, natural, spontaneous way. The Zen master is not interested in *what* questions, for example, whether the target is actually hit. He is interested in *how* questions, for example, how the activity is executed. Competence is reflected in unhesitating, confident, effortless action. In a way, it is all means and no end.

In the West we tend to associate competence with intelligence and with hitting the target rather than with some mysterious way of letting the arrow do its flying. Of course, we do admire masters of their craft who are able to let the *it* within themselves create pots, statues, or paintings. We may even notice the driver who "goes with the flow" and eases his huge bus through a torrent of traffic without rudely blowing his horn. But would we express admiration if the pot were not beautiful (and hence not salable) or if the bus did not eventually reach our destination?

Zen and Balance

Finally, Zen moves the long-term end of harmony and balance into the foreground, ahead of immediate payoffs and the next quarterly bottom line. The Japanese terms *haragei, rikutsu,* and *matomeru* throw some additional light on this Japanese emphasis on harmony and its converse, the fear of disruption and tension.

Haragei can be translated as "art of the belly." The word may remind the reader of *harakiri* ("belly slitting") and *geisha* ("art person"). To the Japanese, the belly is the barometer of harmony and the seat of feeling and intuition. They tend to trust people who operate on the basis of "gut-feeling" and to distrust those who rely too much on logic, analysis, and argument, that is, on the functions represented by the head. Haragei implies communication without elaboration, interaction that does not require constant legalistic clarification of what one said and what one meant.

Rikutsu is in some ways the opposite of haragei. The word can mean reason and/or theory. So far so good. But it can also mean pretext and/ or argument. It thus reflects the negative attitude of the Japanese toward reason or logic. They prefer intuition and feeling to cold logic, they associate reason with finding pretexts and specious arguments, they see it as something that is artificial and used to obscure reality, as a tool of foreign minds (be they Western or Chinese) who are too intolerant of ambiguity, too eager to resolve questions one way or the other and to "hash things out once and for all."

Matomeru (meaning "to gather," "collect," "bring together") is the term the Japanese use to refer to what we call decision making. The English words *decide* and *decision* come from the Latin *decidere*, literally "to cut off." We pride ourselves in our ability to make a decision abruptly, to cut off options and to end debate (Watanabe, 198l; Lewis, 1975). To be called *decisive* is the fondest wish of many a manager; we equate decisiveness with the entrepreneurial spirit, the deft seizing of opportunities, the courageous rejection of anything but the best option. Ichiro is less macho in his decision making than Jack.

The relationship between Zen and the formidable effectiveness of the Japanese workforce should not be underestimated. Zen is an aspect of the Japanese life sphere which has powerful effects on activity in the work sphere and which provides a link between the two to the point where they often appear to be one.

The model of the worker as monk seeking spiritual fulfillment in work activity is not completely foreign to the West. The call to *ora et labora* ("pray and work") of the Benedictine monks is only one example. But even in the West, the idea of work as a religious pursuit is often associated with Zen. Carla Needleman's (1979) description of how she and her fellow craftspeople and artists work as potters and weavers depicts individuals who resemble Buddhist monks in their ability to concentrate on perfection. Pirsig's (1975) description of his competent mechanic comes early in a book called *Zen and the Art of Motorcycle Maintenance,* a book which shows that the classical competence of the mechanic must be synthesized with romantic elements focusing on emotion and experience, before the synthesis or harmonious balance of real competence and quality is attained.

THE WORKER AS CITIZEN

This brings us to a fourth model of the competent worker, one which stresses his or her responsibilities to the community or collectivity, what the Romans called *civitas.* A variety of terms are related to, and sometimes derived from, the Latin civitas: city, citizen, civility, civilization, etc. The fourth model of the worker is that of the worker as citizen, as one of many elements, hopefully civil, comprising a city or civilization.

Working in Groups

Craftsmen, like Pirsig's taciturn mechanic, work alone. So do many workers playing the role of monk who see their work as a way of meeting their spiritual needs. Not only do they work alone, they are not primarily concerned with how others react to their work. As Needleman (1979) observed, prototypical craftsmen make pots which meet their own criteria above all, although they no doubt entertain secondary hopes that others will like and buy them.

Workers functioning primarily as citizens also may work alone, but it is more likely that they are social creatures. The collective rice culture tradition of Japan is a culture of workers who see themselves as citizens cooperating for the good of the group and ultimately of the *civitas.* Gibney (1982) notes, for example, that Eiichi Shibusawa, the founder of the Dai Ichi Bank, "believed that more profit would accrue in the end to the honest businessman who planned wisely . . . and took the long view of development, with the interests of the country as well as the company in mind" (p. 30).

Similarly, the tradition of industrial democracy of Western European countries is likely to foster the worker's role as citizen. The Marxists argue that our ancestors became humans when they learned to cooperate, when some of them actually could be persuaded to drive game *away,* into the hands of their "comrades" waiting at the other end of the clearing or forest (Leontiev, 1981).

Working to Produce Socially Desirable Effects

While workers operating as citizens can conceivably work alone, they must be keenly aware of the effects of their work on the community. They "hate waste" (Whitehead, 1929, p. 23). They minimize pollution. They stress quality of their output, be it goods or services, because such quality is an important contribution to the quality of life offered by their community. This social awareness is the distinguishing and necessary condition of being a worker who is also a citizen.

The four models of the competent worker presented here are offered as devices which can serve as starting points from which to approach a clearer understanding of the objective of the various activities that fall under the rubric "upgrading people." They are relevant to women as well as men, although the worker as craftsman and as warrior are models which reflect patriarchal traditions and which require reinterpretation and adaptation in the present context of changing sex roles.

It seems clear that the activities which upgrade people are largely initiated by individuals who upgrade themselves, that upgrading people is not something a society or work organization can decide to do in the manner of a marine drill sergeant approaching his recruits. It also seems clear that the models suggested here are in a way variants on a single theme, and that the competent worker is a competent person for whom there is no real gap between work and life.

12

The Interaction
Between Upgraded
Jobs and Upgraded
People

Like Chapter 1, this final chapter looks at the work and life spheres on both the macro- and micro-levels. It recapitulates the arguments of the book and looks at common elements in the relationships between work and life. It reviews the options presented and speculates briefly on the interaction we might expect between upgraded jobs and competent workers.

RECAPITULATION

Throughout the book an attempt has been made to relate the different chapters to each other by means of Exhibit 1–1, the skeleton intended to provide structure. The chapters fall into two categories: those dealing with the macro-level of society, and those dealing with the micro-level of the individual. The two levels interface on the level of the work organization where the demands of society meet the expectations and personal needs of individuals.

Part 1 deals with the work and life spheres on the level of society. It does so in three stages. First, the work sphere is examined in Chapters 2 to 5. Chapter 2 deals with the development of the work sphere as society evolved through the pre-industrial, the industrial, and into the post-industrial stage. Chapters 3, 4, and 5 look at the demand for, and the supply of, human resources within the work sphere.

The work sphere on the macro-level of society is a complex entity, but among its important aspects are the material and cultural conditions which characterize it. The two material conditions listed in Exhibit 1–1 are the constraints dictated by the collective objective of meeting primarily material needs and the demands of the productive system for specific human resources, that is, for personnel with given abilities and motivational dispositions. Collective industrial values and materialistic determinism exemplify the cultural conditions of society's work sphere, but since the work sphere is essentially concerned with material needs, the material conditions loom larger and the focus in Chapters 2 to 5 is on the two material conditions.

In Chapter 6 attention shifts to the life sphere. This is the second stage of the analysis on the macro-level of society. Again, there is more to the life sphere than its material and cultural conditions, but they provide a starting point for discussion. Where the work sphere is generally concerned with the material, the life sphere comprises values and is generally cultural in nature. In Chapter 6, the focus is thus on cultural conditions. Three such conditions are listed in Exhibit 1–1. The focus is on collective post-industrial values and, to a lesser degree, on the cultural conditions conducive to educational activity. The third cultural condition, cultural determinism, is a way of looking at the world as well as a substantive characteristic of the life sphere, and it has been discussed in Chapter 1.

The last two chapters of Part 1 consider possibilities for changing the climates prevailing in the work and life spheres, to make them more supportive of efforts designed to bridge the gap between them. Chapter 7 focuses on the possibilities for creating a climate for upgrading jobs so they demand behavior more similar to what is expected of workers as individuals in the life sphere. The modest thesis of this chapter is that by being open to ideas of other cultures, we can redefine work and create a climate that encourages actions to upgrade jobs. This involves primarily a shift of emphasis from the efficiency and productivity orientation to the human growth and development orientation, from basic industrial values and their implications of high achievement levels, hierarchical structures, and strong leadership to post-industrial values and resulting emphases on self-actualization, worker participation, and maintenance-oriented management style. In terms of Exhibit 1–1, interest here focuses on collective industrial and post-industrial values.

Where Chapter 7 looks at the climate for changes in the work environment, Chapter 8 ultimately deals with changes in people. In short, the focus shifts from upgrading jobs to upgrading people. The thesis of Chapter 8 is that any step which brings the egalitarian society closer is also a step which makes it easier for people to upgrade themselves. Such steps involve a shift of emphasis from power to equality, from artificial constraints based on race, sex, and other irrelevant factors to freedom from such constraints. In terms of Exhibit 1–1, interest here focuses on the cultural conditions conducive to educational activity.

This brings us to Part 2. Chapter 9 provides an overview of possible relationships between the work and life spheres of individuals. Psychological conditions enter the picture on this level; they are analogues of cultural conditions on the level of society.

Chapters 10 and 11 in some ways take the issues of Chapters 7 and 8 from the macro-level to the micro-level. They focus on opportunities for changing jobs and for helping people to change themselves. Chapter 10 reviews the ways for upgrading jobs through the traditional means of organizational development and job design. The focus is on the work sphere on the level of the organization. How can it be moved closer to the life sphere of the individual? That's what upgrading jobs is all about. We are dealing here with the interface of work (shaped by society) and the life sphere (originating in the higher-level, personal, or growth needs of individuals).

The life sphere of the individual is once again the subject in Chapter 11. Some models are suggested which have inspired individuals to reintegrate their work and life spheres and to deal effectively with both their life and work concerns. Chapter 11 implies such questions as: How can individuals upgrade themselves? What conditions are optimal? Can these optimal conditions be arranged by others, by the organization, by society?

PARALLELS BETWEEN MODELS OF THE WORK/LIFE RELATIONSHIP ON THE MICRO- AND MACRO-LEVELS

Chapter 9 dealt with the models of the relationship between work and life on the level of the individual. These models are listed in Exhibit 12–1 in the rows labeled *micro-level*. It is possible to find analogues of these models on the macro-level. These analogues have been listed in the rows labelled *macro-level*. A noncausal model on the macro-level is Dubin's segmentation model mentioned in Chapter 1. The search for analogues is a little more difficult in the case of the one-way causal models; however, the economic determinism of Marx and Harris implies causation in the direction from work to life, while the cultural determinism of Weber, Tawney and others implies causation in the opposite direction, from life to work. Generalization and compensation are likely to result as work affects the life sphere, or vice versa.

On the micro-level, the final model is one which implies interaction, reciprocal causation, either manifesting itself in generalization or compensation. The macro-level equivalent of this systems approach, of course, also leads one to see the work and life spheres of society as parts of a larger whole. That larger whole is not necessarily society or

Exhibit 12–1
Overview of Models of Work/Life Relationships

Level	Class of Model
	Noncausal Models
	No assumption that one sphere affects the other
Macro-level	Segmentation: multi-equal institutions (Dubin, 1973)
Micro-level	Segmentation: ego-defensive origins Congruence: common underlying factor(s) Noncausal identity model
	One-Way Causal Work -> Life Models
	Assumption that the work sphere affects the life sphere
Macro-level (economic determinism)	Generalization and/or compensation models (Marx, 1859; Harris, 1981)
Micro-level (environment affects person)	Generalization from work to life (Wilensky, 1960) Compensation for work in life (Wilensky, 1960)
	One-Way Causal Life -> Work Models
	Assumption that the life sphere affects the work sphere
Macro-level (cultural determinism)	Generalization and/or compensation models (Weber, 1958; Tawney, 1952; Widmer, 1984)
Micro-level (person affects environment)	Generalization from life to work (Schein, 1981; Neff, 1985) Compensation for life in work (Lehr, 1974)
	Two-Way Causal Work <-> Life Models
	Assumption that each sphere affects the other, and that many effects are feedback effects.
Macro-level	Systems theory: work and life sphere as subsystems of society or culture in the anthropological sense
Micro-level	Reciprocal generalization: causal identity model Reciprocal compensation Reciprocal generalization **and** compensation

society's culture in the broad anthropological sense, but it overlaps to a great extent with both. The next section will take a closer look at the macro-level analogue of the micro-level systems view.

Exhibit 12–1 also clarifies a difference in emphasis between the two levels. On the macro-level, it is primarily the status of material and cultural determinants which differentiates the one-way causal models of the relationship between work and life. Sometimes economic determinants are seen as the ultimate and primary causes. At other times, especially under conditions of affluence, the cultural determinants acquire that status. On the micro-level of the individual, the emphasis is on the effects of work on life, and vice versa. On this level we have models postulating effects of work on life which correspond to materialistic or economic determinism. These are usually effects of the environment on the person. We also have models which postulate effects of life on work. These correspond to cultural determinism on the macro-level of society and they tend to imply effects of the person—who holds certain values—on the environment.

WORK AND LIFE AS PARTS OF A LARGER SYSTEM

On one hand, there is a marked gap between work and life in industrial societies like the United States; on the other, it is often difficult to draw a precise line between them. There are no infallible criteria with which we can identify all activity that falls within the work sphere and differentiate it from all activity which belongs in the life sphere.

Some life activities imply effort and extrinsic motivation, just like work. Raising a family may require more effort than many jobs. Organizing a stamp collection could be motivated by extrinsic factors such as the money received for duplicates discovered. In other words, differences between a mother and a child care worker, or between a stamp collector and a stamp dealer, are not always obvious. They are probably matters of degree, although they usually have something to do with whether an activity is pursued as a means (e.g., the work activity of cleaning commercial premises) or as an end in itself (e.g., the nonwork activity of cleaning one's own house for the sheer pleasure of rediscovering that cleanliness is indeed next to godliness).

The Work and Life Spheres as Subsystems

The distinction between work and life spheres is not always clear because they are subsystems of the same larger system. This larger system assumes somewhat different forms depending on one's perspective. On the macro-level it can be the society, consisting of work-related institutions (corporations, unions, employer associations, training institutions) and institutions related to family life, leisure, politics, and religion.

Still on the macro-level, but from a slightly different perspective, the larger whole can be the culture in the broad sense of the anthropologist. Brian Fagan (1980) for example, defines this larger whole as "the distinctive adaptive system used by human beings . . . to maintain a community in a state of equilibrium with its environment" (pp. 4–5). Culture in this sense is an interrelated set of ways a society has worked out collectively and in the course of centuries to establish at least a working relationship with its physical environment and other cultures.

On the micro-level of the individual, personality plays a role which is in some ways analogous to that of the culture on the macro-level of society. It is a set of ways of coming to terms with the environment. A person works out or learns these ways in the course of years or decades of development and maturation.

Some of these ways of coping and maintaining a workable relationship with the environment lead to changes of the individual or society, others lead to changes of the environment. Ultimately it is always interrelated changes of both the adjusting entity and the adjusted environment that are involved in the process of maintaining a working relationship between the two.

Individuals can adapt by way of *accomodation*, involving changes of their own attitudes, skill levels, etc., and *assimilation*, involving changes they make in their environments (Piaget, 1952). On the level of the culture it is said that oriental cultures tend to either be part of the cyclical universe (as in India) or to "go with the flow" (as in Japan), while occidental cultures are said to focus on changing the environment, a focus which has led to modern technology as well as to ecological problems (Campbell, 1962).

The Work and Life Spheres as Interacting Subsystems

To say that the work and life spheres are subsystems of the same larger system, such as a society's culture, implies that they interact either directly or indirectly. They may conflict, they may enhance each other, they may be separated by a wide gap. Even the gap between them in the industrial society constitutes a type of relationship, one which is the result of, and which leads in turn to, particular interactions. One would expect the life sphere of a society whose work sphere is highly routinized to offer a huge entertainment sector designed to afford workers outlets for frustration and aggression generated by the work they do. The entertainment offered would probably include more *Wrestlemania* spectaculars than pianists playing Chopin's *Etudes*, more demolition derbies than actors reciting lines from Sophocles' *Antigone*.

The work and life spheres of individuals are also interacting subsystems. From the perspective of the larger system of personality, self-actualization might be a central growth need originating in the life sphere, in the interaction between a person's genetic predispositions and family and peers. Furthermore, this need for self-actualization might manifest itself in high expectations that the work sphere will provide opportunities to acquire new insight, broaden one's horizon, and test one's skills. Such opportunities in turn, when dealt with successfully, might increase self-confidence and self-efficacy, that is, expectations of further success. These person characteristics have implications beyond the work sphere and are of primary relevance to the life sphere.

The Work and Life Spheres as Integrated Subsystems

In many societies the work and life spheres do more than interact: They interact harmoniously as integrated subsystems which enhance each other. There is a marked contrast, for example, between the prehistoric hunters, fishers, and gatherers on one hand, and the workers of industrialized societies today.

Industrial workers clearly distinguish their work, which they do for someone who pays them wages, from their personal life, in which they do what is important to them rather than to their employer. Our early ancestors, in contrast, worked while living and lived while working. While making a spear, that is, while working on a tool to be used in subsequent work, they might add a few ornaments to make it beautiful. Prehistorians seem to agree that during most of their existence, human beings found it relatively easy to feed and shelter themselves (Sahlins, 1972). Work played a minor role and there was ample time to pursue other activities such as religious and courtship rituals.

The gap which developed between work and life is a recent phenomenon and a deviation from the norm. Most societies—ranging from those of prehistoric hunters, gatherers, and fishers to medieval craftsmen and peasants—did not exhibit such a gap. Thus on the macro-level the task is one of *re*integration rather than integration, of bringing about something for which we have models, not of creating something new and utterly unheard of.

On the level of the individual, particularly among individuals who occupy complex jobs likely to fulfill higher level needs, we may also find exemplars of integrated goals and expectations relating to the work and life spheres. Such individuals may act as craftsmen, warriors, monks, or citizens in a work sphere they can barely distinguish from the life sphere. Of the models discussed in Chapter 9, the noncausal congruence and the identity models best describe the intimate relationship between work and life in these cases. Just as other societies of the past and present may serve as models in the quest for reintegrated work and life spheres on the macro-level of society, so such individuals may serve as models for integrating them on the micro-level.

The Work and Life Spheres Under Changing Conditions

Finally, the degree to which they are integrated and the scope of the two systems into which we have divided the larger system—the society, its culture, the life space, the personality—change with time. This brings us back to a question alluded to in the beginning of the book: How does the relationship between work and life change as a society evolves, for example, through the pre-industrial and industrial stages into the post-industrial stage?

In the traditional industrial society, the work sphere dominated. In early nineteenth-century Britain, children worked in mines and the twelve-hour day was the norm. In the turbulent 1960s it looked to many as if robots and computers would shrink the work sphere, perhaps make work unnecessary for many. The life sphere dominated, the focus was on self-expression, beards sprouted and flower-power flourished. More recently, the pendulum has swung back toward work in many ways. Inflation and unemployment (not the fully paid kind of unemployment envisioned by the optimists in the 1960s) sharpened interest in work, in careers, in earning substantial amounts of money. Teenagers spend more time passing out hamburgers in part-time jobs than on homework, and it seems to take two wage earners to support the model family.

On the level of the individual, different priorities arise in the course of development through the life span. Childhood is largely dominated by the life sphere. Young adulthood and perhaps also the middle years are dominated by concerns about earning a living, training to make a living, and planning one's career. The retirement years are once again a time dedicated to the life sphere. On the level of the individual, conditions thus also change over time.

Such changes in the relative dominance of the two spheres with time underline the usefulness of a flexible systems perspective which views the two spheres as sometimes conflicting and as sometimes integrated subsystems which are part of a larger system. The systems perspective always implies a larger whole. Given that implication, reintegrating the work and life spheres of society and integrating those of the individual appear to be less formidable tasks.

THE OPTIONS FOR REINTEGRATING WORK AND LIFE

The four chapters which suggest options for narrowing the gap between work and life call for scrutiny that goes beyond recapitulation. They constitute the core of the book.

Exhibit 12–2 identifies the options discussed and attempts to relate them to each other and to their context. The main distinction made is that between the macro-level of society, on which we diagnose the problem of the gap between work and life as a major issue going far beyond particular individuals, and the micro-level of the individual on which specific action is ultimately initiated in modest steps.

On both the macro-level of society and the micro-level of the individual a fundamental choice is between pursuing strategies that seek to upgrade jobs and strategies that seek to upgrade people, where "up-

Exhibit 12–2
Options for Reintegrating Work and Life

Level	Upgrading jobs versus upgrading people (task- versus person-centered action)	Focus	
		Focus on task outcomes (work sphere)	Focus on person outcomes (life sphere)
Macro-level (society) Diagnosis	Upgrading jobs	Redefined work: changing the climate of the work sphere [Chapter 7] Japanese collectivism, worker participation -->	
	Upgrading people	<--	Equal opportunities: changing the climate of the life sphere [Chapter 8] meritocracy versus egalitarianism
Micro-level (organi- zation and individual) Action	Upgrading jobs	Redesigned jobs [Chapter 10] humanistic organization theory, organizational --> develoepement, job (re)design	
	Upgrading people	<--	Competent workers [Chapter 11] worker as craftsman, warrior, monk, and citizen

grading people" is a label that really refers to creating conditions which encourage and enable people to upgrade themselves.

We can make the choice between upgrading jobs and "upgrading people" based on our perception of a given situation at a particular time. Of course, in the real world the two can usually not be kept separate for long. As we saw in Chapter 9, environment and person (and behavior too, for that matter) always interact.

These two, at least conceptually distinct, choices constitute the relevant context of the four options discussed earlier and presented in the overview in Exhibit 12–2. Upgrading jobs is, by definition, task-centered and it is likely to focus on the work sphere and on task outcomes such as producing more and better widgets. It is necessary to distinguish between what is changed and what one ultimately expects to change. Jobs are usually changed for their own sake, in the sense that they can be done more efficiently and more effectively. But from the humanistic perspective, we are likely to change jobs not for the sake of changed jobs, but so they will afford people opportunities to change.

Upgrading people, on the other hand, is obviously people- or person-centered and it is likely to focus on the life sphere and on person outcomes. Here too, however, it is possible that we may see the upgraded person as someone who will do a better job. In that less likely case, it may be the job that we ultimately expect to change. Again we have to distinguish between what our actions are expected to change in the short run and what we expect to change in the long run.

Up to this point in the book, the level of the work organization appeared as the level on which the demands of society and the expectations of individuals meet and usually clash. In Exhibit 12–2, the work organization is treated as part of the micro-level because it affords a view of sufficiently high resolution to identify variables precisely, manipulate them, and produce controlled changes. On the micro-level we thus have two loci of specific change: The work organization is the locus of change as far as the work sphere and its jobs are concerned, while individuals are the locus of change within the life sphere.

This brings us to the specific options. Redefining work to create a suitable climate in the work sphere, largely by reconsidering worker participation as a right and as a means for normal development as adults in a democratic society, appears to be a prerequisite for successful job design and job redesign efforts. The focus of redefining work is thus on creating a better climate for upgrading jobs.

Working toward more equal opportunities implies efforts that aim beyond the work sphere at the life sphere. The object is to improve the climate in which people develop and mature. Attention has focused on equal opportunities in the work sphere, largely because this is the public sphere more likely subject to legislation than the personal life sphere. The gains made by means of equal employment opportunity legislation in the area of personnel decisions are crucial. They enable many to assure themselves of the material conditions necessary for personal growth and development. Of course, the ultimate goal should be decisions we make about each other which are fair because we have reflected on them and are doing the "right thing," and not only because we are afraid of an interminable and costly judicial contest.

That leaves the two options on the micro-level. Redesigning jobs to increase their scope is an activity in which work organizations in the United States have been engaged for decades. Given a better climate, it is likely to be more successful in the future than it has been in the past.

The process by which individuals upgrade themselves is definitely less well understood. Education, it was argued, is not something that can be planned, arranged, and provided by means of a structured system of institutions and programs. The best this book could do is suggest some models that might encourage education and personal growth leading toward integrated work and life spheres for particular individuals: the models of the worker as craftsman, as warrior, as monk, and as citizen. Such models may be starting points; the end might be individuals who, in terms of the models discussed in Chapter 9, experience the work and life spheres as congruent or even identical.

The arrows in Exhibit 12–2 suggest that the options for upgrading jobs seek to move the work sphere toward the life sphere, while those for upgrading people seek to move the life sphere toward the work sphere. As noted above, what we change now is not necessarily what we expect to be different in the future. For example, job redesign to increase job scope within the framework of humanistic, or person-oriented, organization theory focuses on satisfied and intellectually active workers likely to stay with the organization and able to contribute materially to its productivity in the long run. Here we change jobs in order to change people. Similarly, an individual's development must obviously take into account the demands of the work sphere.

The four options presented are points for further discussion. Small changes in our behavior and attitudes may produce meaningful effects in the course of time. They could bring a future in which upgraded jobs, upgraded people, and the behavior of upgraded people in upgraded jobs and in their life spheres interact with each other to form a progressive system. Such systems are dynamic and changing, and they seek to maintain a stable flow rather than a stable or even steady state (Waddington, 1977). One can envisage a system which promotes a stable flow of interactions and activities leading toward better jobs, more competent persons, more highly integrated work and life spheres, and higher satisfaction levels in work and life for both the 50 percent of the American population at work, and the 100 percent of the American population dependent on the products of work.

Bibliography

Alioth, A. 1980. *Entwicklung und Einführung alternativer Arbeitsformen* [Development and implementation of alternative forms of work]. Berne, Switzerland: Huber.

Arendt, H. 1958. *The human condition*. Chicago: University of Chicago Press.

Argyle, M. 1972. *The social psychology of work*. New York: Taplinger Publishing.

Argyris, C. 1964. *Integrating the individual and the organization*. New York: Wiley.

Baitsch, C. & Frei, F. 1980. *Qualifizierung in der Arbeitstätigkeit* [The development of ability and personality on the job]. Berne, Switzerland: Huber.

Baitsch, C., Frei, F., Duell, W., & Casanova, R. 1986. *Qualifizierende Arbeitsgestaltung—Bericht über zwei Veränderungsprojekte* [Qualifications-enhancing job design: Two case studies.] BMFT-FB-HA 86–006. Eggenstein-Leopoldshafen, Federal Republic of Germany: Fachinformationszentrum.

Bandura, A. 1977. *Social learning theory*. Englewood Cliffs, N.J.: Prentice-Hall.

Bandura, A. 1986. *Social foundations of thought and action*. Englewood Cliffs: Prentice-Hall.

Barling, J. & Abel, M. 1983. Self-efficacy beliefs and tennis performance. *Cognitive Therapy and Research*. 7: 265–272.

Barling, J. & Beattie, R. 1983. Self-efficacy beliefs and sales performance. *Journal of Organization Behavior Management* 5: 41–51.

Barzun, J. 1954. *Teacher in America*. Garden City, N.Y.: Doubleday (Anchor Books).

Bass, B. M. & Rosenstein, E. 1978. Integration of industrial democracy and participative management: U.S. and European perspectives. In B. King, S. Streufert, and F. E. Fiedler (Eds.). *Managerial control and organizational democracy*. New York: Wiley.

Bass, B. M., Shackleton, V. J., & Rosenstein, E. 1979. Industrial democracy and participative management: What's the·difference? *International Review of Applied Psychology* 28(2): 82–92.

Bell, D. 1973. *The coming of post-industrial society.* New York: Basic Books.

Bell, D. 1976. *The cultural contradictions of capitalism.* New York: Basic Books.

Berg, I. 1971. *Education and jobs: The great training robbery.* Boston: Beacon Press.

Berger, B. (May 1976). The coming age of people work. *Change,* Pp. 24–30.

Bolman, L. G. & Deal, T. E. 1984. *Modern approaches to understanding and managing organizations.* San Francisco: Jossey-Bass.

Bowen, H. R. (January 1974a). The manpower vs. the free-choice principle. *University Affairs* (Ottawa, Canada), p. 2.

Bowen, H. R. 1974b. Eight misconceptions about the labor market. *Journal of Teacher Education* 25(3): 213–215.

Bramel, D. & Friend, R. 1981. Hawthorne, the myth of the docile worker, and class bias in psychology. *American Psychologist* 36: 867–878.

Braverman, H. 1977. *Labor and monopoly capital.* New York: Monthly Review Press.

Brown, I. (October 6, 1984). Thinking without a brain. *Globe and Mail,* P. 10.

Buchanan, D. A. 1979. *Development of job design theories and techniques.* New York: Praeger.

Burke, R. J. & Greenglass, E. R. 1987. Work and family. In G. L. Cooper and I. T. Robertson (Eds.). *International Review of Industrial and Organizational Psychology.* New York: Wiley.

Campbell, J. 1962. *The masks of god: oriental mythology.* New York: Penguin Books. Vol. 2.

Celine, L. F. 1934. *Journey to the end of the night.* (J. H. P. Marks, Trans.). Boston: Little, Brown and Co.

Certo, S. C. & Appelbaum, S. H. 1983. *Principles of modern management.* Dubuque, Iowa: Wm. C. Brown.

Clavell, J. 1976. *Shogun.* New York: Dell.

Corn, D. (September, 1986). Dreams gone to rust. *Harper's Magazine,* Pp. 56–64.

Crandall, R. (1984). Work and leisure in the life space. In M. D. Lee and R. N. Kanungo (Eds.). *Management of work and personal life: Problems and opportunities.* New York: Praeger.

Dachler, H. P. 1978. The problem nature of participation in organizations: A conceptual evaluation. In B. King, S. Streufert, and F.E. Fiedler (Eds.). *Managerial control and organizational democracy.* New York: Wiley.

Dachler, H. P. & Wilpert, B. 1978. Conceptual dimensions and boundaries of participation in organizations: A critical evaluation. *Administrative Science Quarterly* 23: 1–39.

Dahrendorf, R. (November 28, 1982). Die Arbeitsgesellschaft ist am Ende. *Die Zeit.*

De Grazia, S. 1964. *Of time, work, and leisure.* Garden City: N.Y.: Doubleday (Anchor Books).

DeMente, B. 1981. *The Japanese way of doing business.* Englewood Cliffs, N.J.: Prentice-Hall.

de Tocqueville, A. 1963. *Democracy in America.* (H. Reeve and F. Bowen, Trans.; P. Bradley, Ed.). New York: Knopf. Vol. 1.

Dubin, R. 1965. Supervision and productivity: Empirical findings and theoretical considerations. In R. Dubin (Ed.). *Leadership and productivity*. San Francisco: Chandler.

Dubin, R. 1973. Work and nonwork: Institutional perspectives. In M. D. Dunnette (Ed.). *Work and nonwork in the year 2001*. Monterey, Calif.: Brooks/Cole.

Dubin, R. & Champoux, J. E. 1977. Central life interests and job satisfaction. *Organizational Behavior and Human Performance* 18: 366–377.

Dumezil, G. 1973. *Gods of the ancient Northmen*. (E. Haugen, Ed.). Berkeley, Calif.: University of California Press.

Emery, F. E. & Emery, M. 1974. Participative design: Work and community life. Centre for Continuing Education, Canberra. Reprinted in Emery, F., & Thorsrud, E. *Democracy at work*. Leiden, Holland: Nijhoff, 1976.

Emery, F. E. & Thorsrud, E. 1976. *Democracy at work*. Leyden, Holland: Nijhoff.

Engels, F. 1892. *The condition of the working class in England in 1844*. (F. K. Wischnewetsky, Trans.). London: Allen & Unwin.

Fagan, B. M. 1980. *People of the earth: An introduction to world prehistory*. Boston: Little, Brown and Co.

Farber, J. 1969. *The student as nigger: Essays and stories*. New York: Contact Books.

Fayol, H. 1949. *General and industrial management*. (C. Stours, Trans.). London: Pittman.

Fiske, E. B. (January 4, 1987a). Searching for the key to science literacy. *New York Times Education Life*, Pp. 21–23.

Fiske, E. B. (January 4, 1987b). U.S. Pupils lag in math ability, 3 studies find. *New York Times*, Pp. 6, 10.

Flanagan, J. C. 1978. A research approach to improving our quality of life. *American Psychologist* 33: 138–147.

Freeman, R. B. 1976. *The overeducated American*. New York: Academic Press.

Frei, F. 1986. Worker participation and personality development. In M. Morf (Chair). Towards the reintegration of work and life. Symposium, 21st Congress of the International Association of Applied Psychology, Jerusalem, July 13–18.

Frese, M. 1982. Occupational socialization and psychological development: An underemphasized research perspective in industrial psychology. *Journal of Occupational Psychology* 55: 209–224.

Freud, S. 1957. On Narcissism: An introduction. *Standard Edition of the Complete Works of Sigmund Freud* (James Strachey, general editor). Vol. 14. London: Hogarth Press.

Frisch, G. R., Morf, M. E., & Libby, W. L., Jr. 1975/76. The Sandstone experiment: Values of a post-industrial community. *Interpersonal Development* 6: 192–202.

Fromm, E. 1941. *Escape from freedom*. New York: Rinehart.

Gibney, F. 1982. *Miracle by design: The real reasons behind Japan's economic success*. New York: Times Books.

Gifford-Jones, W. (May 17, 1979). Dental x-rays shouldn't be a matter of routine. *Globe and Mail*.

Gilder, G. 1981. *Wealth and poverty*. New York: Basic Books.

Gillingham, P. Introduction to Schumacher, E. F. (1979), *Good work*. New York: Harper & Row.

Gimbutas, M. 1977. The first wave of Eurasian steppe pastoralists into copper age Europe. *Journal of Indo-European Studies* 5: 277–338.

Gist, M. E. 1987. Self-efficacy: Implications for organizational behavior and human resource management. *Academy of Management Review* 12: 472–485.

Goodall, K. (November 1972). Shapers at work. *Psychology Today,* Pp. 53ff.

Gottfredson, L. S. 1986. Societal consequences of the g factor in employment. *Journal of Vocational Behavior* 29: 379–410.

Greenberg, E. S. 1975. The consequences of worker participation: A clarification of the theoretical literature. *Social Science Quarterly* 56: 191–209.

Hacker, W. 1986. *Arbeitspsychologie: Psychische Regulation von Arbeitstätigkeiten.* [The psychology of work: Cognitive regulation of work activity]. Berne, Switzerland: Huber.

Hackman, J. R. & Oldham, G. R. 1975. Development of the job diagnostic survey. *Journal of Applied Psychology* 60: 159–170.

Hackman, J. R. & Oldham, G. R. 1980. *Work redesign*. Reading, Mass.: Addison-Wesley.

Hall, R. H. 1975. *Occupations and the social structure*. (2d ed.). Englewood Cliffs, N.J.: Prentice-Hall.

Hall, E. (November 1972). Will success spoil B. F. Skinner? (Interview). *Psychology Today,* Pp. 65–72, 130.

Hall, O. & Carlton, R. 1977. *Basic skills at school and work*. Toronto: Ontario Economic Council, Occasional Paper 1.

Hanihara, K. 1985. Origins and affinities of Japanese as viewed from cranial measurements. In R. Kirk and E. Szathmary (Eds.). *Out of Asia: Peopling the Americas and the Pacific*. Canberra: Journal of Pacific History, Pp. 123–131.

Hardwick, M. 1976. *The world of Upstairs Downstairs*. New York: Holt, Rinehart and Winston.

Harris, J. (April 1977). Literacy and liberal education. *Canadian Forum,* Pp. 7–12.

Harris, M. 1977. *Cannibals and kings: The origins of culture*. New York: Vintage Books.

Harris, M. 1981. *America now: The anthropology of a changing culture*. New York: Simon and Schuster.

Harvey, E. B. 1975. *Industrial society: Structures, roles and relations*. Homewood, Ill.: Dorsey Press.

Hawkesworth, J. 1973. *Upstairs, Downstairs*. New York: Dell Publishing.

Heers, J. 1965. *Le travail au moyen age* [Work in the Middle Ages]. Paris: Presses Universitaires de France.

Herzberg, F., Mausner, B., & Snyderman, B. 1959. *The motivation to work*. New York: Wiley.

Hoff, E.-H. 1986. *Arbeit, Freizeit und Persönlichkeit* [Work, leisure, and personality]. Berne, Switzerland: Huber.

Holt, J. 1970. *What do I do Monday?* New York: Dutton.

Huizinga, J. 1968, c1950. *Homo ludens: A study of the play-element in culture*. Boston: Beacon Press (Beacon Paperback).

Hunter, J. E. 1986. Cognitive ability, cognitive aptitudes, job knowledge, and job performance. *Journal of Vocational Behavior* 29: 340–362.

Hunter, J. E. & Hunter, R. F. 1984. Validity and utility of alternative predictors of job performance. *Psychological Bulletin* 96: 72–98.

Huxley, A. 1946. *Brave new world.* New York: Harper & Row.

Is a board liable for student outcome? (August 1973). *American School Board Journal,* p. 13–14.

Ishida, E. 1974. *Japanese culture: A study of origins and characteristics.* T. Kachi (Trans.). Tokyo: University of Tokyo Press.

Jencks, C. and collaborators. 1972. *Inequality.* New York: Harper & Row.

Kabanoff, B. & O'Brien, G. E. 1980. Work and leisure: A task attributes analysis. *Journal of Applied Psychology* 65: 596–609.

Kando, T. M. & Summers, W. C. 1971. The impact of work on leisure: Toward a paradigm and research strategy. *Pacific Sociological Review* 14: 310–327.

Katz, D. R. (September 1981). Ruthless mothers: Money, values and the gimme decade. *Playboy Magazine,* Pp. 94ff.

Katz, D. & Kahn, R. L. 1978. *The social psychology of organizations.* (2d ed.). New York: Wiley.

Keats, J. 1963. *The sheepskin psychosis.* New York: Dell.

Kingsley, C. 1969. *The works of Charles Kingsley.* Hildesheim, Federal Republic of Germany: Georg Olms.

Koestler, A. 1960. *The lotus and the robot.* New York: Macmillan.

Kohn, M. L. & Schooler, C. 1973. Occupational experience and psychological functioning: An assessment of reciprocal effects. *American Sociological Review* 38: 97–118.

Kohn, M. L. & Schooler, C. 1983. *Work and personality: An inquiry into the impact of social stratification.* Norwood, N.J.: Ablex Publishing.

Landy, F.J. 1985. *Psychology of work behavior.* Homewood, Ill.: Dorsey Press.

Lasch, C. 1978. *The culture of narcissism: American life in an age of diminishing expectations.* New York: Norton.

Lee, M. D. & Kanungo, R. N. (Eds.). 1984. *Management of work and personal life: Problems and opportunities.* New York: Praeger.

Lehr, U. 1974. Freizeit und Beruf [Leisure and vocation]. In R. Schmitz-Scherzer (Ed.). *Freizeit.* FRG: Frankfurt/M.: Akademische Verlagsgesellschaft.

Leonard, G. B. 1968. *Education and ecstasy.* New York: Dell Publishing.

Leontiev, A. N. 1981. *Problems of the development of the mind.* Moscow: Progress Publishers.

Lewis, A. 1975. *Saints and samurai.* New Haven: Yale University Press.

Locke, E. A. 1982. The ideas of Frederick W. Taylor: An Evaluation. *Academy of Management Review* 7: 14–24.

Locke, E. A., Frederick, R., Lee, C., & Bobko, P. 1984. Effect of self-efficacy, goals, and task strategies on task performance. *Journal of Applied Psychology* 69: 241–251.

Locke, E. A. & Schweiger, D. M. 1979. Participation in decision-making: One more look. In Barry M. Staw (Ed.). *Research in organizational behavior.* Vol. 1. Greenwich, Conn.: Jai Press.

Locke, E. A., Schweiger, D. M., & Latham, G. P. 1986. Participation in decision making: When should it be used? *Organizational Dynamics* 14(3): 65–79.

London, H. (September 16, 1972). University without walls. *Saturday Review/Education*, Pp. 62–65.

Lyons, G. (September 1976). The higher illiteracy. *Harper's Magazine*, Pp. 33–40.

Maccoby, M. 1976. *The gamesman*. New York: Simon and Schuster.

MacMichael, D. C. 1974. Occupational bias in formal education and its effect on preparing children for work. In James O'Toole (Ed.). *Work and the quality of life*. Cambridge, Mass: MIT Press.

Mankin, D. 1978. *Toward a post-industrial psychology*. New York: Wiley.

Marx, K. 1859. Preface to a contribution to the critique of political economy. Cited from R. C. Tucker (Ed.). *The Marx-Engels Reader*. New York: Norton, 1972.

Marx, K. 1975. *Economic and philosophic manuscripts of 1844*. In Karl Marx/Friedrich Engels Collected Works, Vol. 3. New York: International Publishers.

Marx, K. 1977, Capital. Vol. 1. (B. Fowkes, Trans.). New York: Random House (Vintage Books).

Marx, K. 1981. Capital. Vol. 3. (D. Fernbach, Trans.). New York: Random House (Vintage Books).

Maslow, A. 1954. *Motivation and personality*. New York: Harper.

McEvedy, C. 1967. *The Penguin atlas of medieval history*. New York: Penguin Books.

McLeod, W. E. 1974. *Investor's guide to a successful retirement in Canada*. Toronto: International Self-Counsel Press.

McLuhan, M. 1964. *Understanding media: The extensions of man*. New York: McGraw Hill.

Meakin, D. 1976. *Man and work: Literature and culture in industrial society*. New York: Holmes and Meyer.

Michener, J. A. 1974. *Centennial*. New York: Random House.

Miller, R. A. 1980. *Origins of the Japanese language*. Seattle: University of Washington Press.

Mischel, W. 1968. *Personality and assessment*. New York: Wiley.

Misumi, J. 1982. Meaning of working life: An international comparison. Paper presented at the 20th International Congress of Applied Psychology. Edinburgh.

Morf, M. 1986. *Optimizing work performance: A look beyond the bottom line*. Westport, Conn.: Greenwood Press (Quorum Books).

Morf, M. E. & Alexander, P. 1984. *The electronic cottage*. Knoxville: University of Tennessee (Office for Research in High Technology Education). Report R01–1565–44–007–85.

Mortimer, J. T., Lorence, J., & Kumka, D. S. 1986. *Work, family, and personality: Transition to adulthood*. Norwood, N.J.: Ablex.

Mossé, C. 1969. *The ancient world at work* (J. Lloyd, Trans.). New York: Norton.

Musashi, Miyamoto. 1982. *The book of five rings*. New York: Bantam Books.

National Commission on Excellence in Education. 1983. *Nation at risk: The imperative for educational reform*. Washington, D.C.: U.S. Government Printing Office.

Near, J. P., Rice, R. W., & Hunt, R. G. 1980. The relationship between work and nonwork domains: A review of empirical research. *Academy of Management Review* 5: 415–429.

Needleman, C. 1979. *The work of craft.* New York: Knopf.

Neff, W. S. 1985. *Work and human behavior.* (3d ed.). New York: Aldine.

Newman, P. C. 1975. *The Canadian establishment.* Vol. 1. Toronto: McClelland and Stewart.

Nilles, J. M., Carlson, F. R., Gray, P., & Hanneman, G. J. 1976. *The telecommunications-transportation tradeoff: Options for tomorrow.* New York: Wiley.

O'Brien, G. E. O. 1986. *Psychology of work and unemployment.* New York: Wiley.

O'Toole, J. 1977. *Work, learning and the American future.* San Francisco: Jossey-Bass.

O'Toole, J. (March/April 1979). What's ahead for the business-government relationship? *Harvard Business Review.* 57(2): 94–105.

O'Toole, J. 1985. *Vanguard management: Redesigning the corporate future.* Garden City, N.Y.: Doubleday.

Ong, W. J. 1958. *Ramus: Method, and the decay of dialogue.* Cambridge, Mass.: Harvard University Press.

Parker, S. R. & Smith, M. A. 1976. Work and leisure. In R. Dubin (Ed.). *Handbook of work, organization, and society.* Chicago: Rand McNally.

Pascale, R. T. & Athos, A. G. 1981. *The art of Japanese management.* New York: Warner Books.

Peters, R. S. 1965. Education as initiation. In R. D. Archambault (ed.). *Philosophical analysis and education.* New York: Humanities Press.

Piaget, J. 1952. *The origins of intelligence in children.* New York: International University Press.

Pirsig, R. M. 1975. *Zen and the art of motorcycle maintenance.* New York: Bantam Books.

Postman, N. 1980. *Teaching as a conserving activity.* New York: Dell Publishing (Delta Books).

Postman, N. & Weingartner, C. 1969. *Teaching as a subversive activity.* New York: Dell Publishing.

Preston, L. E. & Post, J. 1974. The third managerial revolution. *Academy of Management Journal* 17: 476–486.

Ravitch, D. & Finn, C. R. 1987. *What do our 17–year olds know? The first national assessment of what American students know about history and literature.* New York: Harper & Row.

Raymond, H. A. (September-October 1986) Management in the third wave. *The Futurist,* Pp. 15–17.

Reich, C. 1970. *The greening of America.* New York: Random House.

Reischauer, E. O. 1981. Introduction to E. Yoshikawa. *Musashi.* New York: Harper & Row/Kodansha International.

Riesman, D. 1953. *The lonely crowd: A study of the changing American character.* Garden City, N.Y.: Doubleday (Anchor Books). With N. Glazer and R. Denney.

Riesman, D. (September 1978). The anti-organisational syndrome. *Encounter,* Pp. 52–68.

Roethlisberger, F. J. & Dickson, W. J. 1939. *Management and the worker.* Cambridge, Mass.: Harvard University Press.

Rohter, L. (April 13, 1986). The scourge of adult illiteracy. *New York Times Education Life*, Pp. 33–37.

Rokeach, M. 1973. *The nature of human values.* New York: Free Press.

Roseman, E. (April 20, 1977). Advice on vitamins called irresponsible in pharmacies and health food stores. *Globe and Mail.*

Roszak, T. 1973. *Where the wasteland ends.* Garden City, N.Y.: Doubleday (Anchor Books).

Rotter, J. B. 1966. Generalized expectancies for internal versus external control of reinforcement. *Psychological Monographs* 80: 1, Whole No. 609.

Rouse, I. 1986. *Migrations in prehistory: Inferring population movement from cultural remains.* New Haven, Conn.: Yale University Press.

Rubinstein, S. L. 1977. *Grundlagen der allgemeinen Psychologie.* [Foundations of general psychology] 9th ed. (H. Hartmann, trans.). Berlin, German Democratic Republic: Volk und Wissen.

Sahlins, M. 1972. Stone Age economics. Chicago: Aldine.

Sashkin, M. 1984. Participative management is an ethical imperative. *Organizational Dynamics* 12 (4): 5–22.

Sashkin, M. 1986. Participative management remains an ethical imperative. *Organizational Dynamics* 14 (4): 62–75.

Schein, E. H. (Fall 1981). Does Japanese management style have a message for American managers? *Sloan Management Review,* Pp. 55–68.

Schneider, J. & Locke, E. A. 1971. A critique of Herzberg's incident classification system and a suggested revision. *Organizational Behavior and Human Performance* 6: 441–457.

Schumacher, E. F. 1973. *Small is beautiful.* New York: Harper & Row (Perennial Library).

Servan-Schreiber, J.-J. 1968. *The American challenge.* (D. Steel, Trans.). New York: Athenaeum House.

Silvestri, G. T. & Lukasiewicz, J. M. 1987. A look at occupational employment trends to the year 2000. *Monthly Labor Review* 110(9): 46–63.

Skinner, B. F. 1971. *Beyond freedom and dignity.* New York: Knopf.

Spearman, C. 1927. *The abilities of man.* New York: Macmillan.

St. John Hunter, C. & Harman, D. 1979. *Adult literacy in the United States: A report to the Ford Foundation.* New York: McGraw Hill.

Stafford, E. M. & Jackson, P. R. 1983. Job choice or job allocation? Work aspirations and job seeking in an area of high unemployment. *International Review of Applied Psychology* 32: 207–232.

Tausky, C. 1978. *Work organizations: Major theoretical perspectives.* (2d ed). Itasca, Ill.: Peacock Publishers.

Tawney, R. H. 1952. *The acquisitive society.* London: Bell.

Teilhard de Chardin, P. 1959. *The phenomenon of man.* New York: Harper & Row (Harper Torchbooks).

The new economy. (May 30, 1983). *Time,* Pp. 60–72.

Toffler, A. 1980. *The third wave.* New York: William Morrow.

Toynbee, A. 1955. *A study of history.* Vol. 5. New York: Oxford University Press.

Trist, E. L. 1973. Aspects of the transition to post-industrialism. In F. E. Emery and E. L. Trist. *Toward a social ecology.* New York: Plenum Publishing.

Trist, E. L. & Bamforth, K. W. (February 1951). Some social and psychological consequences of the longwall method of coal getting. *Human Relations* 4: 3–38.

Tucker, R. C. (Ed.). 1972. *The Marx-Engels reader.* New York: Norton.

Turner II, C. G. 1985. The dental search for native American origins. In R. Kirk and E. Szathmary (Eds.). *Out of Asia: Peopling the Americas and the Pacific.* Canberra: Journal of Pacific History.

Tyler, L. E. 1978. *Individuality.* San Francisco: Jossey-Bass.

Tyler, L. E. 1986. Back to Spearman? *Journal of Vocational Behavior* 29: 445–450.

U.S. Bureau of Labor Statistics. 1983. Handbook of Labor Statistics. Bulletin 2175. Washington, D.C.

U. S. Bureau of Labor Statistics. 1986. *Occupational projections and training data.* 1986 Edition. A statistical and research supplement to the 1986–1987 Occupational Outlook Handbook. Washington, D.C.

U.S. Department of Labor. 1977. *Dictionary of Occupational Titles.* (4th ed.). Washington, D.C.

Ulich, E. 1974. Neue Formen der Arbeitsstrukturierung. [New ways of structuring work]. *Fortschrittliche Betriebsführung* 23(3): 187–196.

Ulich, E. 1981. Subjektive Tätigkeitsanalyse als Voraussetzung autonomieorientierter Arbeitsgestaltung. [Subjective activity analysis as necessary condition of autonomy-oriented job design]. In F. Frei & E. Ulich (Eds.). *Beiträge zur psychologischen Arbeitsanalyse.* Berne, Switzerland: Huber.

Ulich, E. & Ulich, H. (1977). Über einige Zusammenhänge zwischen Arbeitsgestaltung und Freizeitverhalten. [On some relationships between job design and leisure behavior]. In Th. Leuenberger und K.-H. Ruffmann (Hrsg.). *Bürokratie: Motor oder Bremse der Entwicklung?* Berne, Switzerland: Peter Lang.

UNESCO Statistical Yearbook 1985. Paris: United Nations Educational, Scientific and Cultural Organization.

Vonnegut, K. 1952. *Player piano.* New York: Dell Publishing.

Waddington, C. H. 1977. *Tools for thought: How to understand and apply the latest scientific techniques of problem solving.* New York: Basic Books.

Wain, J. (July 1973). Swing high, swing low: Reflections on a Saturday night out. *Encounter,* Pp. 3–12.

Watanabe, T. 1981. The internationalization of Japanese industries: The view from political economy. Unpublished master's thesis. York University. Toronto, Canada.

Watson, J. B. 1930. *Behaviorism.* Chicago: University of Chicago Press)

Weber, M. 1947. *The theory of social and economic organization.* (A. M. Henderson and T. Parsons, Trans. and Eds.). New York: Oxford University Press.

Weber, M. 1958. *The Protestant ethic and the spirit of capitalism.* (T. Parsons, trans.). New York: Charles Scribner's Sons.

White, R. 1959. Motivation reconsidered: The concept of competence. *Psychological Review* 66: 297–333.

Whitehead, A. N. 1929. *The aims of education and other essays.* London: William & Norgate.

Whyte, Jr., W. H. 1956. *The organization man.* New York: Simon & Schuster.

Widmer, S. 1984. *Zürich, eine Kulturgeschichte* [Zürich: a cultural history]. Band 2. 2d ed. Zürich: Artemis Verlag.

Wilensky, H. L. 1960. Work, careers, and social integration. *International Social Science Journal* 12: 543–560.

Wilson, S. 1956. *The man in the grey flannel suit.* London: Cassell.

Wisdom, J. O. (August 18, 1966a). The social pathology of Great Britain. *Listener* 76(1951): 223–225.

Wisdom, J. O. (August 25, 1966b). The social pathology of Great Britain-II. *Listener* 76(1952): 265–266.

Wiseman, F. J. 1956. *Roman Spain.* London: G. Bell and Sons.

Wittfogel, K. A. 1957. *Oriental despotism: A comparative study of total power.* New Haven: Yale University Press.

Woodward, J. 1958. *Management and technology.* London: Her Majesty's Stationary Office.

Yankelovich, D. 1981. *New rules: Searching for self-fulfillment in a world turned upside down.* New York: Random House.

Yoshida, Y., Saji, K., & Nishide, I. 1969. *The first step to kanji: Part I.* Osaka, Japan: Osaka University of Foreign Studies.

Yoshikawa, E. 1981. *Musashi.* (C. S. Terry, Trans.). New York: Harper & Row/Kodansha International.

Young, M. 1958. *The rise of the meritocracy: 1870–2033.* London: Thames and Hudson.

Subject Index

Author Index

ABOUT THE AUTHOR

MARTIN MORF is Associate Professor on faculty of the Applied Social Psychology Program, Department of Psychology at the University of Windsor, Ontario, Canada. His previous works include *Optimizing Work Performance* (Quorum, 1986).